High Score
iBT TOEFL LISTENING
For Junior

Intermediate

Dear Teachers and Parents,

Welcome to Darakwon's *High Score iBT TOEFL Listening for Junior* series.

Today, many English textbooks focus on the same topics and follow similar study patterns. Students are able to learn basic conversation skills, but too often, that is about it. They are limited because many texts do not allow students the opportunity to take it to the next level. *The High Score iBT TOEFL Listening* for Junior series has been created to change the way students study English. This wonderful series focuses on teaching students English by introducing them to an exciting variety of topics. By studying fascinating subjects and topics, students will become more interested in the English language, enhance their English vocabulary, and broaden their overall knowledge.

The *High Score iBT TOEFL Listening for Junior* series is written as a junior iBT TOEFL textbook. The books in this series cover topics that appear on the actual iBT TOEFL test. The questions in the books are also phrased just like those that students will find on the iBT TOEFL test. This should help familiarize students with the iBT TOEFL test and prepare them for when they take it in the future. By learning as much as they can about the iBT TOEFL test prior to taking it, the students will ensure that they will have some knowledge of many of the topics on the test and will be comfortable with the style of the test and the questions on it. All of these factors should lead to higher scores for the students.

Students will be able to use this series as a kind of stepping-stone for the actual iBT TOEFL test. The lectures and conversations have been written at a level they will be able to understand and follow. They are also filled with real-world situations and interesting facts and information. I believe that students will find the content stimulating, and it will help them become familiar and comfortable with what to expect on the actual iBT TOEFL test. Furthermore, I hope this series will ignite a passion for the English language, one which will remain with each student for a lifetime.

Henry William Link, VI

Table of CONTENTS

About the TOEFL 4

How to Use This Book 8

Chapter 1   **Architecture** (Focusing on Content Words) 13

Chapter 2   **Office Hours** (Linking) 29

Chapter 3   **The History of English** (Focusing on Structure Words) 45

Chapter 4   **Service Encounters** (Chunking) 61

Chapter 5   **Office Hours** (Pitch and Intonation) 77

Chapter 6   **Physiology** (Signal Words and Phrases) 93

Chapter 7   **Oceanography** (Distinguishing Consonants) 109

Chapter 8   **Endangered Animals** (Listening for Numbers) 125

Actual Test 141

Appendix: Dictation Exercises 155

About the TOEFL

The TOEFL iBT

TOEFL is the Test of English as a Foreign Language. It measures the test taker's ability in English. Foreign students often need to take the TOEFL to get into an American college or university. For that reason, the TOEFL exam is very important.

The TOEFL iBT is an Internet-based test (iBT). Students take the TOEFL iBT on a computer at one of the test centers.

The TOEFL iBT tests four language skills. These skills are reading, listening, speaking, and writing. There are many different kinds of passages, lectures, conversations, and questions. Many sections combine two or more of these skills. So students must be capable in several English skills to get high scores on the exam.

The Format of the TOEFL iBT

There are four sections on the TOEFL iBT. These sections are Reading, Listening, Speaking, and Writing.

The Reading section has two passages. These passages are around 700 words long with 10 questions per passage. The Reading section of the test takes 35 minutes.

The Listening section has two types of passages. They are lectures and conversations. Each Listening section has 3 lectures. The lectures are 3-5 minutes each with 6 questions per lecture. Each listening section has 2 conversations. The conversations are 3 minutes each with 5 questions per conversation. The Listening section of the test takes 36 minutes.

The Speaking section has two types of questions. They are independent and integrated questions. There is 1 independent question. The independent question asks about your own ideas, opinions, and experiences. There are 3 integrated questions. The integrated questions consist of conversations, reading passages, lectures, or combinations of them—just as you would see in or out of a classroom. They ask questions based on the reading and listening passages. The Speaking section of the test takes 16 minutes.

The Writing section has two types of questions: 1 integrated task and 1 academic discussion task. The integrated task combines a short reading passage and a short lecture. The test taker must then write an essay about these two. The academic discussion task asks a question about a personal experience or opinion. The test taker must then write an essay about this question. The Writing section of the test takes 29 minutes.

The Test Format

Test Section	Number of Questions	Timing	Score
Reading	• 2 passages, 10 questions each	35 minutes	30
Listening	• 3 lectures, 6 questions each • 2 conversations, 5 questions each	36 minutes	30
Speaking	• 1 independent task • 3 integrated tasks	16 minutes	30
Writing	• 1 integrated task • 1 academic discussion task	29 minutes	30

The Listening Section

There are 8 different kinds of questions in the Listening section. Each question appears a different number of times.

The different kinds of questions are:

1 Gist-Content Questions

   These ask about the main idea of the lecture.
   There is one of these questions for each lecture.

2 Gist-Purpose Questions

   These ask about the reason why the speakers are talking.
   There is one of these questions for each conversation.

3 Detail Questions

   These ask about the main facts in the lecture or conversation.
   There are 0-2 of these questions in each lecture or conversation.

4 Understanding Function of What Is Said Questions

   These ask about the reason why the speaker says or mentions something.
   There are 0-1 of these questions in each lecture or conversation.

5 Understanding Speaker's Attitude Questions

   These ask about the attitude of the speaker.
   There are 0-1 of these questions in each lecture or conversation.

About the TOEFL

6 Understanding Organization Questions
These ask about the overall organization of the lecture.
There are 0-1 of these questions in each lecture.

7 Connecting Content Questions
These ask about the understanding of the relationships among ideas in a lecture.
There are 0-1 of these questions in each lecture.

8 Making Inferences Questions
These ask about the conclusion based on information.
There are 0-1 of these questions in each lecture or conversation.

How to Use This Book

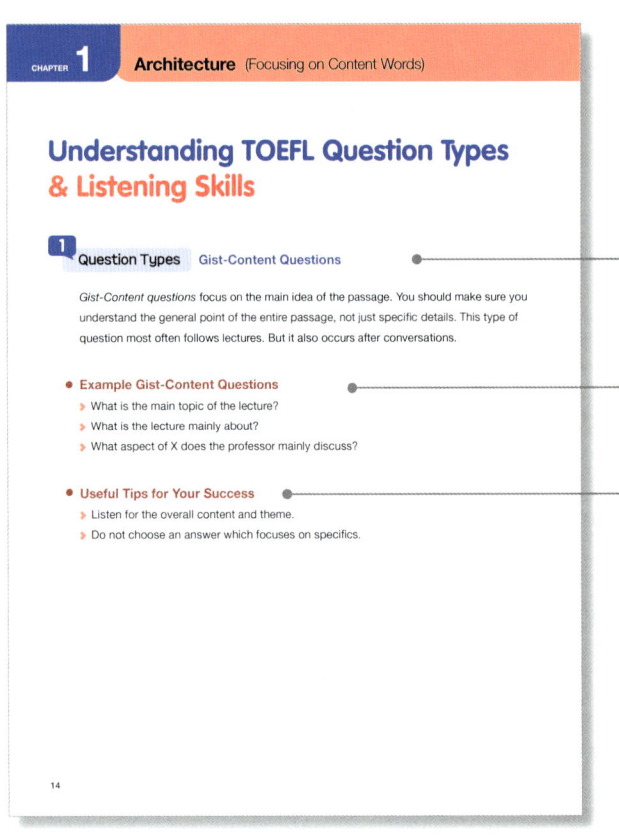

Question Types
This section describes the question or questions covered in the chapter. It provides an explanation of each question and how to try to answer it.

Example Questions
This section shows the different ways that the questions appear on the TOEFL test. Students can learn how to recognize the different types of question in this section.

Useful Tips for Your Success
This section provides various tips on how to answer the questions properly. It also provides hints on the right and wrong approaches to answering each question.

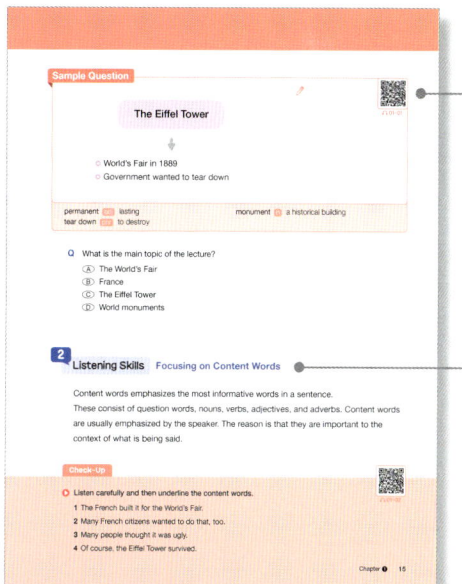

Sample Lecture or Conversation
This is a short 25-30 second lecture or conversation on one of the topics in the unit. It has one TOEFL question and one listening skills question.

Listening Skills
This is an explanation of the listening skill that the chapter covers.

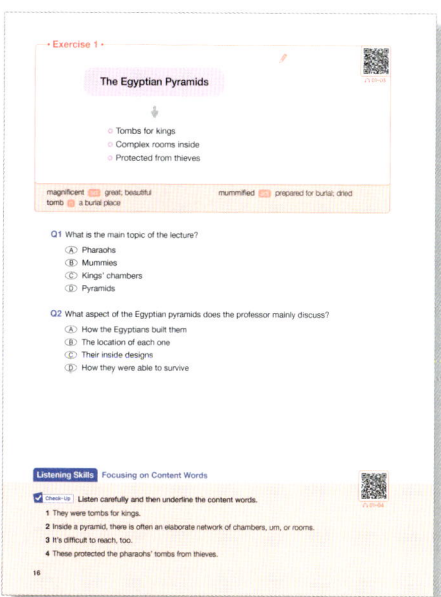

Mid-Length Lectures or Conversations
There are four mid-length lectures or conversations. The conversations are between 45 and 60 seconds long. The lectures are 45 to 65 seconds long. Each passage is on a topic that concerns the subject of the unit and has two TOEFL questions and one listening skills question.

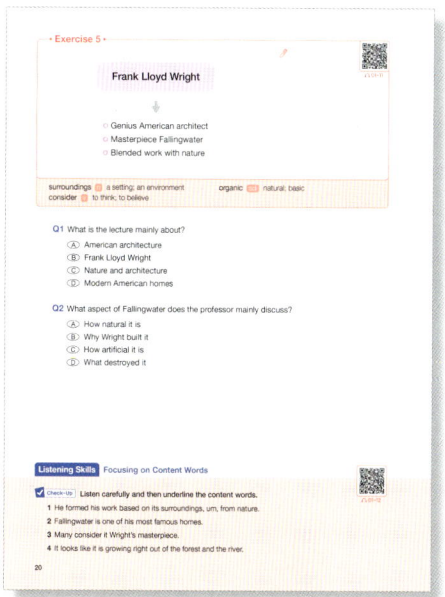

Long Lectures or Conversations
There are four long lectures or conversations. The conversations are between 80 and 100 seconds long. The lectures are 80 to 105 seconds long. Each passage is on a topic that concerns the subject of the unit and has two TOEFL questions and one listening skills question.

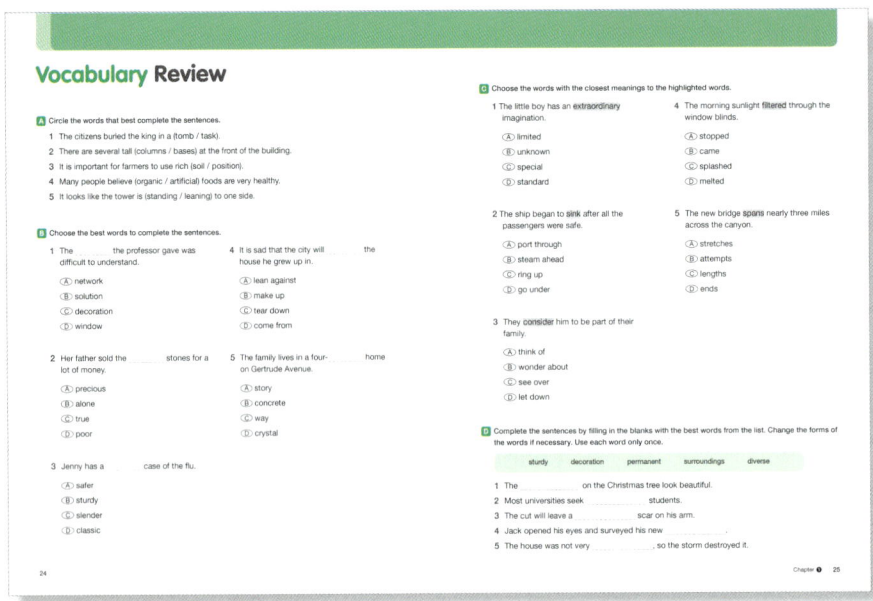

Vocabulary Review

This section provides a comprehensive review of the vocabulary found in the various passages in the unit. Each unit has twenty vocabulary review questions, and all of the answer choices are words that appear in the passages in the unit.

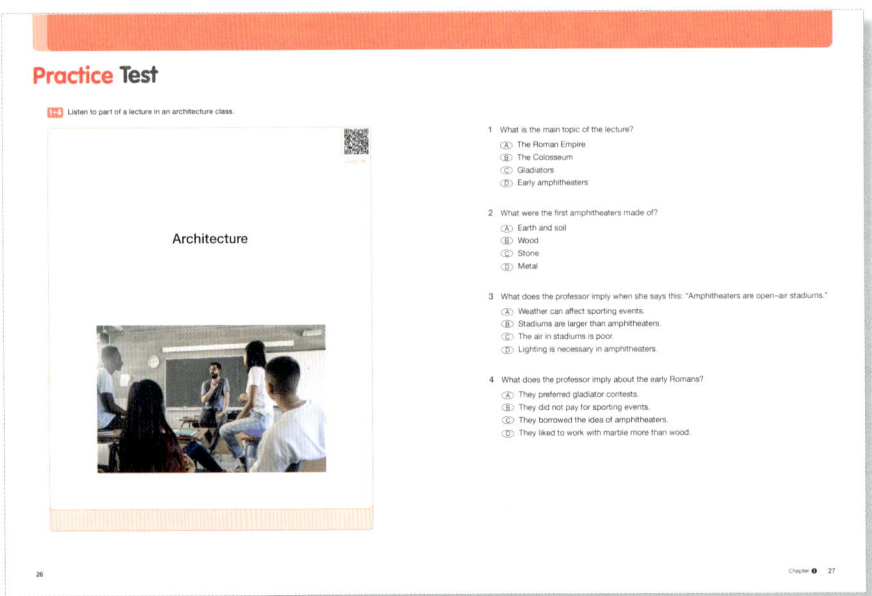

Practice Test

There is one lecture or conversation with 180-190 words. The lecture or conversation is on a topic that concerns the subject of the unit and has three or four TOEFL questions.

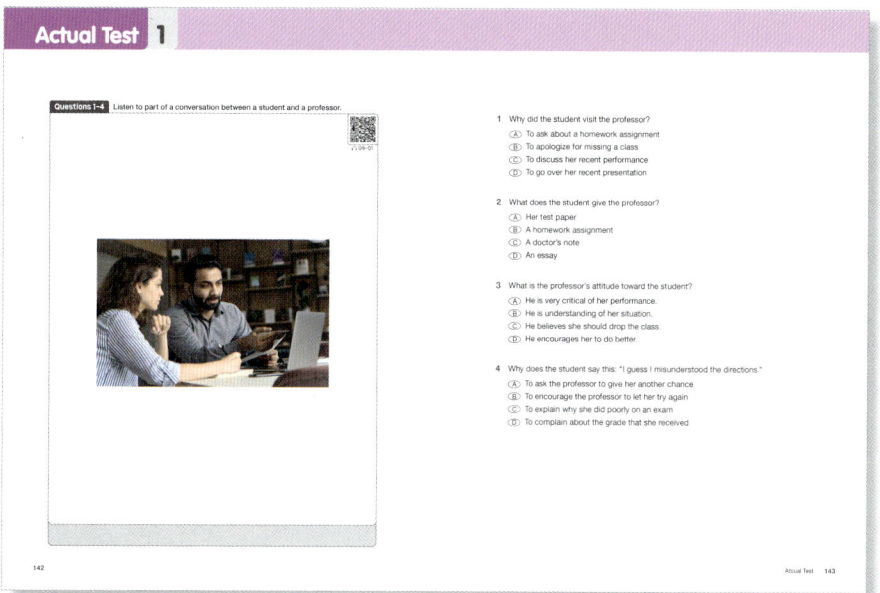

Actual Test

The actual test includes both lectures and conversations. The lectures are between 85 and 125 seconds long and include 5 questions each. The conversations are between 80 and 115 seconds long and include 4 questions each. There are different types of questions for each lecture or conversation. The questions are from all 8 types found in the listening section. Additionally, the lectures are from topics that appear in the book while the conversations are new office hours or service encounters. These lectures and conversations as well as the questions are shorter versions of a typical TOEFL iBT Listening section.

CHAPTER 01

Architecture
(Focusing on Content Words)

CHAPTER 1 Architecture (Focusing on Content Words)

Understanding TOEFL Question Types & Listening Skills

1 Question Types — Gist-Content Questions

Gist-Content questions focus on the main idea of the passage. You should make sure you understand the general point of the entire passage, not just specific details. This type of question most often follows lectures. But it also occurs after conversations.

- **Example Gist-Content Questions**
  - What is the main topic of the lecture?
  - What is the lecture mainly about?
  - What aspect of X does the professor mainly discuss?

- **Useful Tips for Your Success**
  - Listen for the overall content and theme.
  - Do not choose an answer which focuses on specifics.

Sample Question

The Eiffel Tower

- World's Fair in 1889
- Government wanted to tear down

permanent *adj* lasting			**monument** *n* a historical building	
tear down *phr* to destroy				

Q What is the main topic of the lecture?

Ⓐ The World's Fair
Ⓑ France
Ⓒ The Eiffel Tower
Ⓓ World monuments

2 Listening Skills — Focusing on Content Words

Content words emphasize the most informative words in a sentence. These consist of question words, nouns, verbs, adjectives, and adverbs. Content words are usually emphasized by the speaker. The reason is that they are important to the context of what is being said.

Check-Up

▶ Listen carefully and then underline the content words.

1 The French built it for the World's Fair.
2 Many French citizens wanted to do that, too.
3 Many people thought it was ugly.
4 Of course, the Eiffel Tower survived.

Chapter ❶ 15

• **Exercise 1** •

The Egyptian Pyramids

- Tombs for kings
- Complex rooms inside
- Protected from thieves

magnificent adj great; beautiful
tomb n a burial place

mummified adj prepared for burial; dried

Q1 What is the main topic of the lecture?
- Ⓐ Pharaohs
- Ⓑ Mummies
- Ⓒ Kings' chambers
- Ⓓ Pyramids

Q2 What aspect of the Egyptian pyramids does the professor mainly discuss?
- Ⓐ How the Egyptians built them
- Ⓑ The location of each one
- Ⓒ Their inside designs
- Ⓓ How they were able to survive

Listening Skills — Focusing on Content Words

 Check-Up Listen carefully and then underline the content words.

1. They were tombs for kings.
2. Inside a pyramid, there is often an elaborate network of chambers, or rooms.
3. It's difficult to reach, too.
4. These protected the pharaohs' tombs from thieves.

• **Exercise 2** •

 01-05

Greek Columns

- Doric: simple and thick
- Ionic: base and some decorations
- Corinthian: the most decorations

remains n pieces of something that was once larger
structure n a building; something people make
decoration n an ornament; something that makes another thing look better

Q1 What is the lecture mainly about?
- Ⓐ Greek buildings
- Ⓑ Greek columns
- Ⓒ Athens and other Greek cities
- Ⓓ Greece and Rome

Q2 What aspect of Greek architecture does the professor mainly discuss?
- Ⓐ Building methods
- Ⓑ Building materials
- Ⓒ Its influence on Rome
- Ⓓ Different columns

Listening Skills — Focusing on Content Words

 01-06

✓ **Check-Up** Listen carefully and then underline the content words.

1 The ancient Greeks were great architects.
2 Greek architecture is known for its columns.
3 A column is a slender, tall, circular structure.
4 Corinthian columns had lots of decorations.

• Exercise 3 •

The Great Wall of China

⬇

- Protected China from invaders
- Built of stone, rock, and bricks
- Longest manmade structure

soil n earth; dirt
sturdy adj strong; solid
span v to cross or stretch

Q1 What is the lecture mainly about?
  Ⓐ The Mongols
  Ⓑ The early fifth century
  Ⓒ The Chinese Empire
  Ⓓ The Great Wall of China

Q2 What aspect of the Great Wall of China does the professor mainly discuss?
  Ⓐ Who thought of making it
  Ⓑ Who it protected the Chinese from
  Ⓒ How long it took to build
  Ⓓ What the Chinese used to build it

Listening Skills Focusing on Content Words

 **Check-Up** Listen carefully and then underline the content words.

1 The Chinese built it to protect their empire.
2 The stones were hard to work with.
3 Later, they used bricks to construct it.
4 Bricks also made the wall stronger and sturdier.

• Exercise 4 •

Gothic Architecture

- Began in France in the twelfth century
- Notre Dame Cathedral in Paris
- Towers, huge front, stained-glass windows

classic adj typical; popular for a long time
spire n a pointed roof
filter v slowly to pass through

Q1 What is the main topic of the lecture?
- Ⓐ Gothic authors
- Ⓑ Notre Dame Cathedral
- Ⓒ Paris in the twelfth century
- Ⓓ Gothic churches

Q2 What aspect of Gothic architecture does the professor mainly discuss?
- Ⓐ Its earliest architects
- Ⓑ Its main features
- Ⓒ Its influences
- Ⓓ Its problems

Listening Skills Focusing on Content Words

 Listen carefully and then underline the content words.

1 It is a classic example of Gothic architecture.
2 This is the facade.
3 Look at the massive open space.
4 Look at how the light filters through.

• **Exercise 5** •

Frank Lloyd Wright

- Genius American architect
- Masterpiece Fallingwater
- Blended work with nature

surroundings n a setting; an environment
organic adj natural; basic
consider v to think; to believe

Q1 What is the lecture mainly about?
- Ⓐ American architecture
- Ⓑ Frank Lloyd Wright
- Ⓒ Nature and architecture
- Ⓓ Modern American homes

Q2 What aspect of Fallingwater does the professor mainly discuss?
- Ⓐ How natural it is
- Ⓑ Why Wright built it
- Ⓒ How artificial it is
- Ⓓ What destroyed it

Listening Skills Focusing on Content Words

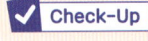 Listen carefully and then underline the content words.

1 He formed his work based on its surroundings, from nature.
2 Fallingwater is one of his most famous homes.
3 Many consider it Wright's masterpiece.
4 It looks like it is growing right out of the forest and the river.

• **Exercise 6** •

The Leaning Tower of Pisa

⬇

- Inexperienced architects
- Weak foundation
- Poor location

lean v to tilt; to slant to one side **sink** v to go under; to descend
foundation n a base; a bottom part

Q1 What is the main topic of the lecture?
- Ⓐ Cathedral bell towers
- Ⓑ Early design faults
- Ⓒ The Leaning Tower of Pisa
- Ⓓ Church foundations

Q2 What aspect of the Leaning Tower of Pisa does the professor mainly discuss?
- Ⓐ Why one side sank
- Ⓑ Its strong foundation
- Ⓒ How it continues to stand
- Ⓓ When construction began

Listening Skills Focusing on Content Words

Check-Up Listen carefully and then underline the content words.

1 It looks like it might fall over at any minute.
2 It does not stand alone.
3 The location wasn't the best.
4 Even today, it continues to lean more and more.

• **Exercise 7** •

The Taj Mahal

- Indian domed structure
- White marble
- Precious stones from Asia

extraordinary adj special; unique
precious adj rare; expensive
diverse adj various; assorted

Q1 What is the lecture mainly about?
- Ⓐ Buildings in India
- Ⓑ The Taj Mahal
- Ⓒ Indian architects
- Ⓓ Precious stones from Sri Lanka

Q2 What aspect of the Taj Mahal does the professor mainly discuss?
- Ⓐ Many domes it contains
- Ⓑ Why it is important in Indian culture
- Ⓒ The materials used to build it
- Ⓓ How it compares to Chinese temples

Listening Skills Focusing on Content Words

✓ **Check-Up** Listen carefully and then underline the content words.

1 It was a very difficult task, class.
2 The turquoise came from Tibet.
3 The Taj Mahal is a very diverse structure.
4 It is a collection of the most beautiful natural materials available in Asia.

• **Exercise 8** •

Skyscrapers

⬇

○ Nineteenth century in New York and Chicago
○ Steel provided an advantage
○ Built to maximize space

| frame n the main support of a building | solution n an answer |
| story n a level; a floor | |

Q1 What is the main topic of the lecture?

Ⓐ The differences between New York and Chicago architecture
Ⓑ The American skyscraper
Ⓒ The Empire State Building
Ⓓ The Home Insurance Building in Chicago

Q2 What aspect of American architecture does the professor mainly discuss?

Ⓐ The tallest building in the United States
Ⓑ The use of concrete and steel
Ⓒ The earliest skyscrapers
Ⓓ The Empire State Building's influence

Listening Skills Focusing on Content Words

 Listen carefully and then underline the content words.

1 Architects used steel frames to support buildings.
2 Steel allowed architects to design much taller structures.
3 Skyscrapers were their solution.
4 It was completed in 1931.

Vocabulary Review

A Circle the words that best complete the sentences.

1 The citizens buried the king in a (tomb / task).
2 There are several tall (columns / bases) at the front of the building.
3 It is important for farmers to use rich (soil / position).
4 Many people believe (organic / artificial) foods are very healthy.
5 It looks like the tower is (standing / leaning) to one side.

B Choose the best words to complete the sentences.

1 The _____ the professor gave was difficult to understand.
 - Ⓐ network
 - Ⓑ solution
 - Ⓒ decoration
 - Ⓓ window

2 Her father sold the _____ stones for a lot of money.
 - Ⓐ precious
 - Ⓑ alone
 - Ⓒ true
 - Ⓓ poor

3 Jenny has a _____ case of the flu.
 - Ⓐ safer
 - Ⓑ sturdy
 - Ⓒ slender
 - Ⓓ classic

4 It is sad that the city will _____ the house he grew up in.
 - Ⓐ lean against
 - Ⓑ make up
 - Ⓒ tear down
 - Ⓓ come from

5 The family lives in a four-_____ home on Gertrude Avenue.
 - Ⓐ story
 - Ⓑ concrete
 - Ⓒ way
 - Ⓓ crystal

C Choose the words with the closest meanings to the highlighted words.

1. The little boy has an extraordinary imagination.
   - Ⓐ limited
   - Ⓑ unknown
   - Ⓒ special
   - Ⓓ standard

2. The ship began to sink after all the passengers were safe.
   - Ⓐ port through
   - Ⓑ steam ahead
   - Ⓒ ring up
   - Ⓓ go under

3. They consider him to be part of their family.
   - Ⓐ think of
   - Ⓑ wonder about
   - Ⓒ see over
   - Ⓓ let down

4. The morning sunlight filtered through the window blinds.
   - Ⓐ stopped
   - Ⓑ came
   - Ⓒ splashed
   - Ⓓ melted

5. The new bridge spans nearly three miles across the canyon.
   - Ⓐ stretches
   - Ⓑ attempts
   - Ⓒ lengths
   - Ⓓ ends

D Complete the sentences by filling in the blanks with the best words from the list. Change the forms of the words if necessary. Use each word only once.

| sturdy | decoration | permanent | surroundings | diverse |

1. The _____ on the Christmas tree look beautiful.
2. Most universities seek _____ students.
3. The cut will leave a _____ scar on his arm.
4. Jack opened his eyes and surveyed his new _____.
5. The house was not very _____, so the storm destroyed it.

Practice Test

1-4 Listen to part of a lecture in an architecture class.

1. What is the main topic of the lecture?

    Ⓐ The Roman Empire
    Ⓑ The Colosseum
    Ⓒ Gladiators
    Ⓓ Early amphitheaters

2. What were the first amphitheaters made of?

    Ⓐ Earth and soil
    Ⓑ Wood
    Ⓒ Stone
    Ⓓ Metal

3. What does the professor imply about the early Romans?

    Ⓐ They preferred gladiator contests.
    Ⓑ They did not pay for sporting events.
    Ⓒ They borrowed the idea of amphitheaters.
    Ⓓ They liked to work with marble more than wood.

4. What does the professor imply when he says this: "Amphitheaters are open-air stadiums."

    Ⓐ Weather can affect sporting events.
    Ⓑ Stadiums are larger than amphitheaters.
    Ⓒ The air in stadiums is poor.
    Ⓓ Lighting is necessary in amphitheaters.

CHAPTER

02

Office Hours
(Linking)

CHAPTER 2 Office Hours (Linking)

Understanding TOEFL Question Types & Listening Skills

1 Question Types — Gist-Purpose Questions

Gist-Purpose questions ask about the reasons why people are having the conversation. Listen to the reasons why the student and other person are meeting. The reason usually appears at the beginning of the conversation.

● **Example Gist-Purpose Questions**
- Why does the student visit the professor?
- Why did the professor ask to see the student?
- Why does the professor mention X?

● **Useful Tips for Your Success**
- Listen for → the main theme of the conversation.
  → the problem the student is trying to solve.
- Don't → focus on the facts in the conversation.
  → ignore the beginning of the conversation.

Sample Question

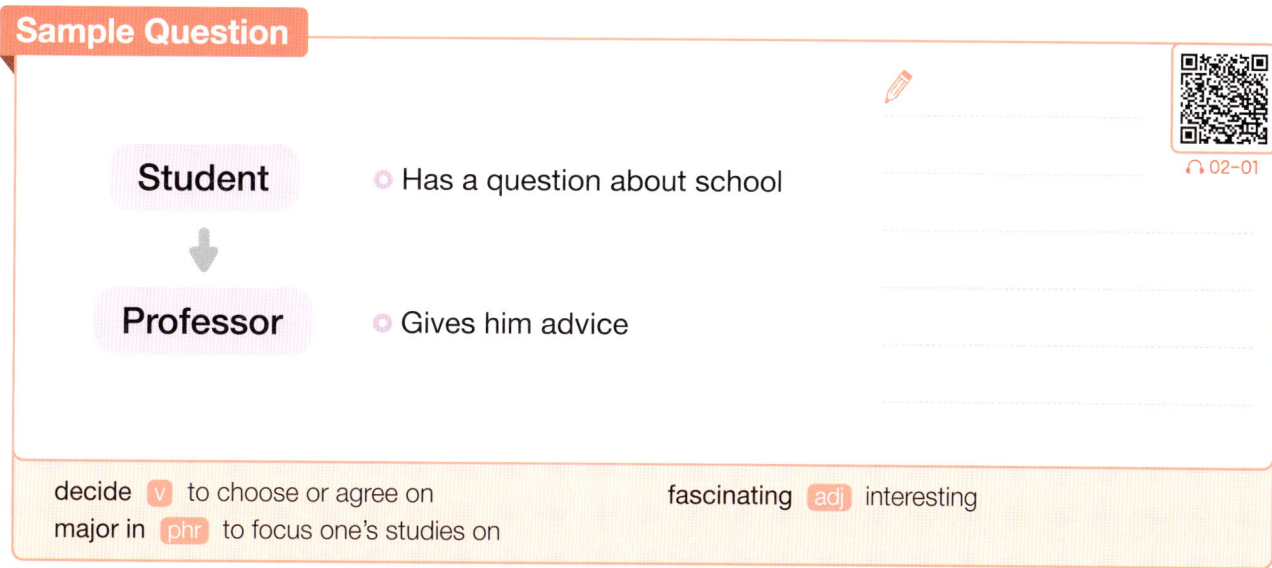

decide [v] to choose or agree on	fascinating [adj] interesting
major in [phr] to focus one's studies on	

Q Why does the professor want to see the student?

- Ⓐ To help him with his homework
- Ⓑ To ask him about his major
- Ⓒ To talk to him about literature
- Ⓓ To see if he wants a job

2 Listening Skills Linking

Linking is joining the pronunciation of two words when speaking. This makes the words easier to speak. In addition, the words flow more smoothly. By using linking, you can speak more clearly and fluently. Learn to recognize linking when people use it. This will allow you to understand people much better.

Check-Up

▶ Listen carefully and write the words you hear.

1 _____
2 _____
3 _____
4 _____

Exercise 1

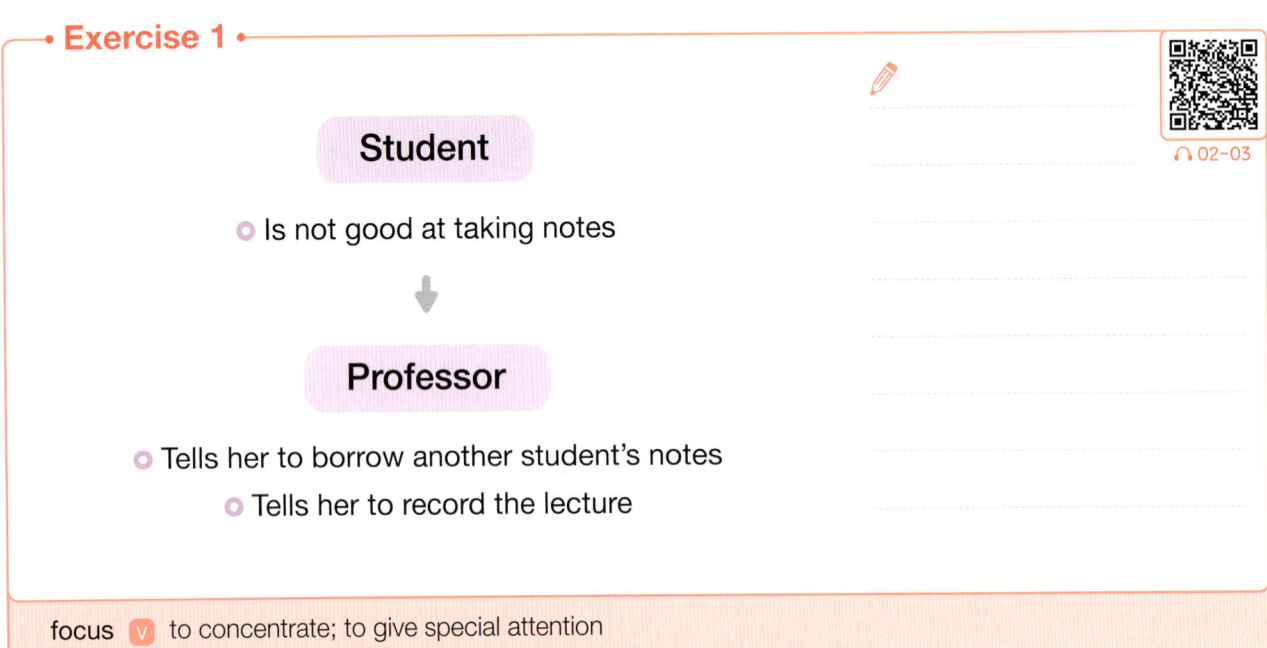

🎧 02-03

focus v to concentrate; to give special attention
borrow v to use something another person has for a short amount of time

Q1 Why does the student visit the professor?
- Ⓐ To pick up her homework assignment
- Ⓑ To talk about the recent lecture
- Ⓒ To ask about the midterm exam
- Ⓓ To mention a problem she has

Q2 Why does the professor mention the student's smartphone?
- Ⓐ To say that students should not use it
- Ⓑ To suggest the student record his lectures
- Ⓒ To ask the student how much it costs
- Ⓓ To compare the student's smartphone with his own

Listening Skills Linking

✓ **Check-Up** Listen carefully and write the words you hear.

🎧 02-04

1 _____
2 _____
3 _____
4 _____

• Exercise 2 •

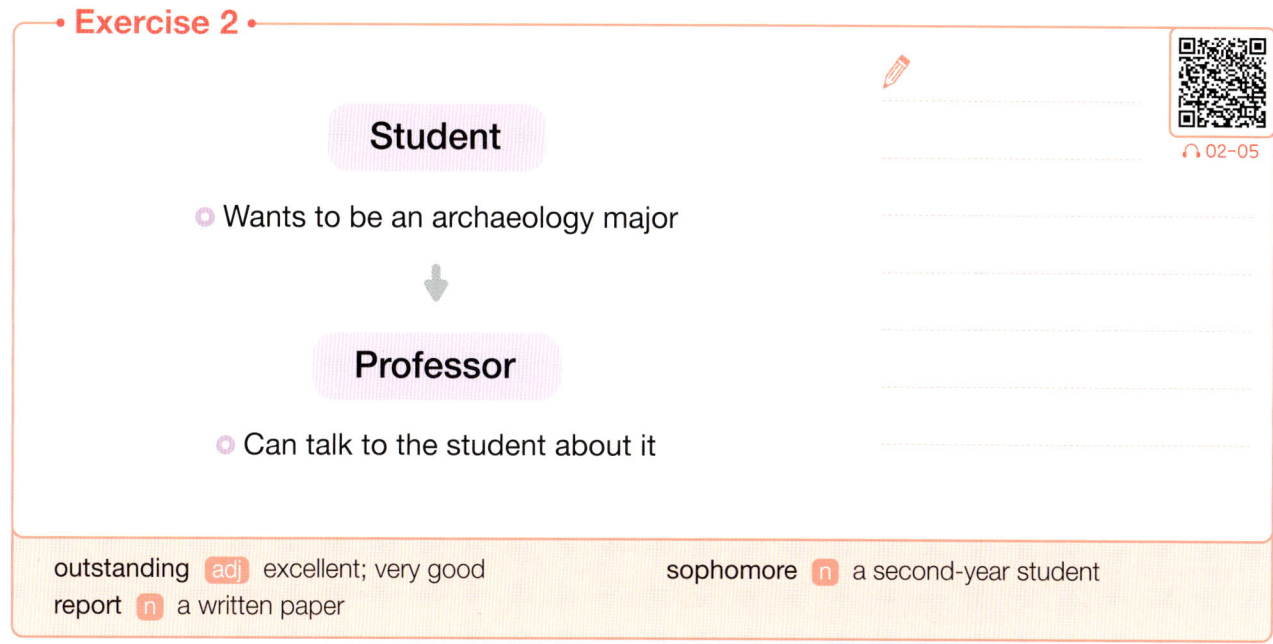

Student
- Wants to be an archaeology major

⬇

Professor
- Can talk to the student about it

outstanding [adj] excellent; very good
report [n] a written paper
sophomore [n] a second-year student

Q1 Why does the student visit the professor?
- Ⓐ To get some help on an assignment
- Ⓑ To ask about his grade on a paper
- Ⓒ To submit a paper to the professor
- Ⓓ To talk about majoring in archaeology

Q2 Why does the professor mention the student's report?
- Ⓐ To tell him he should rewrite it
- Ⓑ To congratulate him on his grade
- Ⓒ To advise him to change the topic
- Ⓓ To say he needs to write better

Listening Skills Linking

☑ Check-Up Listen carefully and write the words you hear.

1 _____
2 _____
3 _____
4 _____

Exercise 3

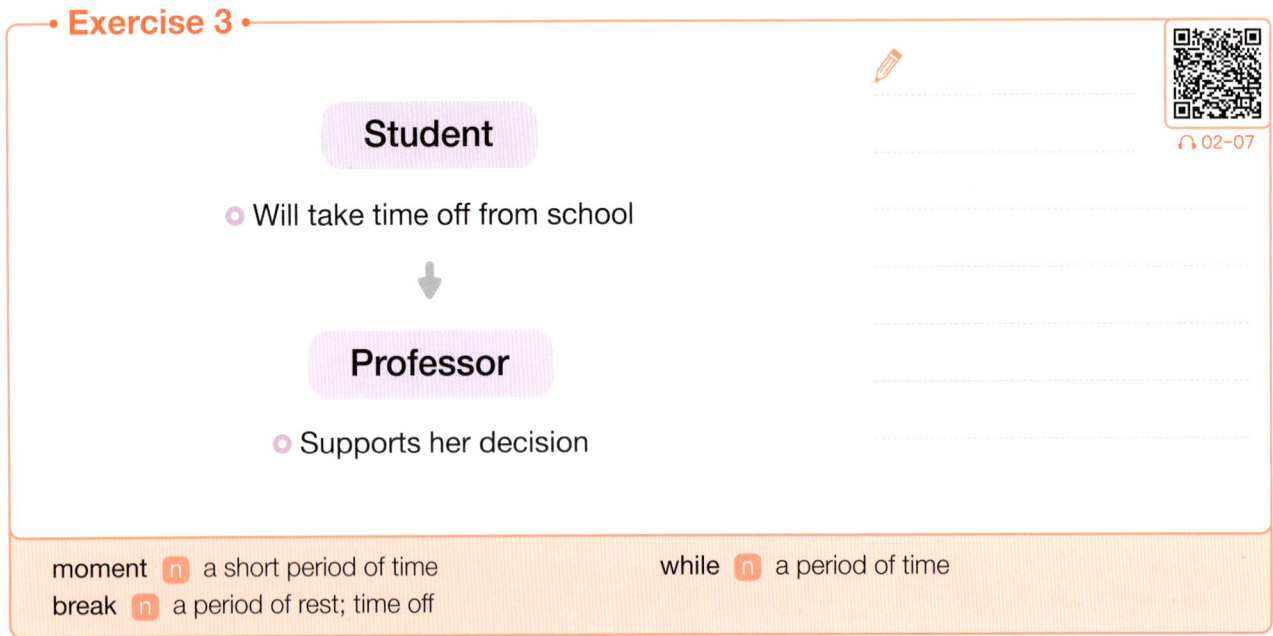

Student
- Will take time off from school

Professor
- Supports her decision

moment n a short period of time
break n a period of rest; time off
while n a period of time

Q1 Why does the professor need to talk to the student?
- Ⓐ To see why she is taking time off
- Ⓑ To have her tutor some students
- Ⓒ To ask her to write an essay on traveling
- Ⓓ To compliment her on her work

Q2 Why does the student mention traveling?
- Ⓐ She has never traveled before.
- Ⓑ She needs a break from school.
- Ⓒ She wants to make it a career.
- Ⓓ She thinks it costs too much.

Listening Skills Linking

✓ **Check-Up** Listen carefully and write the words you hear.

1
2
3
4

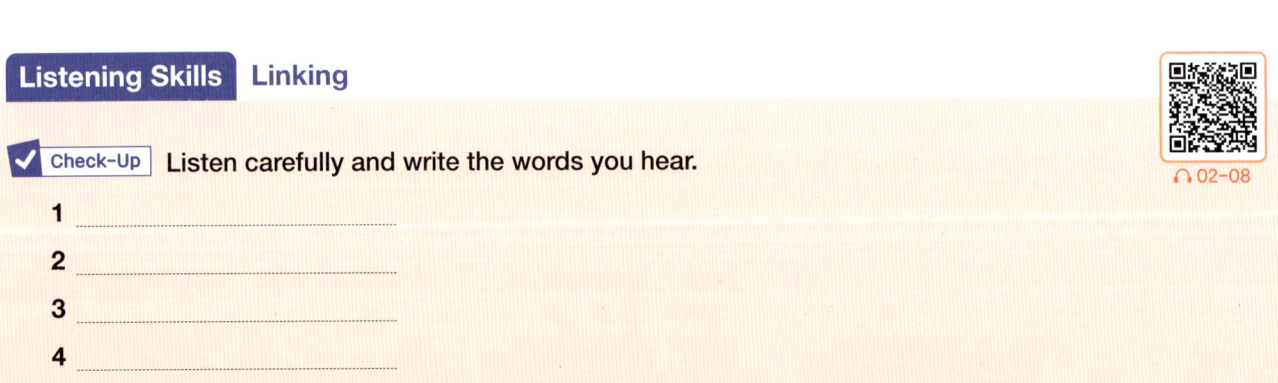

• **Exercise 4** •

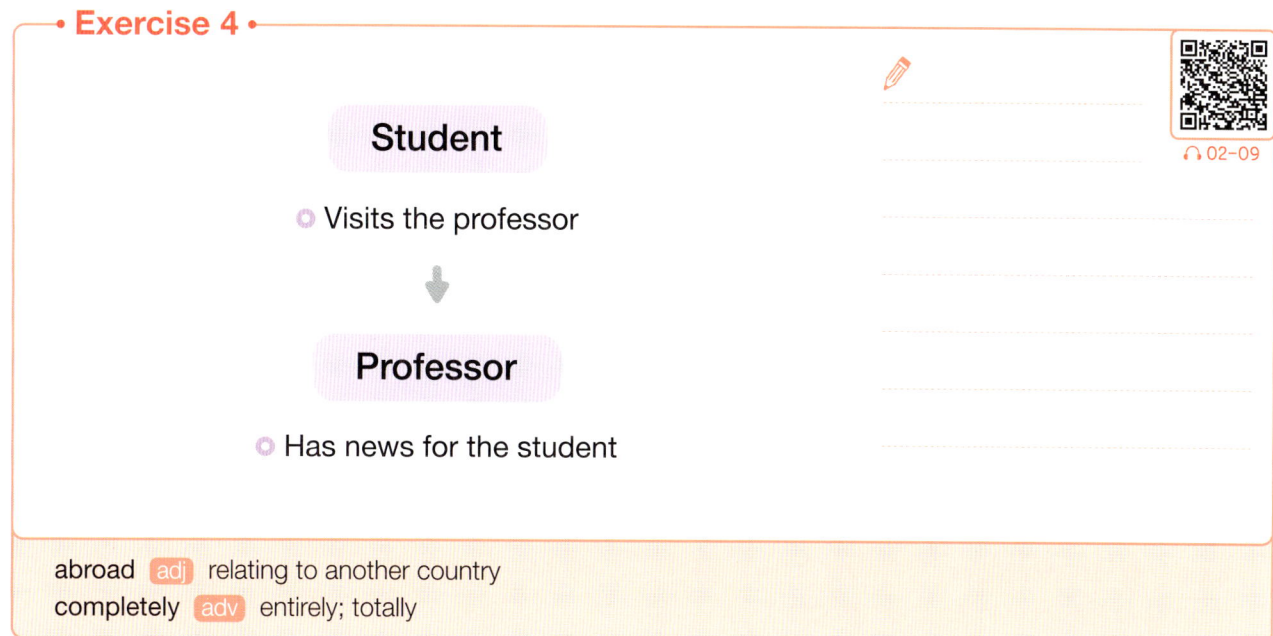

abroad adj relating to another country
completely adv entirely; totally

Q1 Why does the professor want to see the student?
 Ⓐ To talk about the last class
 Ⓑ To discuss her midterm exam score
 Ⓒ To offer her a scholarship
 Ⓓ To congratulate her on her final grade

Q2 Why does the professor mention expenses?
 Ⓐ He thinks education costs too much.
 Ⓑ He wants to discuss a student loan.
 Ⓒ The student will not have to pay to study abroad.
 Ⓓ The student must take class more seriously.

Listening Skills Linking

✓ Check-Up   Listen carefully and write the words you hear.

1 _____
2 _____
3 _____
4 _____

• **Exercise 5** •

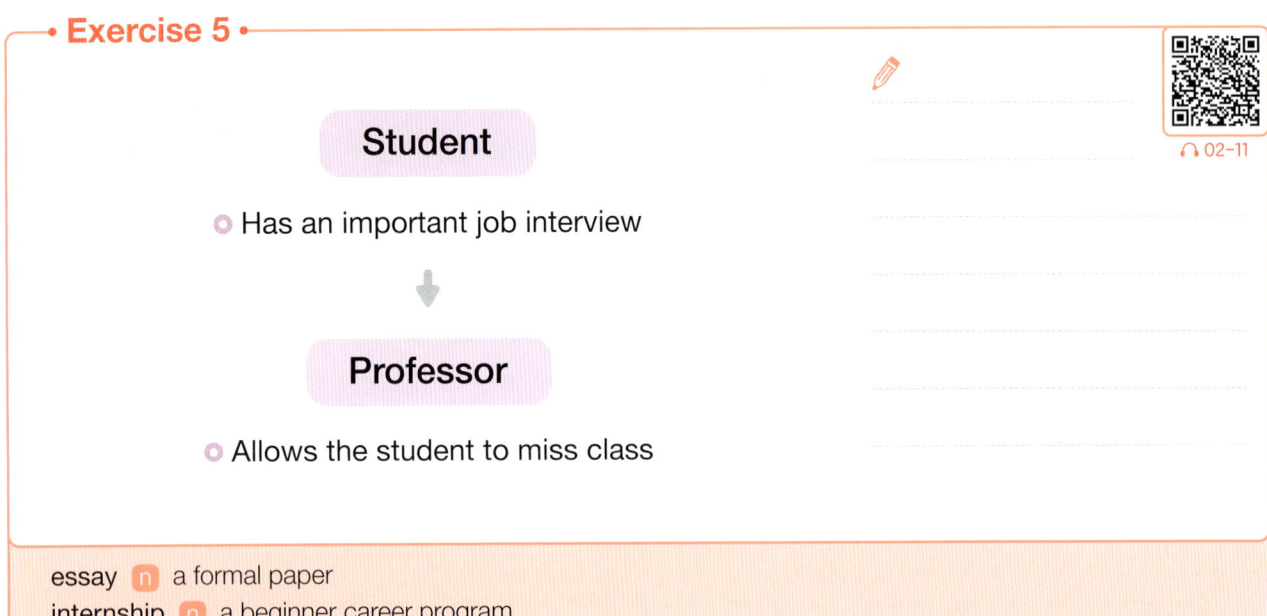

essay n a formal paper
internship n a beginner career program

Q1 Why does the student need to talk to the professor?
- Ⓐ To ask a question about a lecture
- Ⓑ To get more time for an essay
- Ⓒ To pick up a paper he wrote
- Ⓓ To explain why he will miss class

Q2 Why does the student mention the internship?
- Ⓐ He does not have enough time for his classwork.
- Ⓑ He failed to get selected for one.
- Ⓒ He thinks it is a great opportunity.
- Ⓓ He wishes he had never accepted it.

Listening Skills Linking

Check-Up Listen carefully and write the words you hear.

1 _____
2 _____
3 _____
4 _____

• Exercise 6 •

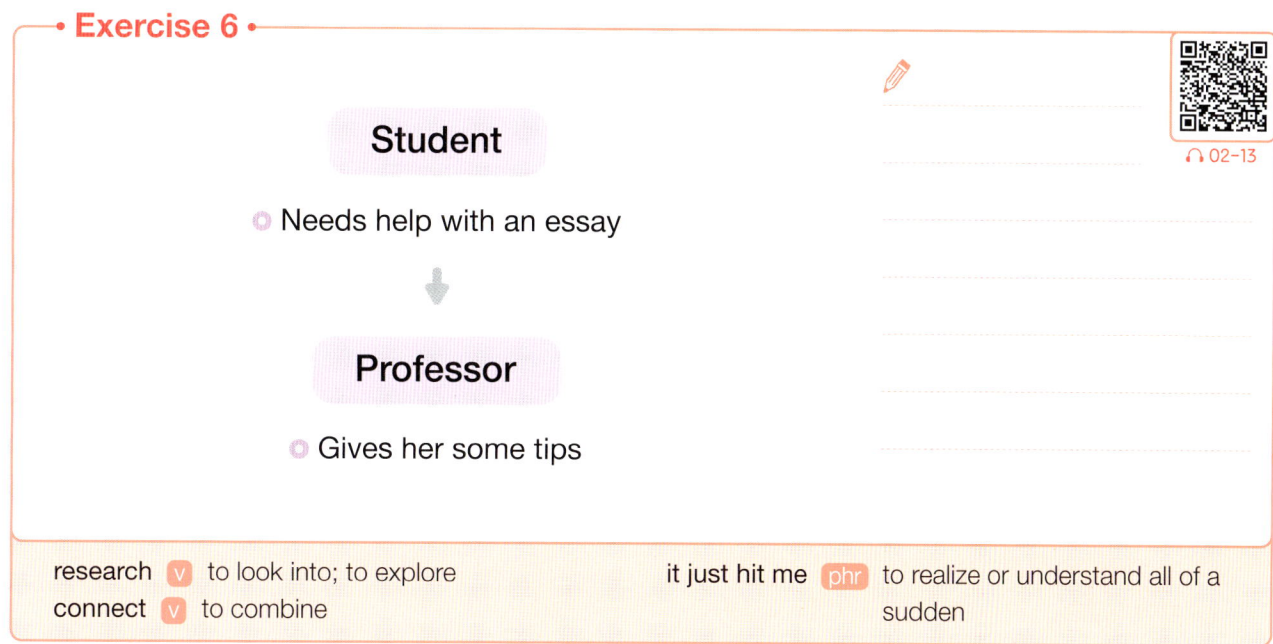

research *v* to look into; to explore	it just hit me *phr* to realize or understand all of a sudden
connect *v* to combine	

Q1 Why does the student visit the professor?

  Ⓐ To pass time between classes
  Ⓑ To get help on a topic for her paper
  Ⓒ To ask for help editing her paper
  Ⓓ To receive a letter of recommendation

Q2 What connection does the professor make between the ambulance driver and the old man?

  Ⓐ He claims they are in the same book.
  Ⓑ He points out that they are main characters.
  Ⓒ He says that they have some similarities.
  Ⓓ He mentions that they are not related.

Listening Skills Linking

Check-Up Listen carefully and write the words you hear.

1 _____
2 _____
3 _____
4 _____

• **Exercise 7** •

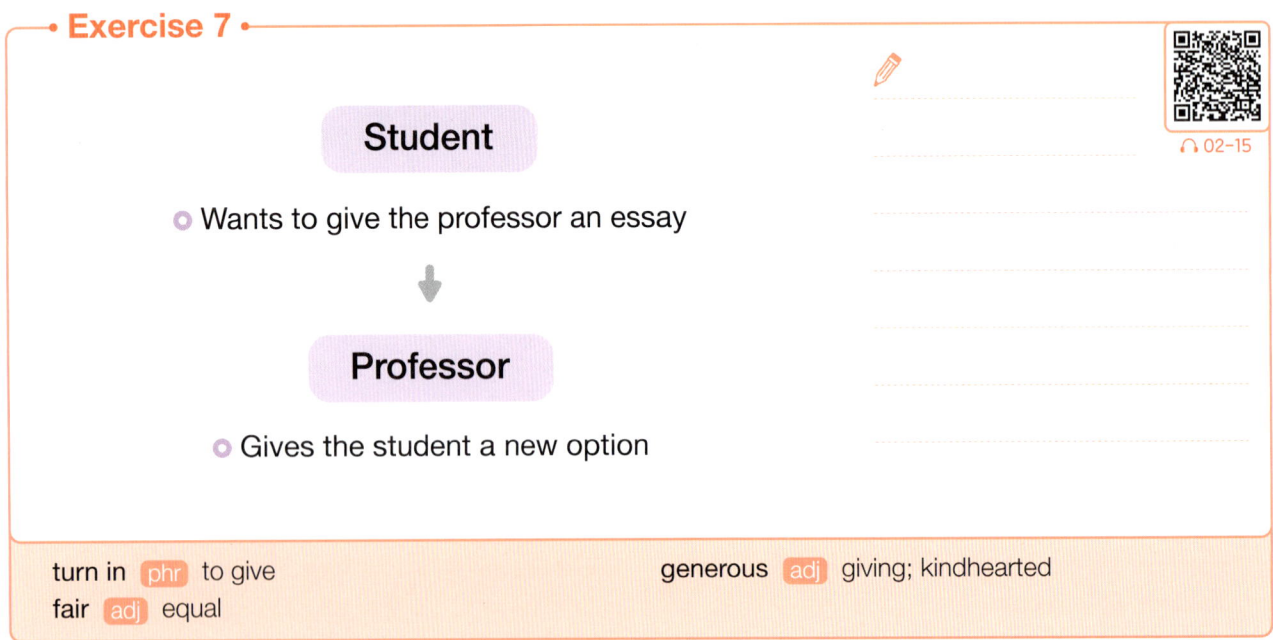

turn in [phr] to give
fair [adj] equal
generous [adj] giving; kindhearted

Q1 Why does the student visit the professor?
- Ⓐ He wants to give her his paper.
- Ⓑ He wants to apologize for being late to class.
- Ⓒ He needs help finding his car.
- Ⓓ He hopes to get some good advice.

Q2 Why does the professor mention the student's next paper?
- Ⓐ To tell the student its due date
- Ⓑ To assign the student a topic
- Ⓒ To explain what she will do
- Ⓓ To encourage the student to try harder

Listening Skills Linking

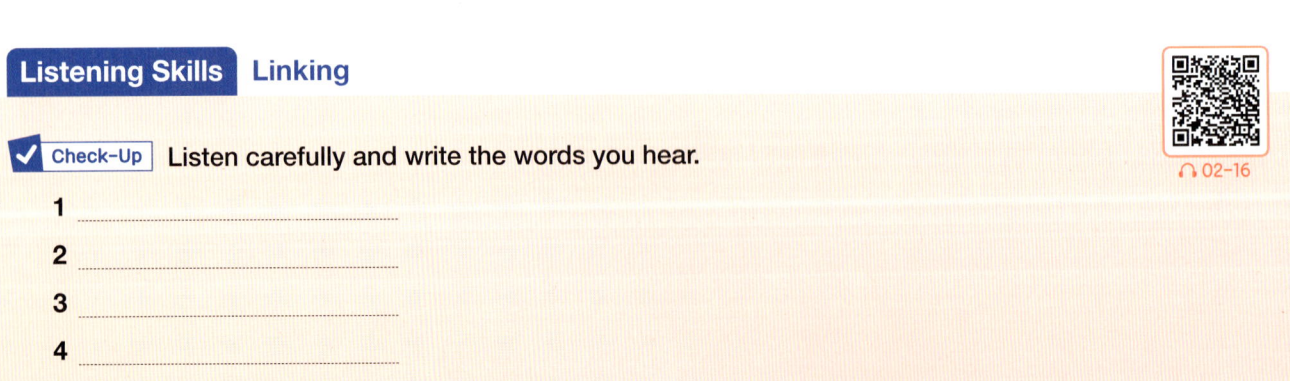

✓ Check-Up Listen carefully and write the words you hear.

1 _____
2 _____
3 _____
4 _____

• Exercise 8 •

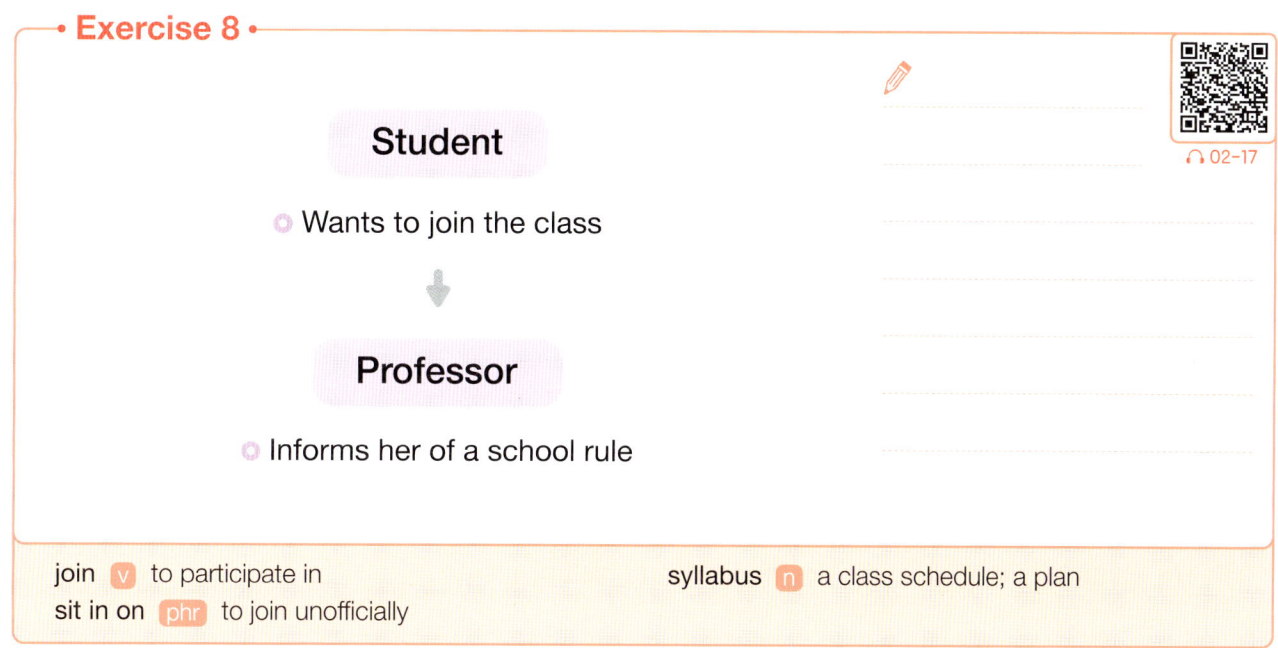

🎧 02-17

| join | v | to participate in | syllabus | n | a class schedule; a plan |
| sit in on | phr | to join unofficially | | | |

Q1 Why does the student visit the professor?
- Ⓐ She wants to interview him.
- Ⓑ She has a question about marine biology.
- Ⓒ She wants to attend his lectures.
- Ⓓ She does not understand the university rules.

Q2 Why does the professor explain the university rules?
- Ⓐ To say why the student cannot attend his lectures
- Ⓑ To state how he feels about them
- Ⓒ To question the university's role
- Ⓓ To prepare the student for the next semester

Listening Skills | Linking

✓ Check-Up | Listen carefully and write the words you hear.

🎧 02-18

1 _____
2 _____
3 _____
4 _____

Chapter ❷ 39

Vocabulary Review

A Circle the words that best complete the sentences.

1 The professor wants us to (join / free) the discussion.
2 Conner thinks his test score is (fail / fair).
3 Students must do their own (research / grade) without help.
4 (Essays / Students) are due on the teacher's desk by 5:00 PM.
5 He wants to (major in / write down) biology at his university.

B Choose the best words to complete the sentences.

1 Students should be able to _____ the two ideas.
   A believe
   B connect
   C search
   D deal

2 The teacher did not prepare a(n) _____ for the class.
   A lesser
   B principal
   C syllabus
   D author

3 An _____ is a good way to gain career experience.
   A understanding
   B accent
   C employer
   D internship

4 The school should pay for all of the _____ on the trip.
   A expenses
   B beverage
   C deliveries
   D parts

5 The _____ drove the injured person to the hospital.
   A train
   B ambulance
   C plane
   D ferry

C Choose the words with the closest meanings to the highlighted words.

1. Everyone thought the new movie was fascinating.
   - Ⓐ slow
   - Ⓑ interesting
   - Ⓒ boring
   - Ⓓ scary

2. We need to decide on a date for the meeting soon.
   - Ⓐ find
   - Ⓑ buy
   - Ⓒ choose
   - Ⓓ drive

3. The teacher gave the student a break and let him write an extra report.
   - Ⓐ chance
   - Ⓑ quit
   - Ⓒ class
   - Ⓓ visit

4. All of the students turned in their reports to the teacher.
   - Ⓐ wrote
   - Ⓑ showed
   - Ⓒ gave
   - Ⓓ saw

5. You must completely finish the test within the next thirty minutes.
   - Ⓐ possibly
   - Ⓑ barely
   - Ⓒ fairly
   - Ⓓ totally

D Complete the sentences by filling in the blanks with the best words from the list. Change the forms of the words if necessary. Use each word only once.

| sophomore | allow | moment | outstanding | note |

1. The work John did on the assignment was _____.
2. It can be hard to take _____ in some lecture classes.
3. We must wait for a(n) _____ until her friend arrives.
4. Martin decided to change his major as a(n) _____.
5. His parents _____ him to stay up late on the weekend.

Practice Test

1-3 Listen to part of a conversation between a student and a fitness center employee.

🎧 02-19

1   Why does the student visit the fitness center?

    A   To pay a late fee
    B   To sign up for it
    C   To ask about a job
    D   To look for a lost book

2   What does the student think of the fitness center map?

    A   It is hard to follow.
    B   It is not complete.
    C   It needs an upgrade.
    D   It is easy to understand.

3   What must the student leave a deposit for?

    A   An aerobics class
    B   A membership card
    C   A locker
    D   A workout uniform

CHAPTER

03

The History of English
(Focusing on Structure Words)

CHAPTER 3 The History of English (Focusing on Structure Words)

Understanding TOEFL Question Types & Listening Skills

1 Question Types — Detail Questions

Detail questions test your understanding of details and facts from the passage. They often support the main idea of the listening passage. However, you may be asked about some details which are not related to the main topic.

- **Example Detail Questions**
  - What is true about X?
  - According to the professor, who is X?
  - What is X?

- **Useful Tips for Your Success**
  - Focus on major points and check your notes for the right answers.
  - Never choose an answer just because it was mentioned in the conversation or lecture.

Sample Question

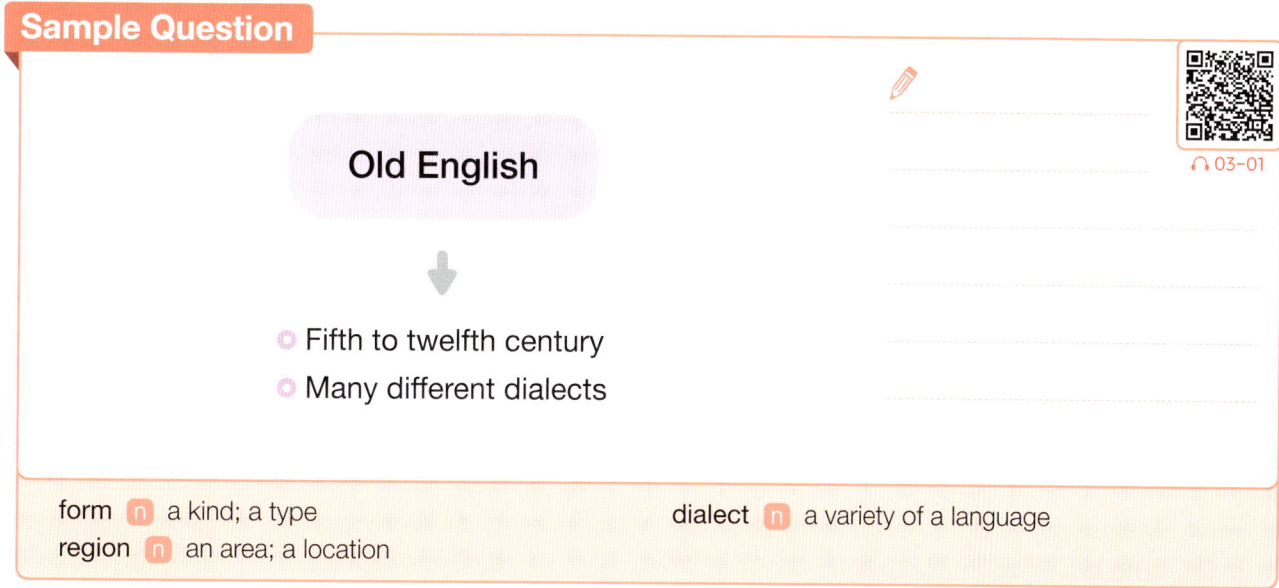

○ 03-01

Old English
- Fifth to twelfth century
- Many different dialects

form n a kind; a type
region n an area; a location
dialect n a variety of a language

Q What is true about Old English?

- Ⓐ It began in Germany.
- Ⓑ It started around the fifth century.
- Ⓒ People speak it today.
- Ⓓ People spoke it in the fifteenth century.

2 Listening Skills   Focusing on Structure Words

Structure words are all of the words in a sentence other than the nouns, the verbs, the adjectives, and the adverbs. They are pronouns, prepositions, conjunctions, be-verbs, and articles. They mostly indicate grammatical relations.

Check-Up

○ 03-02

▶ Listen carefully and underline the structure words.

1 It was an early form of the English language.
2 This was in England.
3 People spoke Old English according to their region.
4 There were four main kingdoms in England.

• **Exercise 1** •

William Caxton

⬇

○ Introduced the first printing press in England
○ Translated books into English

publish v to print a book
translator n a person who changes words to another language
access n a contact; an entry

Q1 Who was William Caxton?
   Ⓐ He was a teacher.
   Ⓑ He was a poet.
   Ⓒ He was a doctor.
   Ⓓ He was a printer.

Q2 According to the professor, what did William Caxton contribute to the English language?
   Ⓐ More words
   Ⓑ A more standard form
   Ⓒ The first magazine
   Ⓓ The first dictionary

Listening Skills Focusing on Structure Words

✓ **Check-Up** Listen carefully and underline the structure words.

1 He's in your textbook.
2 He was also a translator.
3 This was very important.
4 The language began to grow more quickly.

• **Exercise 2** •

Shakespeare
⬇
○ Formed new English words
○ Clichés: common expressions

🎧 03-05

colorful adj full of variety	**vanish** v to disappear; to go away
flesh n skin; the human body	

Q1 According to the professor, what did Shakespeare do?
- Ⓐ He created many dictionaries.
- Ⓑ He mixed other languages with English.
- Ⓒ He confused Latin with English.
- Ⓓ He made English simpler.

Q2 What is a cliché?
- Ⓐ Colorful language
- Ⓑ A work by Shakespeare
- Ⓒ An overused word or phrase
- Ⓓ A word Shakespeare created

Listening Skills Focusing on Structure Words

 Listen carefully and underline the structure words.

1 He also created new words that we continue to use today.
2 Pretty amazing, isn't it?
3 "Flesh and blood" is a cliché.
4 People after Shakespeare borrowed these terms.

🎧 03-06

• **Exercise 3** •

Scandinavian and Latin

↓

- Old Norse influenced early English
- Latin made English specialized

influence n the power of something to make changes
planet n Earth
specialized adj special; unique

🎧 03-07

Q1 According to the professor, what is true about Old English?
- Ⓐ It had two main influences.
- Ⓑ It began in Scandinavia.
- Ⓒ Latin was its main influence.
- Ⓓ It was not similar to Old Norse.

Q2 How did English become more detailed?
- Ⓐ Through the Norwegians
- Ⓑ From the Danish language
- Ⓒ Through Roman influence
- Ⓓ By developing on its own

Listening Skills | Focusing on Structure Words

✓ **Check-Up** | Listen carefully and underline the structure words.

1 These were the Scandinavian influence and the Latin language.
2 They brought their native language with them.
3 They were both Germanic languages.
4 These words allowed English later to become more specialized and specific.

🎧 03-08

• Exercise 4 •

American English

⬇

○ Influenced by Indians / European languages
○ Different dialects in the North and the South

outline v to explain the basics of something	**develop** v to grow; to become more mature
shape v to form; to outline	

Q1 What influenced American English?

- Ⓐ Jamestown
- Ⓑ European languages
- Ⓒ The southern states
- Ⓓ The Civil War

Q2 What is true about American English?

- Ⓐ It has many different varieties.
- Ⓑ It is the same as British English.
- Ⓒ It has the largest vocabulary.
- Ⓓ It began as pidgin English.

Listening Skills   Focusing on Structure Words

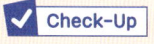 **Check-Up** Listen carefully and underline the structure words.

1 Let me outline it for you.

2 Other European languages took hold on American soil.

3 Different dialects of English began to develop in America.

4 It's true.

• **Exercise 5** •

> **The *Oxford English Dictionary***
>
> ↓
>
> ○ The most comprehensive English dictionary
> ○ Readers sent in words by mail
> ○ Continues to grow

🎧 03-11

comprehensive *adj* full; whole; complete   **emphasis** *n* importance
sophisticated *adj* advanced

Q1 What is the *OED*?

ⓐ A play
ⓑ A style of English
ⓒ A slang word
ⓓ A dictionary

Q2 According to the professor, about how many words does the *OED* have?

ⓐ More than 600 million
ⓑ About 620
ⓒ Around 620,000
ⓓ More than one million

Listening Skills Focusing on Structure Words

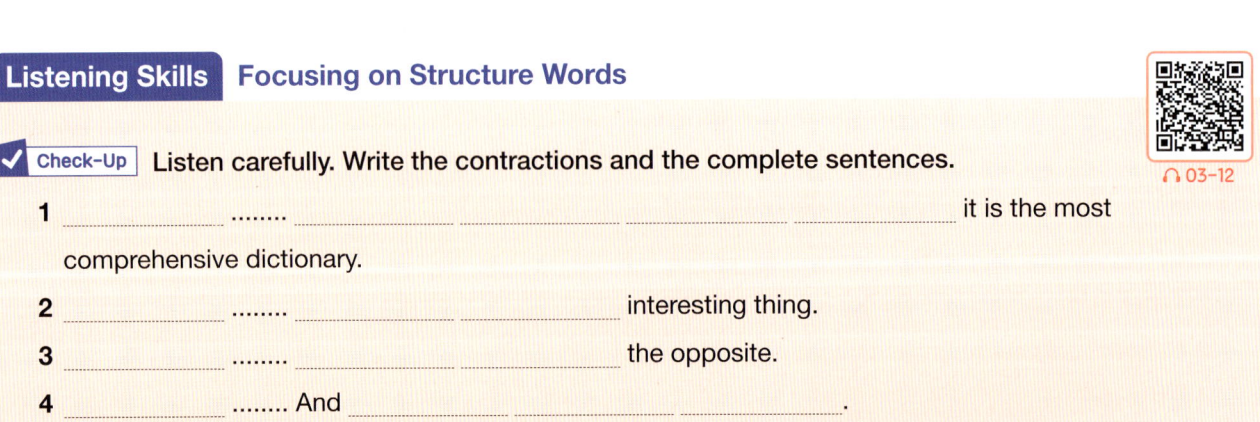

✓ **Check-Up** Listen carefully. Write the contractions and the complete sentences.

1 _____ .... _____ it is the most comprehensive dictionary.

2 _____ .... _____ interesting thing.

3 _____ .... _____ the opposite.

4 _____ .... And _____ .

🎧 03-12

52

• Exercise 6 •

Modern English Influences

- A need for a standard form
- Samuel Johnson and Noah Webster
- World wars and radio / TV

standard `adj` regular; accepted
establish `v` to make; to create
contribute `v` to add; to donate

Q1 Who created one of the first English dictionaries?
- Ⓐ Samuel Johnson
- Ⓑ Noah Webster
- Ⓒ An American university
- Ⓓ A British schoolteacher

Q2 What helped standardize English in the twentieth century?
- Ⓐ Samuel Johnson
- Ⓑ Radio and television
- Ⓒ Harvard University
- Ⓓ The American Revolution

Listening Skills Focusing on Structure Words

 Listen carefully and underline the structure words.

1 Two men helped change this.
2 I'm sure all of you are familiar with Webster.
3 It helped unite European countries with one another.
4 Radio and television contributed to the creation of the most standardized form of English.

• **Exercise 7** •

The British Empire

⬇

- Spread English worldwide
- Wealth and power
- Separation of classes in some countries

---

in a sense *phr* to an extent
wealth *n* money; riches
legacy *n* a tradition; an inheritance

Q1 What helped English spread so quickly?
- Ⓐ Its simplicity
- Ⓑ The British Empire
- Ⓒ Radio
- Ⓓ The Industrial Revolution

Q2 What is true about English in countries like India?
- Ⓐ It is difficult to study.
- Ⓑ It separates classes of people.
- Ⓒ Few people speak the language.
- Ⓓ The poor are beginning to learn English.

Listening Skills | **Focusing on Structure Words**

✓ **Check-Up** Listen carefully. Write the contractions and the complete sentences.

1 _____ .... _____ in history a little.
2 _____ .... _____ .
3 _____ .... _____ , isn't it?
4 _____ .... _____ of the British Empire.

• **Exercise 8** •

Loanwords

⬇

- Many words in English borrowed from other languages
- Ballet = loanword from French
- Sushi = loanword from Japanese

scholar n a person who studies something in depth   **exist** v to be
estimate v to guess; to assume

Q1 According to the professor, about how many words does the English language have?
- Ⓐ 20,000
- Ⓑ 42,000
- Ⓒ 500,000
- Ⓓ 1,000,000

Q2 What is true about loanwords?
- Ⓐ They have new pronunciations in English.
- Ⓑ They come from other languages.
- Ⓒ They are difficult for people to remember.
- Ⓓ They are not considered English words.

Listening Skills   Focusing on Structure Words

Check-Up Listen carefully. Write the contractions and the complete sentences.

1 _____ .... _____ happens.
2 _____ .... _____ _____ from French.
3 _____ .... But everyone thinks _____ .
4 _____ .... Impressive, _____ ?

Vocabulary Review

A Circle the words that best complete the sentences.

1 The camera needs a (specialized / broken) lens to work.
2 Jessie's beautiful garden has many (colorful / dirty) flowers.
3 He knows many languages, so he wants to be a(n) (translator / artist).
4 People speak hundreds of different (dictionaries / dialects) there.
5 Please (outline / unite) your plan for the festival.

B Choose the best words to complete the sentences.

1 The young boy is _____, so he will enter university early.
   A dull
   B intellectual
   C fascinated
   D average

2 The girls want to _____ a new music club on campus.
   A establish
   B delay
   C find
   D require

3 The expert _____ it will take one week to finish the work.
   A shapes
   B helps
   C estimates
   D describes

4 The professor placed a great _____ on Egypt during the class.
   A money
   B emphasis
   C humor
   D enjoyment

5 It can take more a _____ to make buildings like cathedrals.
   A kingdom
   B region
   C century
   D dialect

C Choose the words with the closest meanings to the highlighted words.

1. Wolves live in the coldest region of the country.
   - Ⓐ way
   - Ⓑ part
   - Ⓒ pack
   - Ⓓ purchase

2. The children saw the ghost vanish in the forest.
   - Ⓐ run
   - Ⓑ speak
   - Ⓒ disappear
   - Ⓓ float

3. There are many planets in the universe.
   - Ⓐ worlds
   - Ⓑ space
   - Ⓒ cosmos
   - Ⓓ moons

4. The artist shapes the clay with her hands.
   - Ⓐ wets
   - Ⓑ forms
   - Ⓒ removes
   - Ⓓ bakes

5. The professor wants her students to contribute to the lecture.
   - Ⓐ add
   - Ⓑ leave
   - Ⓒ combine
   - Ⓓ study

D Complete the sentences by filling in the blanks with the best words from the list. Change the forms of the words if necessary. Use each word only once.

| borrow | standard | wealth | comprehensive | access |

1. The _____ documentary about Rome discussed everything.
2. We can gain _____ to the website by paying ten dollars.
3. He gave his _____ response when asked about his early life.
4. Many languages _____ words from other languages.
5. Many people gain _____ by simply saving their money.

Chapter ❸ 57

Practice Test

1-4 Listen to part of a lecture in a literature class.

Literature

1. What aspect of *Beowulf* does the professor mainly discuss?
   - Ⓐ What happens in it
   - Ⓑ Who wrote it
   - Ⓒ Who discovered it
   - Ⓓ Why it is a heroic poem

2. What can be inferred about *Beowulf*?
   - Ⓐ It is the most popular English poem.
   - Ⓑ There are many original texts.
   - Ⓒ The story changed as people retold it.
   - Ⓓ It is a love story.

3. What does the professor think of *Beowulf*?
   - Ⓐ It is overrated.
   - Ⓑ It is not influential.
   - Ⓒ It is incredible.
   - Ⓓ It is too old to understand.

4. Why does the professor mention the oral tradition?
   - Ⓐ To show that singing is important in the poem
   - Ⓑ To note how people passed the story on
   - Ⓒ To contrast *Beowulf* with other poems
   - Ⓓ To suggest that *Beowulf* is a work of nonfiction

CHAPTER

04

Service Encounters
(Chunking)

CHAPTER 4 Service Encounters (Chunking)

Understanding TOEFL Question Types & Listening Skills

1 Question Types — Understanding Function of What Is Said Questions

Understanding Function of What Is Said questions test your understanding of what the speaker is really saying or asking about. It tests your knowledge of the speaker's intention, not simply the statement the person makes.

- **Example Understanding Function of What Is Said Questions**
  - What does the professor imply when he says this: (replay)
  - Why does the student say this: (replay)
  - What is the purpose of the student's response: (replay)

- **Useful Tips for Your Success**
  - What the speaker says and what the speaker really means may be different.
  - Pay close attention to the overall gist of the dialogue.

Sample Question

Student	○ Needs to find the Registrar's office
↓	
Employee	○ Tells her the location

🎧 04-01

junior n a third-year university student
transcript n a record of a student's official grades
hall n a college or university building where students live

Q Why does the student say this: "Yes, um . . . no . . . Well, I'm not sure."

Ⓐ She is unsure about her transcript.
Ⓑ She does not know where Keller Hall is.
Ⓒ She does not know where the admissions office is.
Ⓓ She thinks she could be a junior or senior.

2 Listening Skills   Chunking

Chunking is a way of sorting and organizing information. One way to signal the end of a thought group is to make a pause. A pause gives listeners time to understand what a person just said.

Check-Up

▶ Listen to the sentences and put / marks to divide the sentences into chunks.

1 You look a bit lost.
2 Are you a new student?
3 Where's the Registrar's office?
4 I live in Keller.

🎧 04-02

Exercise 1

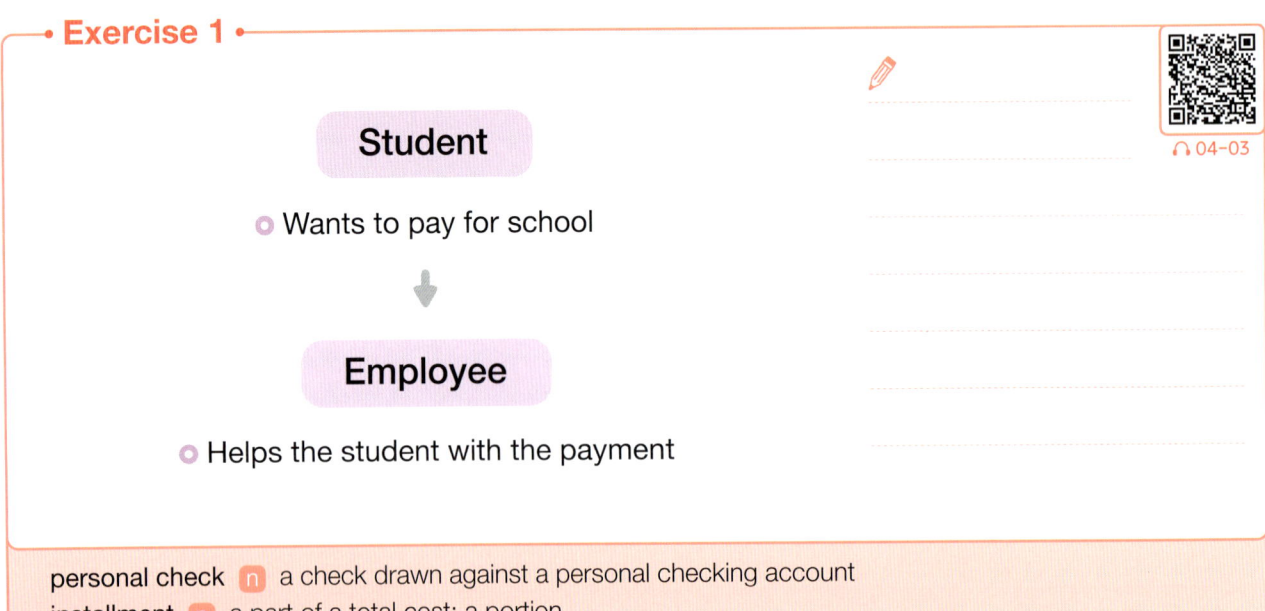

🎧 04-03

Student
- Wants to pay for school

⬇

Employee
- Helps the student with the payment

personal check (n) a check drawn against a personal checking account
installment (n) a part of a total cost; a portion

Q1 Why does the employee say this: "It's okay. I just need your student number."

- Ⓐ The student does not know his number.
- Ⓑ The student does not need to give his name.
- Ⓒ The student lost his ID card.
- Ⓓ The student needs to find a check.

Q2 What can be inferred from the student's response to the employee: "So no personal checks, huh?"

- Ⓐ He prefers to pay at a later date.
- Ⓑ He thinks the fee is very expensive.
- Ⓒ He would rather pay with a check.
- Ⓓ He does not have a credit card.

Listening Skills | Chunking

🎧 04-04

✓ **Check-Up** Listen to the sentences and put / marks to divide the sentences into chunks.

1 I need to pay my tuition, please.
2 What are my options?
3 What's the total, please?
4 Then I guess I'll just pay half of it today.

• **Exercise 2** •

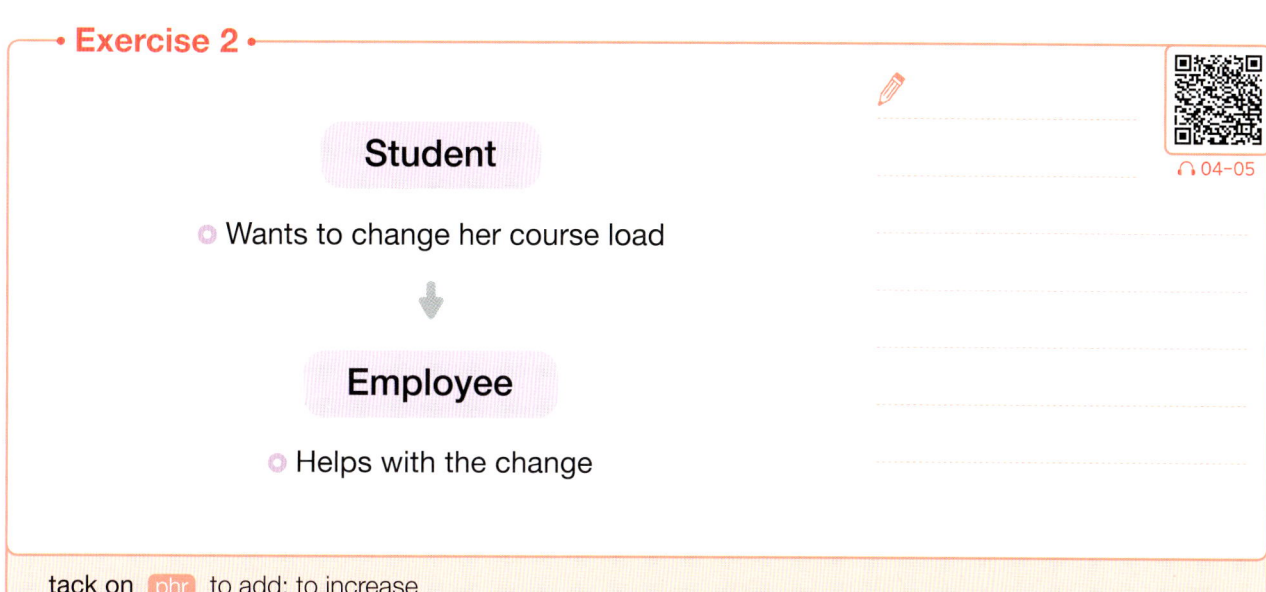

tack on phr to add; to increase

Q1 Why does the student say this: "I'm overloaded."
- Ⓐ She needs some money back.
- Ⓑ She can't carry all of her books.
- Ⓒ She has too much work to do.
- Ⓓ She cannot pay for everything.

Q2 What does the student imply when she says this: "It's killing me."
- Ⓐ She cannot do all of her homework.
- Ⓑ She has a terrible headache.
- Ⓒ The cost of school is too much for her.
- Ⓓ Her chemistry tests are too hard.

 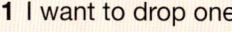 Listen to the sentences and put / marks to divide the sentences into chunks.

1 I want to drop one.
2 I get a refund, right?
3 I don't need it right now.
4 No more chemistry for you.

Chapter ❹   65

• **Exercise 3** •

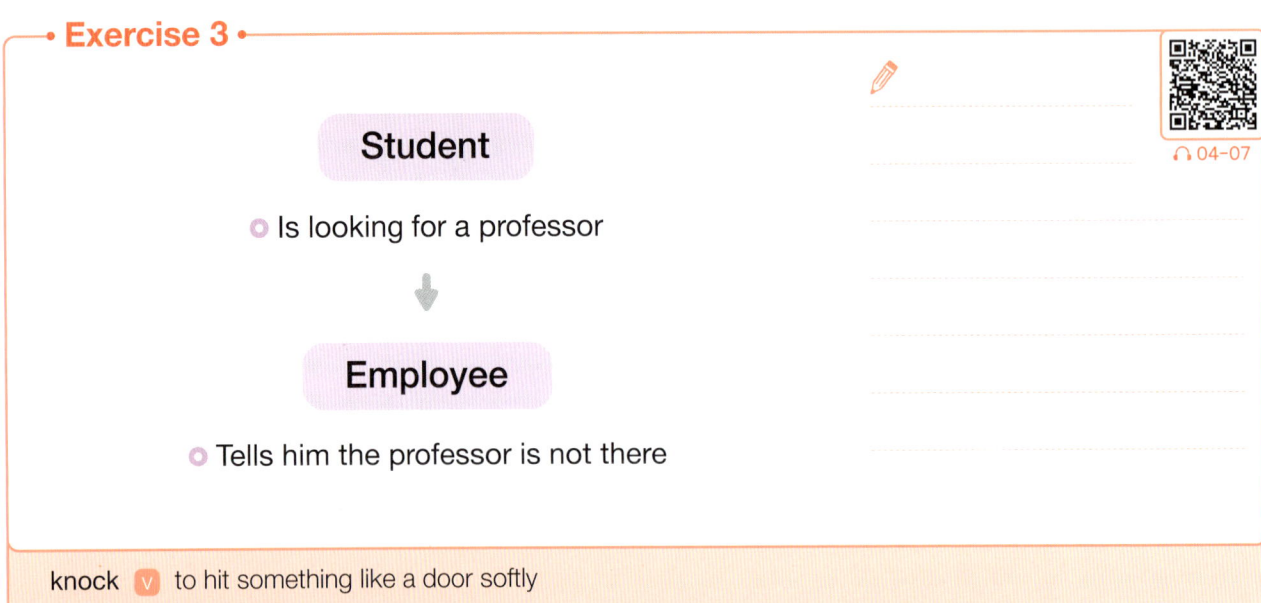

| knock | v | to hit something like a door softly |
| remember | v | to think of again; to recall |

Q1 What does the student imply when he says this: "I already went there."

 Ⓐ He could not find the professor's office.
 Ⓑ He will visit the office in a moment.
 Ⓒ He is pleased with the woman's response.
 Ⓓ Professor Matzek is not in his office.

Q2 Why does the student say this: "Oh, that's too bad."

 Ⓐ To criticize the woman
 Ⓑ To show his disappointment
 Ⓒ To complain about a class
 Ⓓ To ask the woman for advice

Listening Skills   Chunking

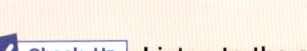 Listen to the sentences and put / marks to divide the sentences into chunks.

1 I'm looking for Professor Matzek.
2 I'm a student in one of his classes.
3 So that's why I came here.
4 Please come back tomorrow morning.

• **Exercise 4** •

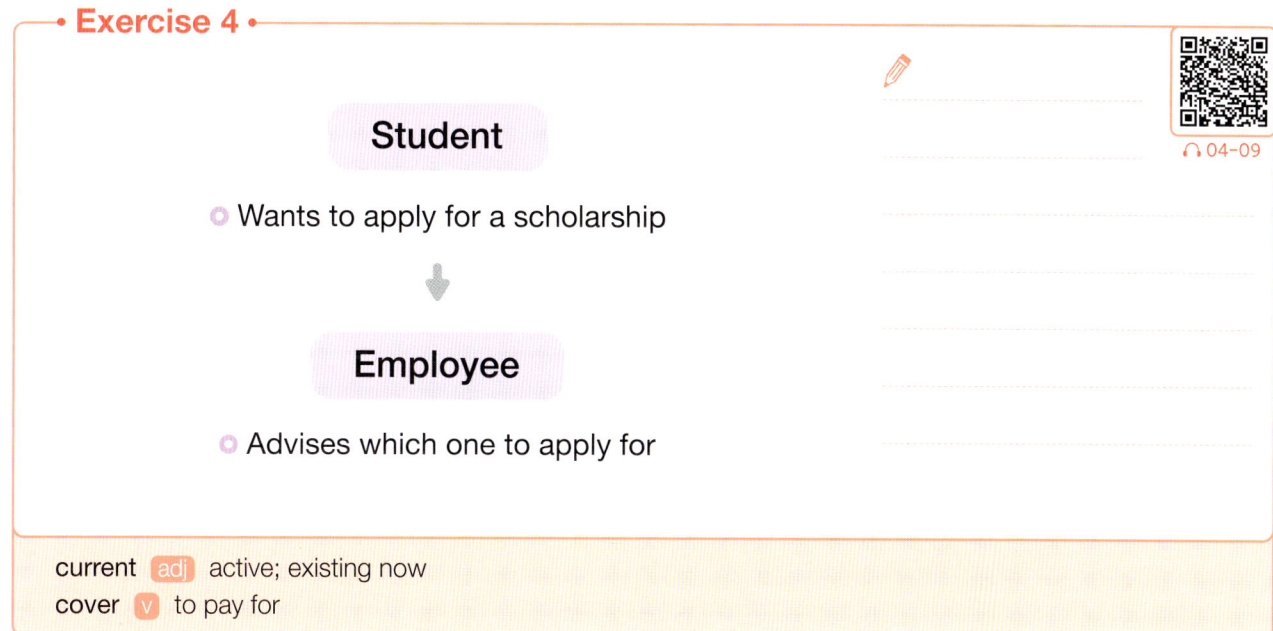

🎧 04-09

current adj active; existing now
cover v to pay for

Q1 Why does the student say this: "High school? Gosh."

  Ⓐ She did well in high school.
  Ⓑ She misses her friends.
  Ⓒ She thinks she looks older.
  Ⓓ She got a scholarship in high school.

Q2 What does the student imply when she says this: "But it only pays for my books and dorm room."

  Ⓐ She is happy with her scholarship.
  Ⓑ She does not have a full scholarship.
  Ⓒ Her scholarship covers tuition.
  Ⓓ Her books and dorm fee are cheap.

Listening Skills Chunking

 **Check-Up** Listen to the sentences and put / marks to divide the sentences into chunks.

🎧 04-10

1 Are you a current student, or are you still in high school?
2 Anyway, I'm a junior.
3 I have a swimming scholarship.
4 Just fill out this form and bring it back to me.

• **Exercise 5** •

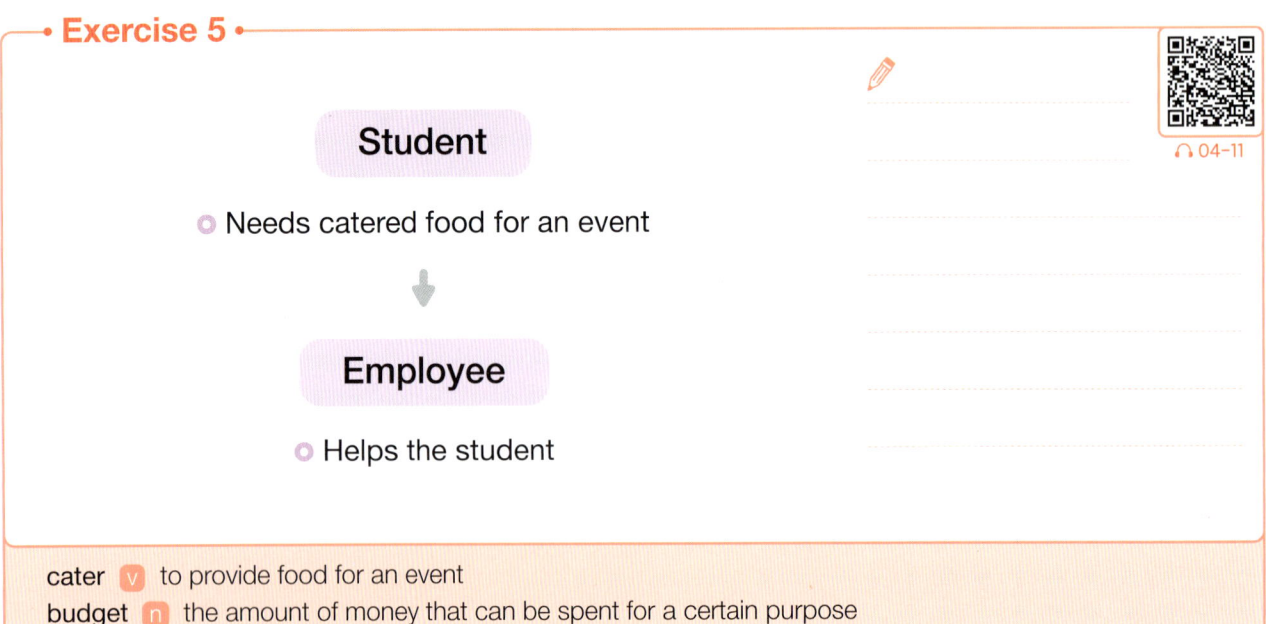

cater v to provide food for an event
budget n the amount of money that can be spent for a certain purpose

Q1 What does the student imply when she says this: "Sandwiches will probably be best."

Ⓐ She does not have much money to spend.
Ⓑ She enjoys eating sandwiches for lunch.
Ⓒ She is not interested in the food choices.
Ⓓ She does not have time to cook any food.

Q2 Why does the student say this: "What a relief."

Ⓐ To ask another question
Ⓑ To prove she has enough money
Ⓒ To show she is concerned
Ⓓ To express her happiness

Listening Skills **Chunking**

✓ Check-Up   Listen to the sentences and put / marks to divide the sentences into chunks.

1 How may I be of assistance?
2 What kind of event do you have?
3 Sandwiches will probably be best.
4 The event isn't for three weeks.

• **Exercise 6** •

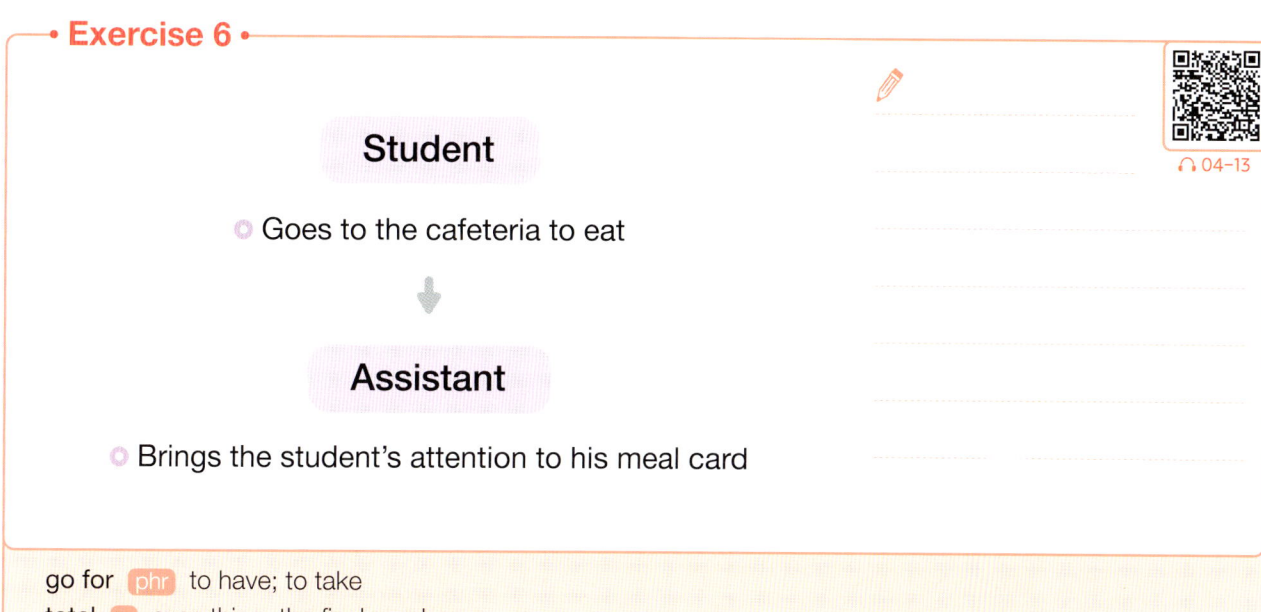

go for **phr** to have; to take
total **n** everything; the final number

Q1 What does the assistant imply when she says this: "You can only add them by the week or month."

Ⓐ Paying by the week is cheaper than by the month.
Ⓑ The student cannot pay day by day.
Ⓒ The student should get a monthly plan.
Ⓓ It is cheaper to add meals by the month.

Q2 What does the student imply when he says this: "Let's make it one week. I don't have that much right now."

Ⓐ He did not realize a price would be so expensive.
Ⓑ He needs to borrow money from a friend.
Ⓒ He only has 128 dollars right now.
Ⓓ He cannot believe the increase in a price.

Listening Skills Chunking

 Listen to the sentences and put / marks to divide the sentences into chunks.

1 You only have one meal left on this card.
2 So that will be sixty-four dollars.
3 Can I help you with anything else?
4 Thanks for everything.

Exercise 7

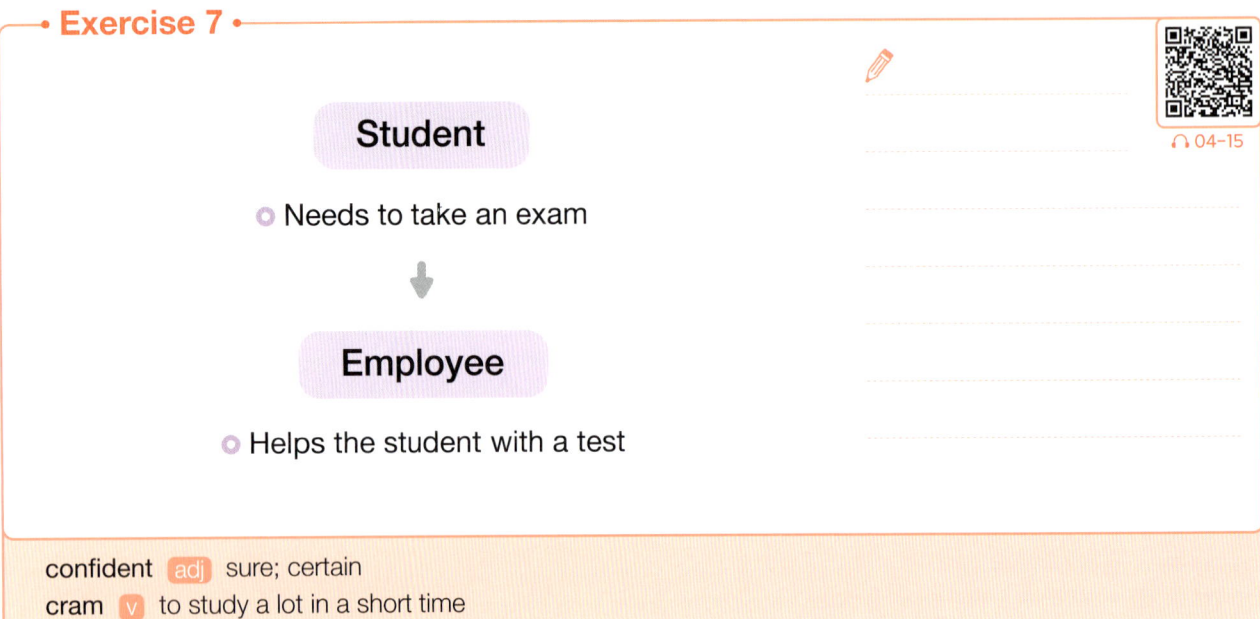

🎧 04-15

Student
- Needs to take an exam
  ↓
Employee
- Helps the student with a test

confident *adj* sure; certain
cram *v* to study a lot in a short time

Q1 What does the student imply when she says this: "A computer?"
- Ⓐ She forgot her computer.
- Ⓑ She does not like math tests.
- Ⓒ She is surprised the test is on a computer.
- Ⓓ She needs her test score.

Q2 What does the employee imply when he says this: "Remember that you can take as long as you like."
- Ⓐ The test has no time limit.
- Ⓑ The student should hurry up.
- Ⓒ The student can finish the test quickly.
- Ⓓ The test has many questions.

Listening Skills Chunking

🎧 04-16

✓ **Check-Up** Listen to the sentences and put / marks to divide the sentences into chunks.

1 When do I get my score?
2 All freshmen math tests are on them.
3 You are in room number two.
4 But most students only require about two hours.

70

• **Exercise 8** •

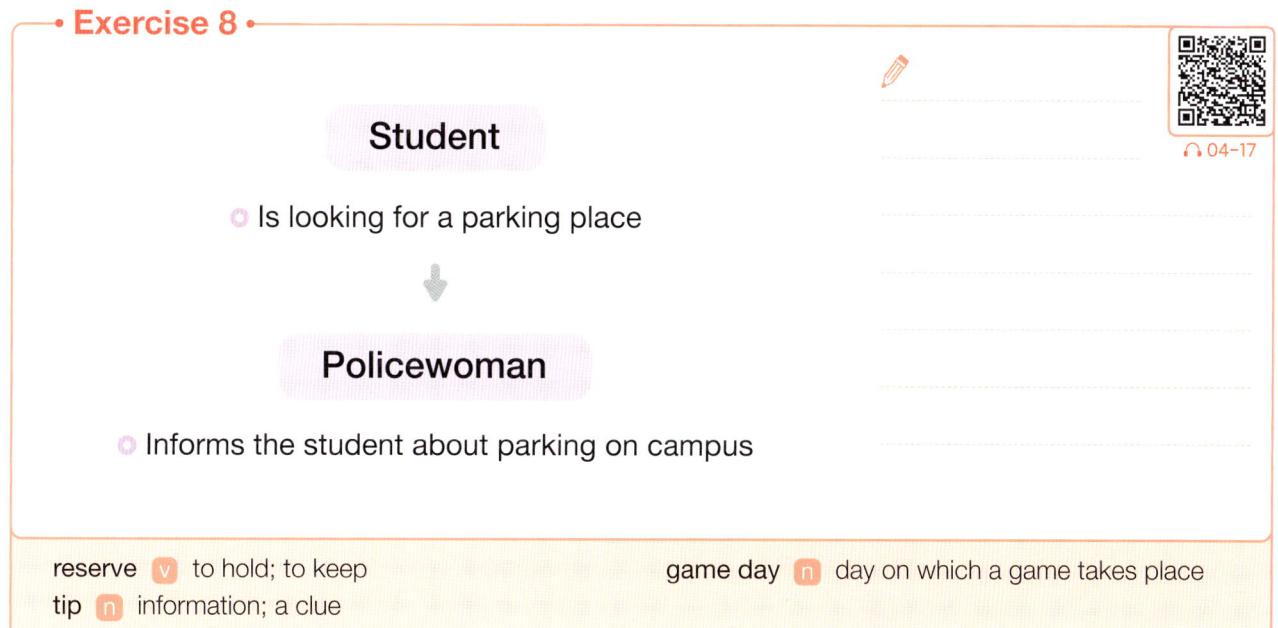

| reserve v to hold; to keep | game day n day on which a game takes place |
| tip n information; a clue | |

Q1 What can be inferred from the policewoman's response to the student: "Don't worry about it. Many people make the same mistake."

- Ⓐ The student is in trouble.
- Ⓑ Everyone parks in a certain spot.
- Ⓒ It happens to lots of people.
- Ⓓ The student should worry.

Q2 What does the policewoman imply when she says this: "If it's full, park at the football stadium."

- Ⓐ The stadium is usually full.
- Ⓑ There are many parking places at the stadium.
- Ⓒ Students can park at the stadium on game day.
- Ⓓ Football stadium parking requires a sticker.

Listening Skills | **Chunking**

✓ **Check-Up** Listen to the sentences and put / marks to divide the sentences into chunks.

1 I'm sorry, but you can't park here.
2 Do I need a sticker for this parking lot?
3 There is a lot behind the library.
4 Well, on any day but a game day.

Vocabulary Review

A Circle the words that best complete the sentences.

1 Devin gave us a lot of good study (tips / reasons).
2 Heather was very (broken / confident), and she got an A+.
3 For lunch, I'll (apply for / go for) two slices of pepperoni pizza.
4 Be sure to (knock / provide) on the door before you enter.
5 They are (current / reserved) members of the health club.

B Choose the best words to complete the sentences.

1 That woman over there is in need of some _____.

  A assistance
  B options
  C budge
  D events

2 Mrs. Adams' son will be a(n) _____ in college this year.

  A English
  B graduate
  C scholarship
  D junior

3 The restaurant will _____ a dinner for fifty people at the school.

  A welcome
  B cater
  C decide
  D tell

4 He wants to get a _____ when he returns the item.

  A refund
  B total
  C tuition
  D service

5 You may _____ one class by the end of this month.

  A practice
  B bet
  C read
  D drop

C Choose the words with the closest meanings to the highlighted words.

1. There will be a big banquet for all of the seniors in the department.
   - A sporting event
   - B dinner party
   - C show
   - D movie

2. So many students cram the night before a big test.
   - A study
   - B relax
   - C remain
   - D create

3. The hostess will reserve a table for us.
   - A keep
   - B release
   - C make
   - D find

4. The theater requires everyone to turn off their smartphones.
   - A questions
   - B asks
   - C sends
   - D treats

5. Sometimes the bookstore tacks on extra charges.
   - A pastes
   - B follows
   - C adds
   - D discounts

D Complete the sentences by filling in the blanks with the best words from the list. Change the forms of the words if necessary. Use each word only once.

| budget | game day | installment | personal check | transcript |

1. Most schools charge a fee for _____.
2. There is not much money left in the _____.
3. Lots of students get excited on _____.
4. The restaurant no longer accepts _____.
5. Customers can pay for the sofa in _____.

Practice Test

1-3 Listen to part of a conversation between a student and a bookstore employee.

1 Why does the student visit the college bookstore?

    A To purchase a book
    B To sell a book
    C To meet a friend
    D To look for a professor

2 How does the employee find the correct textbook?

    A By using the class number
    B By using the professor's name
    C By using the help of Dr. Zephyr
    D By using the name of the author

3 Why does the student say this: "That's a bit steep, isn't it?"

    A She thinks the books are too heavy.
    B It is difficult to find a chemistry book.
    C She believes a textbook is expensive.
    D The clerk is not being very helpful.

CHAPTER

05

Office Hours

(Pitch and Intonation)

CHAPTER 5 Office Hours (Pitch and Intonation)

Understanding TOEFL Question Types & Listening Skills

1 Question Types — Understanding Speaker's Attitude Questions

Understanding Speaker's Attitude questions test how well you understand the attitude or opinion of the speaker. Usually, they are concerned with how the speaker feels or why the speaker is expressing him or herself in a certain way.

- **Example Understanding Speaker's Attitude Questions**
  - What can be inferred about the student?
  - What does the woman mean when she says this: (replay)
  - What is the professor's opinion of the student?

- **Useful Tips for Your Success**
  - Pay attention to the speaker's tone of voice.
  - Pay attention to the speaker's general attitude during the talk.

Sample Question

Student
- Listens to the professor's idea

↓

Professor
- Asks the student about graduate school

05-01

| ace it | phr | to get a perfect score |
| josh | v | to joke with; to trick |

Q What does the professor think about the student?

Ⓐ He should try harder.
Ⓑ He would do well in graduate school.
Ⓒ He does not study for tests.
Ⓓ He is very generous.

2 Listening Skills — Pitch and Intonation

Pitch and intonation are the way that your voice rises and falls as you speak. A fall in pitch helps listeners recognize the end of a thought group. However, a question may end with a rising or falling pitch.

Check-Up

▶ Listen to the following dialogue and underline the high-pitched words.

Student: I hope it is not about the midterm exam.
Professor: Oh, no. Actually, you aced it.
Student: That's wonderful.
Professor: I have a question.

05-02

Chapter ❺ 79

• **Exercise 1** •

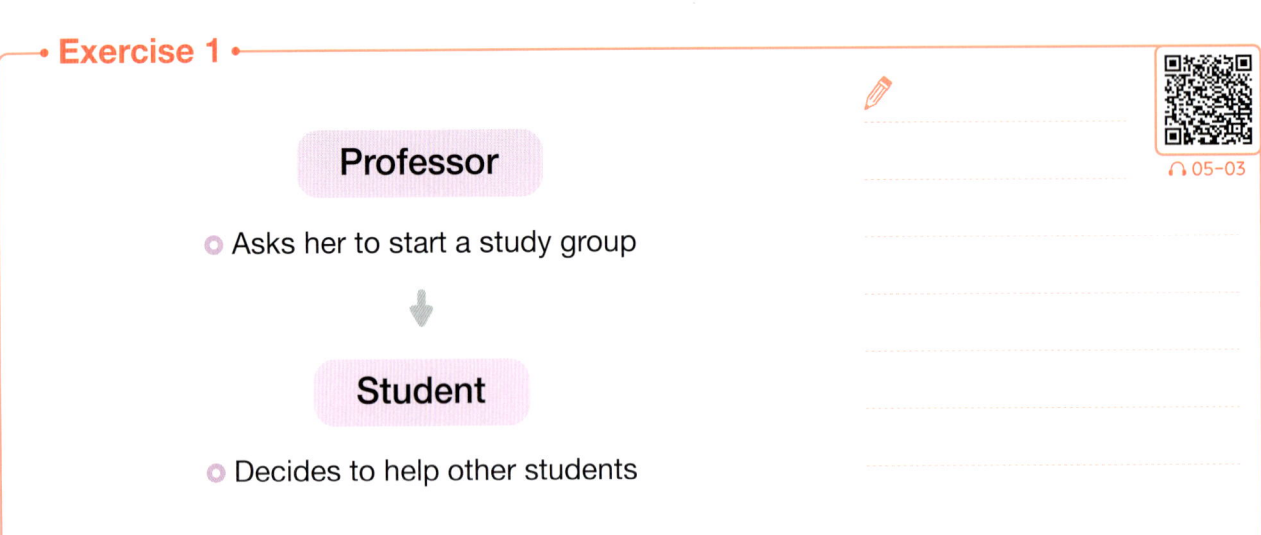

🎧 05-03

| intricate | adj | complex; difficult |
| full plate | phr | a busy schedule |

Q1 What is the student's opinion of the professor?
- Ⓐ He is stubborn.
- Ⓑ She likes his lectures.
- Ⓒ She thinks he is fair.
- Ⓓ He teaches too much.

Q2 What can be inferred about the professor?
- Ⓐ He trusts the student.
- Ⓑ He does not believe the student.
- Ⓒ He thinks the student is lazy.
- Ⓓ He enjoys tutoring students.

Listening Skills Pitch and Intonation

 Listen to the following dialogue and underline the high-pitched words.

Professor: Great. How is your semester going?

Student: Quite well. Is there a problem?

Professor: Well, yes and no.

Student: I see.

🎧 05-04

• **Exercise 2** •

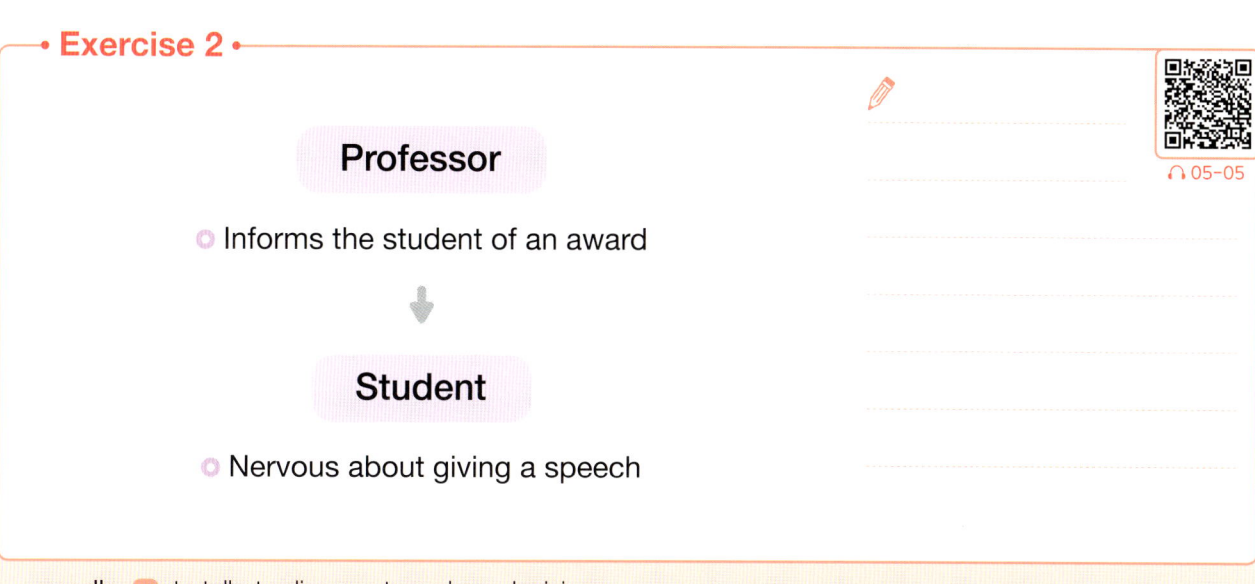

Professor
- Informs the student of an award

Student
- Nervous about giving a speech

noodle v to talk; to discuss; to make a decision
ecstatic adj thrilled; happy

Q1 What does the student mean when he says this: "Um, did I do something?"
- Ⓐ He is confused.
- Ⓑ He is disappointed.
- Ⓒ He made a mistake.
- Ⓓ He is very careless.

Q2 What can be inferred about the student?
- Ⓐ He does not work as hard as he should.
- Ⓑ He needs to improve his writing.
- Ⓒ He is shy in front of big crowds.
- Ⓓ He does not want the award.

Listening Skills Pitch and Intonation

✓ Check-Up Listen to the following dialogue and underline the high-pitched words.

Student: I mean, I'm ecstatic about it, but . . .
Professor: But what?
Student: I'm not very good in front of big audiences.
Professor: Oh, you'll do fine.

Chapter ❺ 81

Exercise 3

Student
- Wants the professor's help

↓

Professor
- Makes an appointment for later

recognize *v* to identify; to know
customary *adj* usual; common

Q1 What can be inferred about the student when she says this: "I like to get a head start."
- Ⓐ She waits until the last minute to write papers.
- Ⓑ She is the top student in the class.
- Ⓒ She plans her school work well.
- Ⓓ She is starting a study group.

Q2 What does the professor mean when he says this: "That's not too customary these days."
- Ⓐ Most students are not competitive.
- Ⓑ Some students visit him these days.
- Ⓒ Few students start their essays early.
- Ⓓ All students should prepare better.

Listening Skills | Pitch and Intonation

✓ Check-Up Listen to the following dialogue and underline the high-pitched words.

Student: Can you look at it now?

Professor: Can you come to my office at 3:00 PM?

Student: I'll be there. Thanks so much.

Professor: I'll see you at three then.

• **Exercise 4** •

Professor
○ Tells the student about a summer job

⬇

Student
○ Is interested in the position

translate v to change from one language to another
set up v to arrange; to schedule

Q1 What can be inferred about the student?

- Ⓐ He is majoring in Italian.
- Ⓑ He wants to take the professor's class.
- Ⓒ He is interested in the summer job.
- Ⓓ He is going to attend a class soon.

Q2 What does the student mean when he says this: "I lived there for six years when I was younger."

- Ⓐ He often returns to Italy.
- Ⓑ He loved living in Italy.
- Ⓒ His family comes from Italy.
- Ⓓ He is able to speak Italian.

Listening Skills Pitch and Intonation

✓ **Check-Up** Listen to the following dialogue and underline the high-pitched words.

Professor: Marty, could I speak with you for a moment, please?
Student: Sure, Professor Watson. What can I do for you?
Professor: Are you still looking for a job for the summer?
Student: Yes, I am. I haven't had any luck so far though.

• **Exercise 5** •

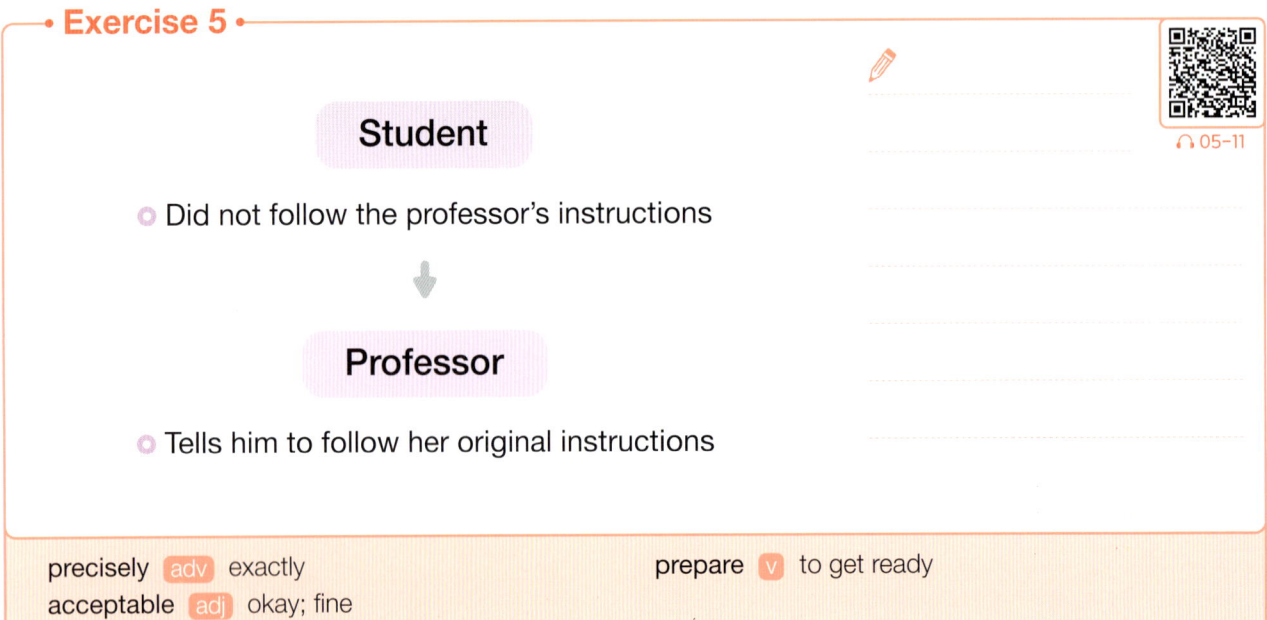

| precisely adv exactly | prepare v to get ready |
| acceptable adj okay; fine | |

05-11

Q1 What can be inferred about the professor?
- Ⓐ She is not happy with the student.
- Ⓑ She approves of the student's presentation.
- Ⓒ She accepts the student's proposal.
- Ⓓ She is the student's advisor.

Q2 What does the professor mean when she says this: "This is not a matter for discussion."
- Ⓐ She wants the student to listen better.
- Ⓑ She does not have time to talk now.
- Ⓒ The student should not talk so much in class.
- Ⓓ The student cannot change the topic.

Listening Skills Pitch and Intonation

✓ Check-Up   Listen to the following dialogue and underline the high-pitched words.

Student: Are you sure I can't keep this topic?

Professor: This is not a matter for discussion.

Student: Okay, but, uh . . . Today is Tuesday. Friday is just three days away.

Professor: Right.

05-12

• **Exercise 6** •

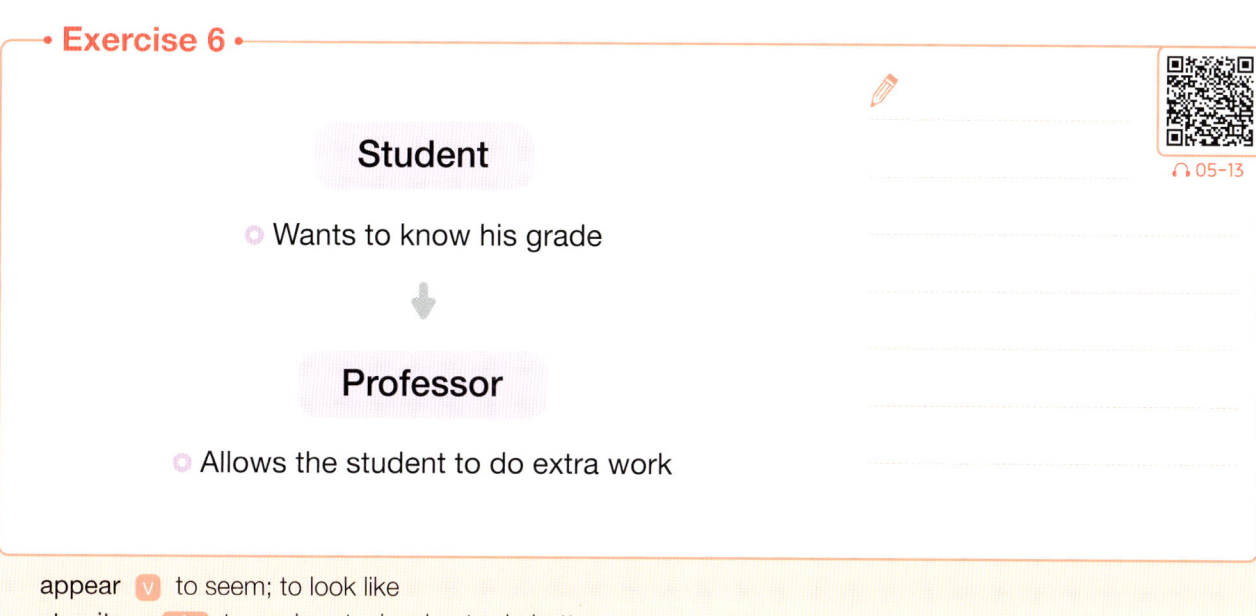

🎧 05-13

Student
○ Wants to know his grade

⬇

Professor
○ Allows the student to do extra work

appear v to seem; to look like
step it up phr to work or try harder; to do better

Q1 What can be inferred about the professor?
- Ⓐ She is very strict.
- Ⓑ She is forgetful.
- Ⓒ She is generous.
- Ⓓ She is very old.

Q2 What is the student's opinion of the professor?
- Ⓐ He thinks she is too demanding.
- Ⓑ He thinks she does not care much about students.
- Ⓒ He believes the professor only cares about tests.
- Ⓓ He thinks she is fair.

Listening Skills Pitch and Intonation

 **Check-Up** Listen to the following dialogue and underline the high-pitched words.

Professor: Your average is about an eighty-eight.
Student: Really? That would be great.
Professor: Give me a four-page paper by Wednesday.
Student: What's the topic?

🎧 05-14

Chapter ❺ 85

• Exercise 7 •

Student
- Cannot find her textbook

⬇

Professor
- Opens the classroom for the student

relief n comfort; ease
run v to hurry

Q1 What does the professor mean when he says this: "I bet it is still there."

Ⓐ Nobody took the book.
Ⓑ He likes to gamble.
Ⓒ The door was not locked.
Ⓓ They must wait for a key.

Q2 What is the professor's opinion of the student?

Ⓐ She is trustworthy.
Ⓑ She is forgetful.
Ⓒ She is diligent.
Ⓓ She is his favorite.

Listening Skills Pitch and Intonation

✓ **Check-Up** Listen to the following dialogue and underline the high-pitched words.

Student: Actually, I'm coming to see you.
Professor: I have class in ten minutes.
Student: This won't take long.
Professor: Okay. What's going on?

• **Exercise 8** •

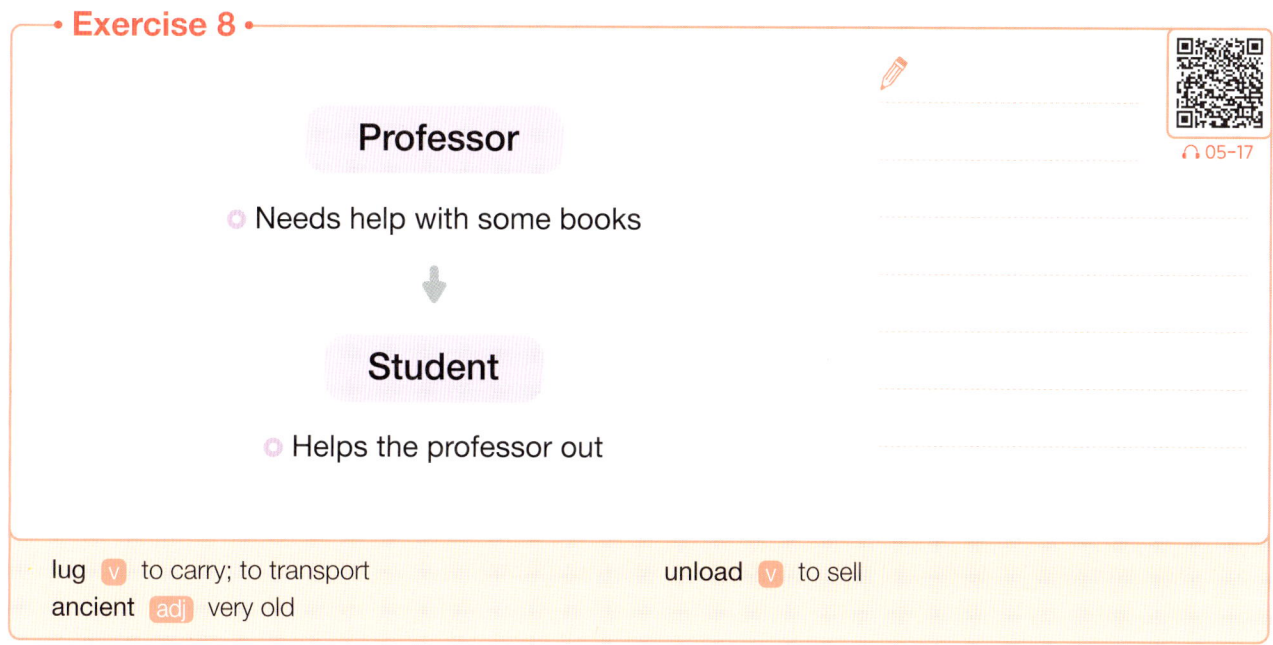

| lug [v] to carry; to transport | unload [v] to sell |
| ancient [adj] very old | |

Q1 What can be inferred about the professor?
- Ⓐ He is new at the university.
- Ⓑ He teaches a science class.
- Ⓒ He exercises a lot.
- Ⓓ He never sells books.

Q2 What does the professor mean when he says this: "You need the cash."
- Ⓐ Most students have enough money.
- Ⓑ Selling books is profitable.
- Ⓒ Many students have little money.
- Ⓓ Books have more value than money.

Listening Skills | **Pitch and Intonation**

✓ **Check-Up** Listen to the following dialogue and underline the high-pitched words.

Student: And you kept it for this long?
Professor: Sure. I keep all the books I buy.
Student: Wow. Your office must be like a library.
Professor: Yes, kind of.

Chapter ❺   87

Vocabulary Review

A Circle the words that best complete the sentences.

1 The crowd was (ecstatic / acceptable) at the rock concert.
2 The old man was (selling / tutoring) her in math and science.
3 Some of the (texts / positions) they are reading are very old.
4 Andrew had to (come / run), so he won't be joining us.
5 The workers must (lock / lug) concrete up the mountain.

B Choose the best words to complete the sentences.

1 It was a _____ to see a familiar face at the party.
   A subject
   B hundred
   C relief
   D discussion

2 Andy did not _____ to be sick yesterday.
   A appear
   B try
   C sleep
   D discover

3 Everyone needs to choose a _____ for the upcoming term paper.
   A direction
   B topic
   C grade
   D room

4 Jason plans to _____ some old stories from ancient Greek.
   A know
   B follow
   C translate
   D keep

5 The professor wants to _____ with Shelby about her research.
   A noodle
   B follow
   C right
   D sign

C Choose the words with the closest meanings to the highlighted words.

1. Trent has a full plate this semester.
   - Ⓐ a busy schedule
   - Ⓑ a hard job
   - Ⓒ an easy class
   - Ⓓ much stress

2. Dr. Lowe likes to josh with his students in class.
   - Ⓐ strict
   - Ⓑ question
   - Ⓒ discuss
   - Ⓓ joke

3. It is customary for students to thank their instructors.
   - Ⓐ common
   - Ⓑ true
   - Ⓒ hard
   - Ⓓ good

4. Please follow the directions precisely so that you do not make any mistakes.
   - Ⓐ fairly
   - Ⓑ exactly
   - Ⓒ nicely
   - Ⓓ slowly

5. The guy tried to unload a broken computer on us.
   - Ⓐ take off
   - Ⓑ fix
   - Ⓒ sell
   - Ⓓ complain

D Complete the sentences by filling in the blanks with the best words from the list. Change the forms of the words if necessary. Use each word only once.

| ancient | step it up | luck | intricate | ace |

1. Sandy _____ her final exam. She was the top student.
2. The team needs to _____ if they want to win.
3. A few students went to Egypt to study _____ history.
4. He needs some _____ to finish first in the race.
5. The design of the building is very _____ and complex.

Practice Test

1-3 Listen to part of a conversation between a student and a professor.

1. Why does the professor want to see the student?

    Ⓐ To discuss the midterm exam
    Ⓑ To help him with his homework
    Ⓒ To offer him a summer job
    Ⓓ To ask him about his future career

2. What does the professor think of the student?

    Ⓐ He does not try hard enough.
    Ⓑ He could be of great help.
    Ⓒ He has trouble making decisions.
    Ⓓ He will become an excellent doctor.

3. What will the student do during the summer?

    Ⓐ He is unsure.
    Ⓑ He will go home.
    Ⓒ He will build a website.
    Ⓓ He will look for a job.

CHAPTER 06

Physiology
(Signal Words and Phrases)

CHAPTER 6 **Physiology** (Signal Words and Phrases)

Understanding TOEFL Question Types & Listening Skills

1 Question Types — Understanding Organization Questions

Understanding Organization questions check how well you understand the overall organization of the passage and the relationship between ideas in the passage. Some questions test general understanding, and others test more detailed understanding.

- **Example Understanding Organization Questions**
    - How does the professor organize the information about X?
    - How is the discussion organized?
    - Why does the professor mention X?

- **Useful Tips for Your Success**
    - Listen carefully for transitions that indicate a sequence.
    - Pay attention to comparisons made by the professor.

Sample Question

The Circulatory System

- Heart and blood vessels
- Arteries: bright red / oxygen
- Veins: dark red / no oxygen

06-01

vessel n a tube; a container	**bright** adj vivid	
pump v to push; to send		

Q How does the professor organize the discussion?

  Ⓐ She refers to a picture in the textbook.
  Ⓑ She compares types of blood vessels.
  Ⓒ She discusses the heart's chambers.
  Ⓓ She draws a picture of the circulatory system.

2 Listening Skills — Signal Words and Phrases

Signal words and phrases are words that provide you with clues. Their purpose is to help you organize information and recognize key ideas. Signal words and phrases also point to concept shifts in the passage.

Check-Up

▶ Listen carefully and fill in the blanks.

1. _____, the heart pumps blood away from the heart in arteries.
2. _____, the heart pumps blood back to it through veins.

06-02

Chapter 6 95

Exercise 1

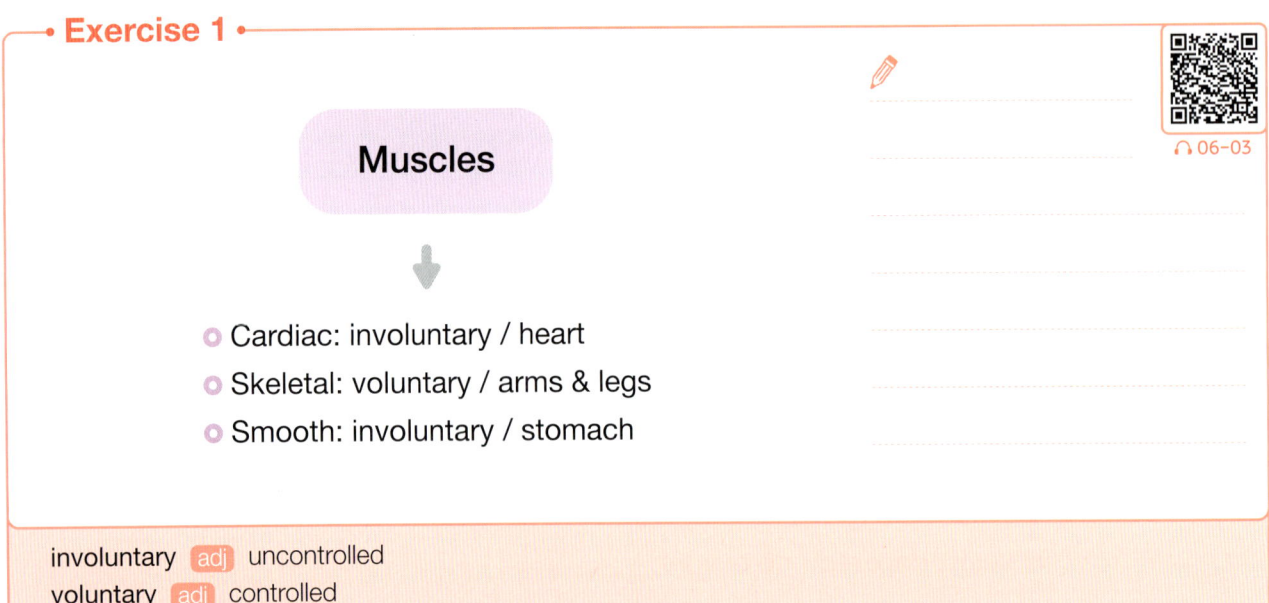

involuntary adj uncontrolled
voluntary adj controlled

Q1 How does the professor organize the information about muscles?

  Ⓐ He focuses on one type of muscle.
  Ⓑ He compares cardiac and smooth muscles.
  Ⓒ He shows the differences in skeletal and smooth muscles.
  Ⓓ He details the traits of three types of muscles.

Q2 Why does the professor discuss skeletal muscles?

  Ⓐ To say that they are in the heart
  Ⓑ To explain how they enable movement
  Ⓒ To compare them with voluntary muscles
  Ⓓ To note that they are involuntary muscles

Listening Skills | Signal Words and Phrases

✓ **Check-Up** | Listen carefully and fill in the blanks.

1 _____, look at this image.

2 Now, the _____ image . . . Okay, next are skeletal muscles.

• **Exercise 2** •

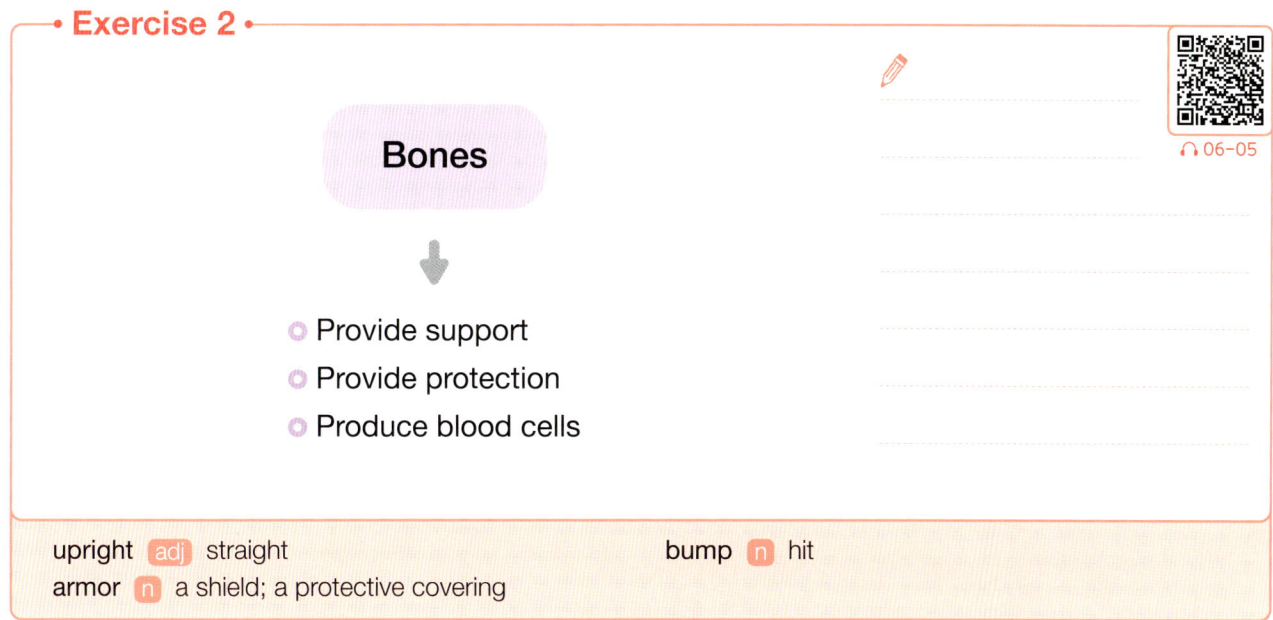

upright adj straight	**bump** n hit
armor n a shield; a protective covering	

Q1 How does the professor organize the discussion?
  Ⓐ She discusses the largest bones in the body.
  Ⓑ She explains the major purposes of bones.
  Ⓒ She compares blood and bones.
  Ⓓ She discusses bone development.

Q2 Why does the professor mention armor?
  Ⓐ To show the strength of the spinal cord
  Ⓑ To illustrate a function of the ribs
  Ⓒ To compare the backbone and the skull
  Ⓓ To disagree with a famous doctor

Listening Skills   Signal Words and Phrases

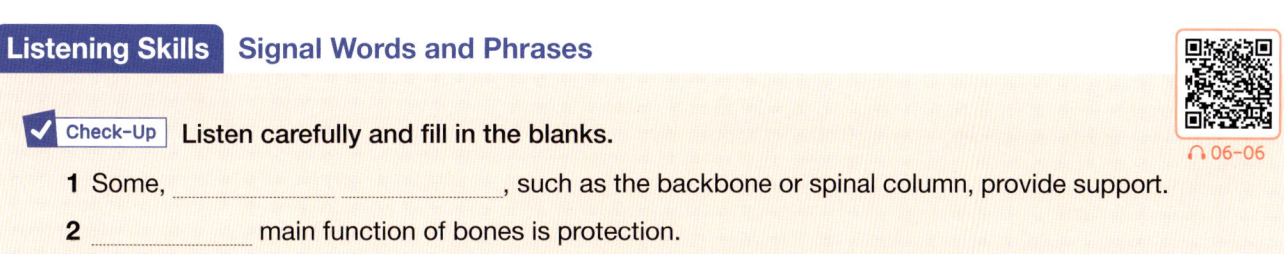

✓ **Check-Up**   Listen carefully and fill in the blanks.
  1 Some, _____ _____, such as the backbone or spinal column, provide support.
  2 _____ main function of bones is protection.

Chapter ❻   97

Exercise 3

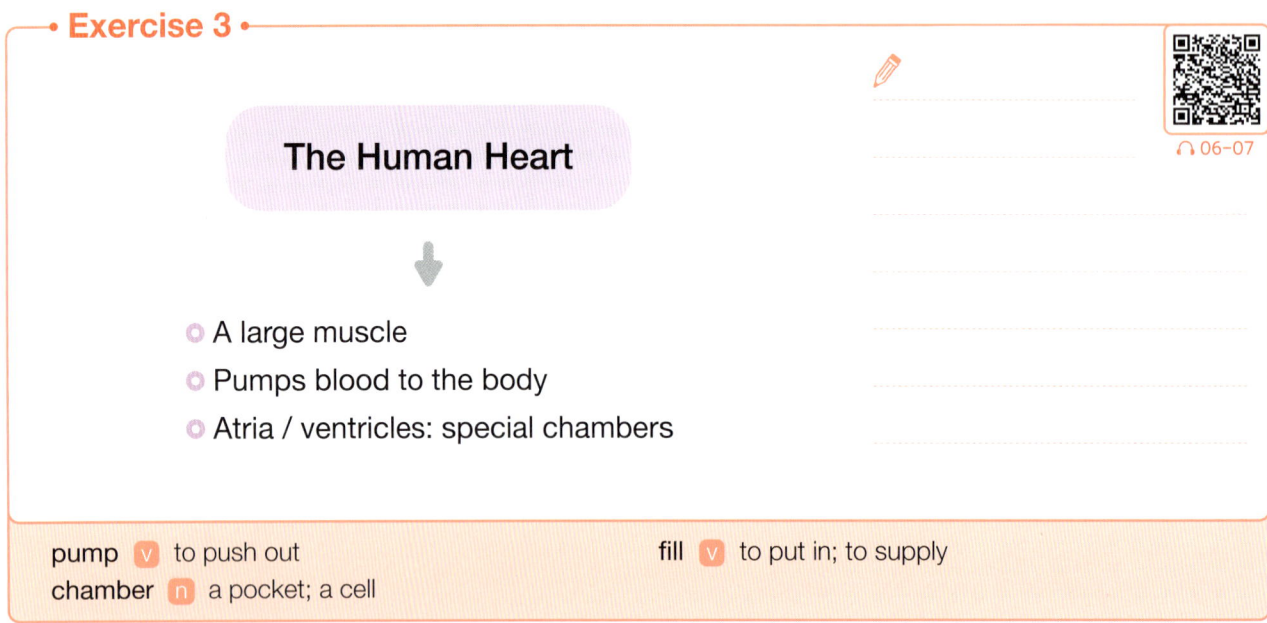

| pump v to push out | fill v to put in; to supply |
| chamber n a pocket; a cell | |

Q1 How does the professor organize the discussion?
- Ⓐ He compares the lungs and the heart.
- Ⓑ He talks about the heart's functions.
- Ⓒ He follows the path of blood in the heart.
- Ⓓ He explores the heart with a microscope.

Q2 Why does the professor mention ventricles?
- Ⓐ To note they are less important than atria
- Ⓑ To illustrate how important they are to the lungs
- Ⓒ To note that they push blood out of the heart
- Ⓓ To explain why they are smaller than atria

Listening Skills Signal Words and Phrases

✓ **Check-Up** Listen carefully and fill in the blanks.

1 Um, _____ _____ a second.

2 _____, _____ _____ a little deeper.

• **Exercise 4** •

The Digestive System

⬇

- Mouth: saliva begins the process
- Esophagus: sends food down
- Stomach: stores and breaks food down

🎧 06-09

---

whatever `pron` anything
break down `phr` to reduce
store `v` to keep for future use

Q1 How does the professor organize the discussion?
- Ⓐ She gives a textbook definition of digestion.
- Ⓑ She follows food from the mouth to the stomach.
- Ⓒ She explains how the stomach digests food.
- Ⓓ She discusses the muscles in the stomach.

Q2 Why does the professor mention pizza and fried chicken?
- Ⓐ To attract the students' attention
- Ⓑ To give examples of foods she dislikes
- Ⓒ To note that the stomach cannot digest them
- Ⓓ To talk about foods that harm the esophagus

Listening Skills | **Signal Words and Phrases**

✓ **Check-Up** Listen carefully and fill in the blanks.

1 _____, the esophagus serves another important purpose.
2 _____, the food enters the stomach.

🎧 06-10

Chapter ❻ 99

• **Exercise 5** •

The Immune System

- Skin: keeps germs out
- Mucus: captures and removes pathogens
- White blood cells: kill pathogens

06-11

harmful adj dangerous; causing damage	**recognize** v to notice; to know
capture v to catch	

Q1 How is the discussion organized?

Ⓐ The professor explains how the body makes antibodies.
Ⓑ The professor compares immune systems in different animals.
Ⓒ The professor discusses different parts of the immune system.
Ⓓ The professor describes the role of white blood cells.

Q2 Why does the professor mention antibodies?

Ⓐ To say that they kill viruses
Ⓑ To explain how they harm the body
Ⓒ To compare them with white blood cells
Ⓓ To talk about their appearances

Listening Skills Signal Words and Phrases

✓ **Check-Up** Listen carefully and fill in the blanks.

06-12

1. _____ cover the immune system now.
2. _____, the immune system has several parts.
3. _____, white blood cells try to kill them.

• **Exercise 6** •

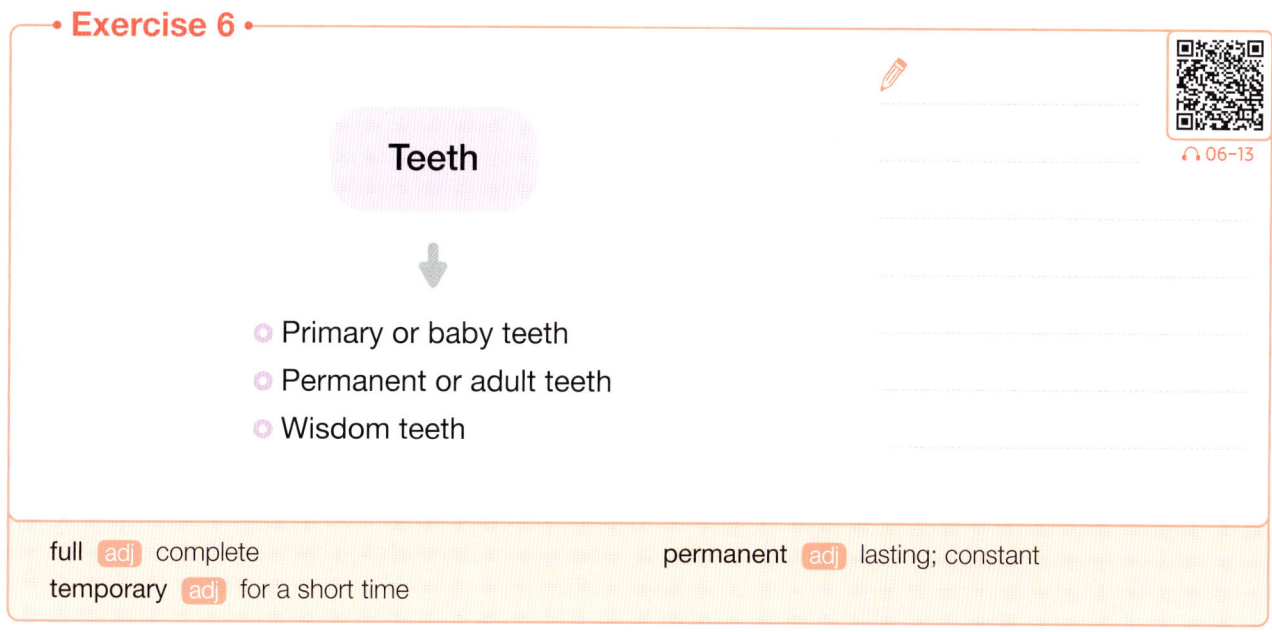

full adj complete
temporary adj for a short time
permanent adj lasting; constant

Q1 How does the professor organize the information about teeth?
- Ⓐ She explains why adults lose their teeth.
- Ⓑ She gives examples of tooth diseases.
- Ⓒ She describes how teeth develop over time.
- Ⓓ She focuses on talking about baby teeth.

Q2 Why does the professor mention wisdom teeth?
- Ⓐ To explain why there are four of them
- Ⓑ To note that some people never get them
- Ⓒ To compare them with permanent teeth
- Ⓓ To show why they can be very painful

Listening Skills   Signal Words and Phrases

✓ **Check-Up** Listen carefully and fill in the blanks.

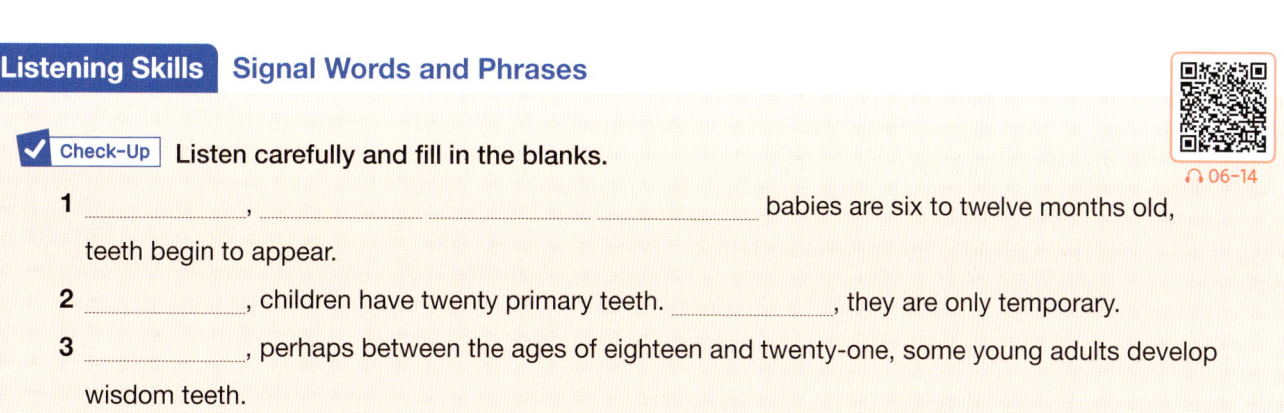

Exercise 7

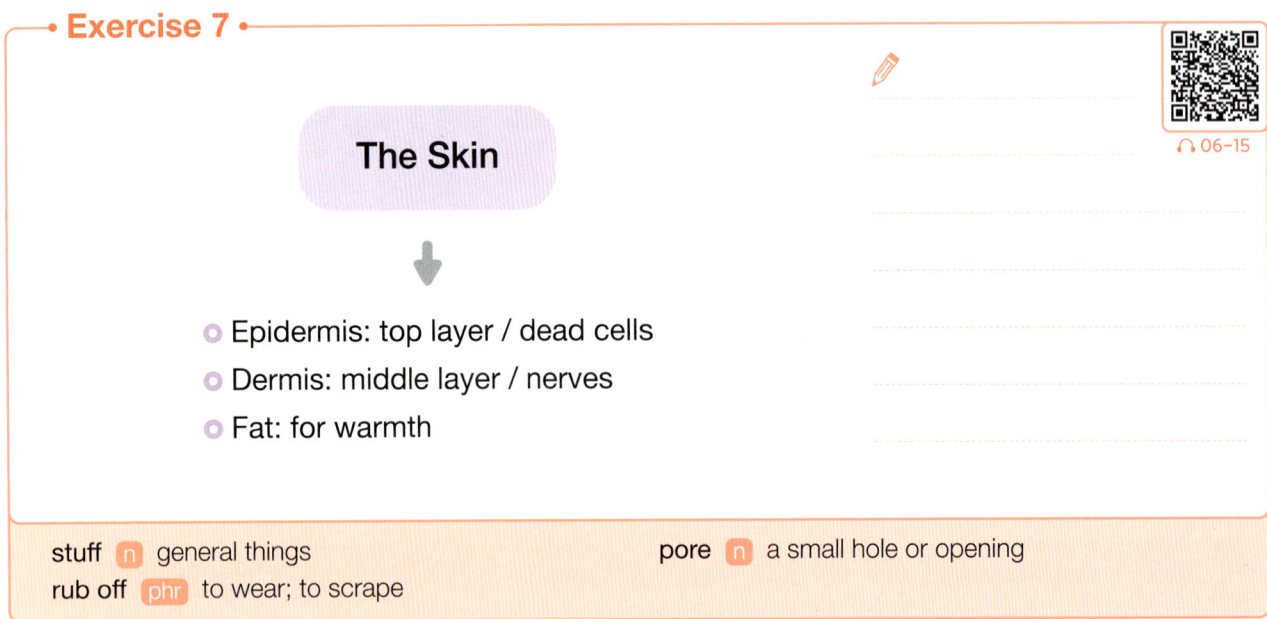

The Skin

- Epidermis: top layer / dead cells
- Dermis: middle layer / nerves
- Fat: for warmth

🎧 06-15

stuff n general things	**pore** n a small hole or opening
rub off phr to wear; to scrape	

Q1 How does the professor organize the discussion?

- Ⓐ He discusses the deadliest skin diseases.
- Ⓑ He describes the layers of the skin from the surface down.
- Ⓒ He tells a personal story about his skin.
- Ⓓ He compares the skin to other organs in the body.

Q2 Why does the professor discuss pores?

- Ⓐ To illustrate how hair develops
- Ⓑ To note the number of pores in the body
- Ⓒ To talk about the purpose of sweat
- Ⓓ To explain how they are not part of the skin

Listening Skills Signal Words and Phrases

✓ **Check-Up** Listen carefully and fill in the blanks.

1 _____ _____ with the top layer.
2 _____, it is made up of dead skin cells.
3 _____ is a layer of fat.

🎧 06-16

• **Exercise 8** •

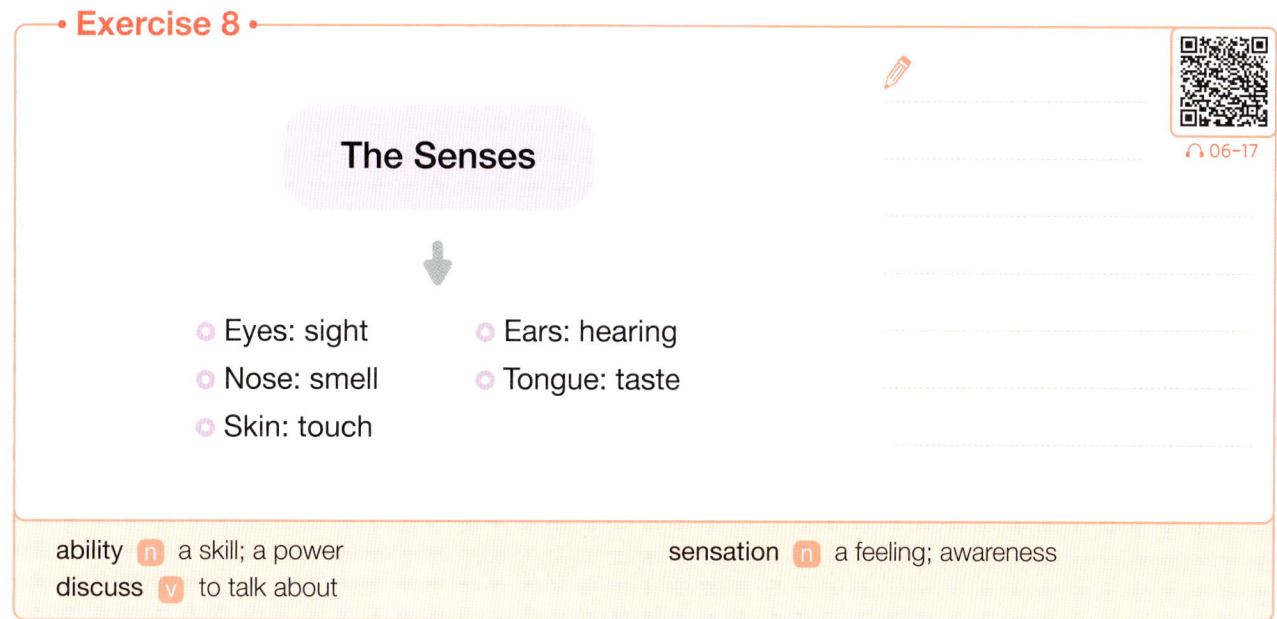

The Senses

- Eyes: sight
- Nose: smell
- Skin: touch
- Ears: hearing
- Tongue: taste

ability n a skill; a power
discuss v to talk about

sensation n a feeling; awareness

Q1 How does the professor organize the discussion?

Ⓐ She ranks the five senses from the most to least important.
Ⓑ She talks about each sense and the organ necessary for it.
Ⓒ She explains how senses travel to the brain.
Ⓓ She focuses on the sense of smell over the other senses.

Q2 Why does the professor mention the tongue?

Ⓐ To show how it relates to the sense of taste
Ⓑ To contrast it with the mouth
Ⓒ To note it is the most sensitive organ
Ⓓ To explain how it is not necessary for speech

Listening Skills   Signal Words and Phrases

✓ **Check-Up**   Listen carefully and fill in the blanks.

1 We _____ _____ _____ senses to discuss.
2 _____ _____ the sense of taste.
3 _____ , we have the sense of touch.

Vocabulary Review

A Circle the words that best complete the sentences.

1 Andrea had a strange (sensation / wisdom) in her hands.
2 Roland's mother wants him to pick up all the (stuff / organs) in his room.
3 The students have a (layer / full) day of tests ahead.
4 The dog (recognized / removed) the sound of its owner's voice.
5 (Whatever / Something) you want to do on Saturday is fine.

B Choose the best words to complete the sentences.

1 The waiter quickly _____ Jen's glass with water.

   A ran
   B placed
   C filled
   D drank

2 Many animals have a kind of _____ for protection.

   A armor
   B sleep
   C habitat
   D far

3 The wild animals are difficult to _____.

   A allow
   B work
   C control
   D stand

4 The student used a small _____, or tube, in the experiment.

   A vessel
   B electric
   C wire
   D needle

5 The young boy saw a(n) _____ light in the night sky.

   A invisible
   B place
   C handy
   D bright

C Choose the words with the closest meanings to the highlighted words.

1. Please stand the ladder upright in the corner.
   - Ⓐ straight
   - Ⓑ down
   - Ⓒ across
   - Ⓓ lean

2. There are many secret chambers in the castle.
   - Ⓐ beds
   - Ⓑ rooms
   - Ⓒ stairs
   - Ⓓ doors

3. Many animals store food for the long winter season.
   - Ⓐ search
   - Ⓑ eat
   - Ⓒ save
   - Ⓓ share

4. The hunters are trying to capture the bear in the forest.
   - Ⓐ find
   - Ⓑ catch
   - Ⓒ kill
   - Ⓓ scare

5. Leslie got a temporary job at the new library downtown.
   - Ⓐ new
   - Ⓑ brief
   - Ⓒ rich
   - Ⓓ lucky

D Complete the sentences by filling in the blanks with the best words from the list. Change the forms of the words if necessary. Use each word only once.

> pore   permanent   ability   bump   break down

1. Sylvia has an excellent _____ in science.
2. Washing your face cleans out the tiny _____ .
3. Chase started to _____ his head on the roof of the car.
4. The stomach is a machine. It _____ all kinds of foods.
5. Hope is looking for a(n) _____ job in teaching.

Chapter ❻   105

Practice Test

1-4 Listen to part of a lecture in a biology class.

06-19

Biology

1   What is the main topic of the lecture?

    Ⓐ Muscle injuries
    Ⓑ Types of connective tissue
    Ⓒ The Achilles tendon
    Ⓓ Ligaments

2   Where is the most common tendon injury?

    Ⓐ In the arm
    Ⓑ In the knee
    Ⓒ In the leg
    Ⓓ In the elbow

3   Do the following sentences refer to the characteristics of tendons or ligaments?
    Click in the correct box for each sentence.

	Tendons	Ligaments
1 They connect bone to bone.		
2 The Achilles heel has one of them.		
3 They attach muscles to bones.		
4 The knee is an example of one of them.		

4   What does the professor imply when he says this: "They give us the ability to walk, talk, lift things, move things, and do just about any physical activity."

    Ⓐ Activities would be difficult without tendons.
    Ⓑ Muscles can work by themselves.
    Ⓒ Exercise helps strengthen tendons.
    Ⓓ Tendons are more important than ligaments.

CHAPTER

07

Oceanography
(Distinguishing Consonants)

CHAPTER 7 Oceanography (Distinguishing Consonants)

Understanding TOEFL Question Types & Listening Skills

1 Question Types — Connecting Content Questions

Connecting Content questions test your ability to relate ideas in the passage. The ideas may be obvious or implied. You may also be asked to fill in a chart which classifies items in categories.

- **Example Connecting Content Questions**
  - What can be inferred about X?
  - What does the professor imply about X?
  - Are the following characteristics of X or Y?
    Click in the correct box for each phrase or sentence.

- **Useful Tips for Your Success**
  - Pay close attention to how you organize your notes.
  - Identify terms and details as well as definitions.

Sample Question

The Great Barrier Reef

- The largest coral reef
- In danger of dying
- Relies on fish

🎧 07-01

peril n a danger; a threat; a crisis
cause n a source; a root

Q What will probably happen if the Great Barrier Reef dies?

- Ⓐ The ocean will become polluted.
- Ⓑ Many fish will lose their habitat.
- Ⓒ More divers will go to the area.
- Ⓓ A new reef will replace it.

2 Listening Skills   Distinguishing Consonants

A consonant is a sound such as *p*, *f*, *n*, and *t*. It is important to distinguish some consonants like *r* from *l*, *v* from *b*, and *f* from *p* in lectures and conversations.

Check-Up

▶ Listen carefully and circle the words you hear.

1 leaf – reef
2 think – sink
3 leads – needs
4 fish – pish

🎧 07-02

Chapter ❼   111

• **Exercise 1** •

Underwater Volcanoes

- Their lava cools and hardens
- Can rise above the sea
- Can make islands

erupt v to explode
lava n hot, melted rock that comes from volcanoes

Q1 The professor mentions volcanoes. Are the following sentences true or false?

	True	False
1 They may be found underwater.		
2 They are only in the Pacific Ocean.		
3 They can make islands.		
4 They send lava into the water.		

Q2 What will probably happen if an underwater volcano erupts many times?

- Ⓐ It will cause problems for people.
- Ⓑ It will make another volcano.
- Ⓒ It will destroy some land.
- Ⓓ It will create an island.

Listening Skills Distinguishing Consonants

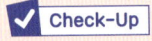 **Check-Up** Listen carefully and circle the words you hear.

1 views – news
2 land – rand
3 harden – pardon
4 rise – vise

• **Exercise 2** •

07-05

> **The Marianas Trench**
>
> ⬇
>
> ○ The deepest on the Earth
> ○ Caused by the shifting ocean floor

| plate [n] a large block of land in the crust | surface [n] a top |
| go up [phr] to ascend | |

Q1 What can be inferred about the ocean floor?
- Ⓐ It is very stable.
- Ⓑ It continues to change.
- Ⓒ It is made of rock.
- Ⓓ It does not have volcanoes.

Q2 Are the following characteristics of the Marianas Trench or Mount Everest?

	Marianas Trench	Mount Everest
① It is greater in height from top to bottom.		
② It is underwater.		
③ It is the tallest mountain on the Earth.		
④ It is not near Guam.		

Listening Skills **Distinguishing Consonants**

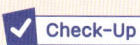 **Check-Up** Listen carefully and circle the words you hear.

1 depth – death   2 bigger – figure

3 plates – planes   4 trash – crash

07-06

Chapter ❼   113

• **Exercise 3** •

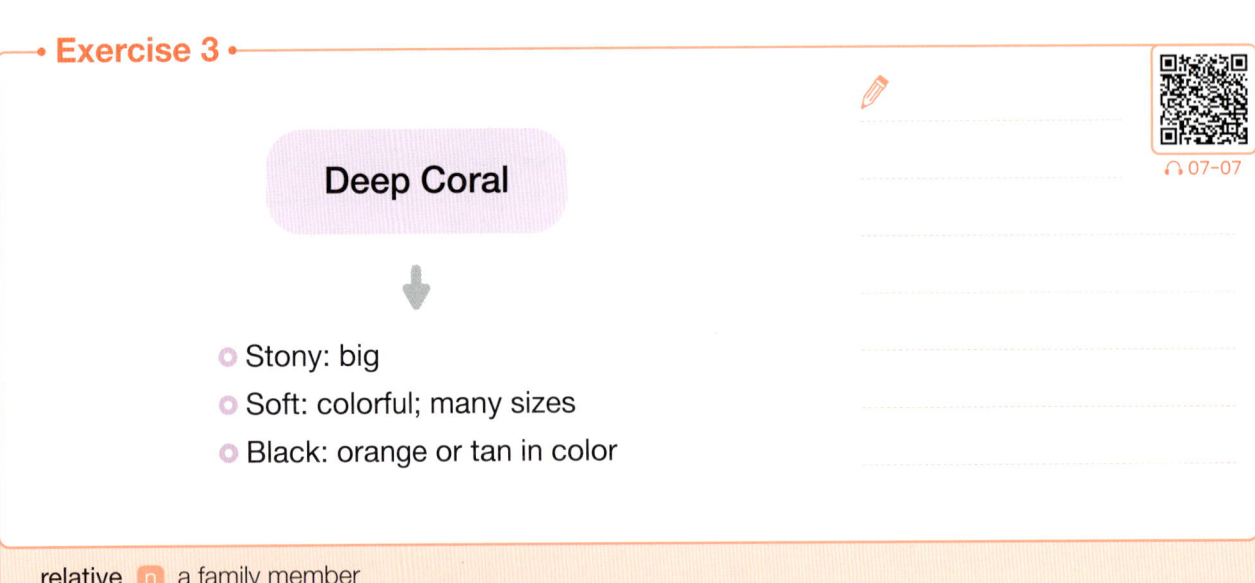

Deep Coral
⬇
- Stony: big
- Soft: colorful; many sizes
- Black: orange or tan in color

relative n a family member
multitude n a large group; a high quantity

Q1 What can be inferred about shallow corals?
- Ⓐ They are smaller than deep corals.
- Ⓑ They do not live very long.
- Ⓒ They need sunlight to survive.
- Ⓓ They are made of one material.

Q2 Are the following characteristics of stony or soft corals?

	Stony	Soft
① They are very colorful.		
② They are large and rocky.		
③ They come in many sizes.		
④ One of them is a sea fan.		

Listening Skills **Distinguishing Consonants**

 Check-Up Listen carefully and circle the words you hear.

1 not – lot
2 freeze – please
3 crass – class
4 right – light

• Exercise 4 •

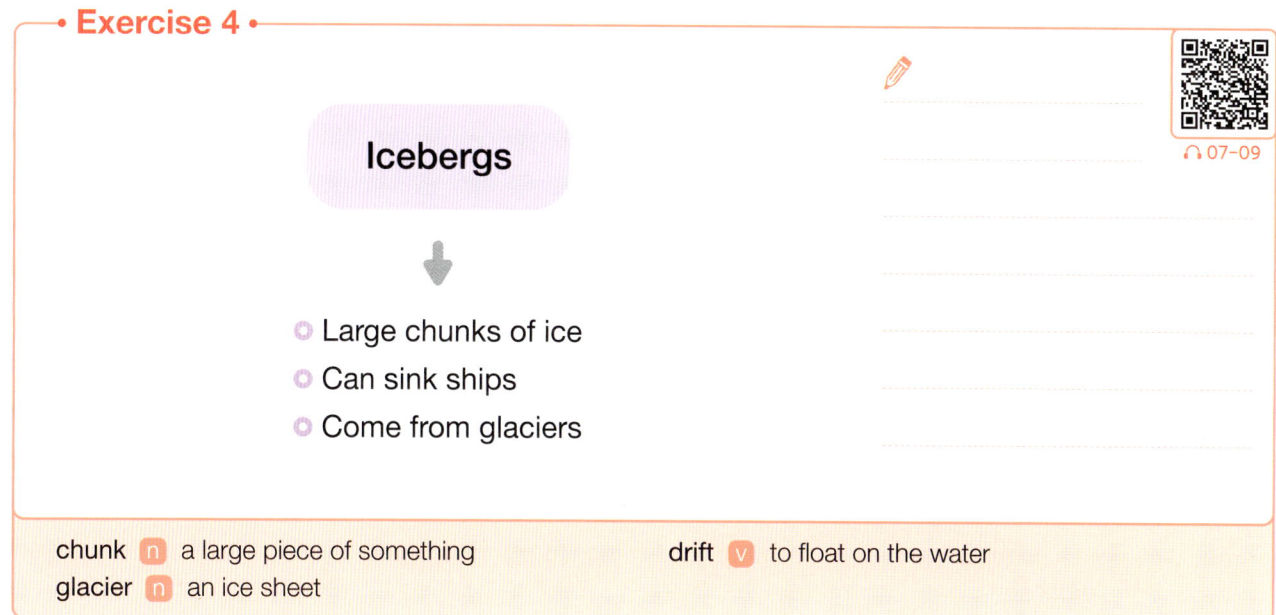

chunk n a large piece of something
glacier n an ice sheet
drift v to float on the water

Q1 What can be inferred about icebergs?

Ⓐ They are only problems in cold water.
Ⓑ They are not very dangerous to ships.
Ⓒ They take a long time to make.
Ⓓ They have killed people in the past.

Q2 The professor discusses icebergs. Are the following sentences true or false?

	True	False
1 They are usually small.		
2 They can sink ships.		
3 They often come from glaciers.		
4 They do not float to warm water.		

Listening Skills Distinguishing Consonants

 Listen carefully and circle the words you hear.

1 visible - risible
2 sunk – sump
3 drift – drip
4 warn - warm

Exercise 5

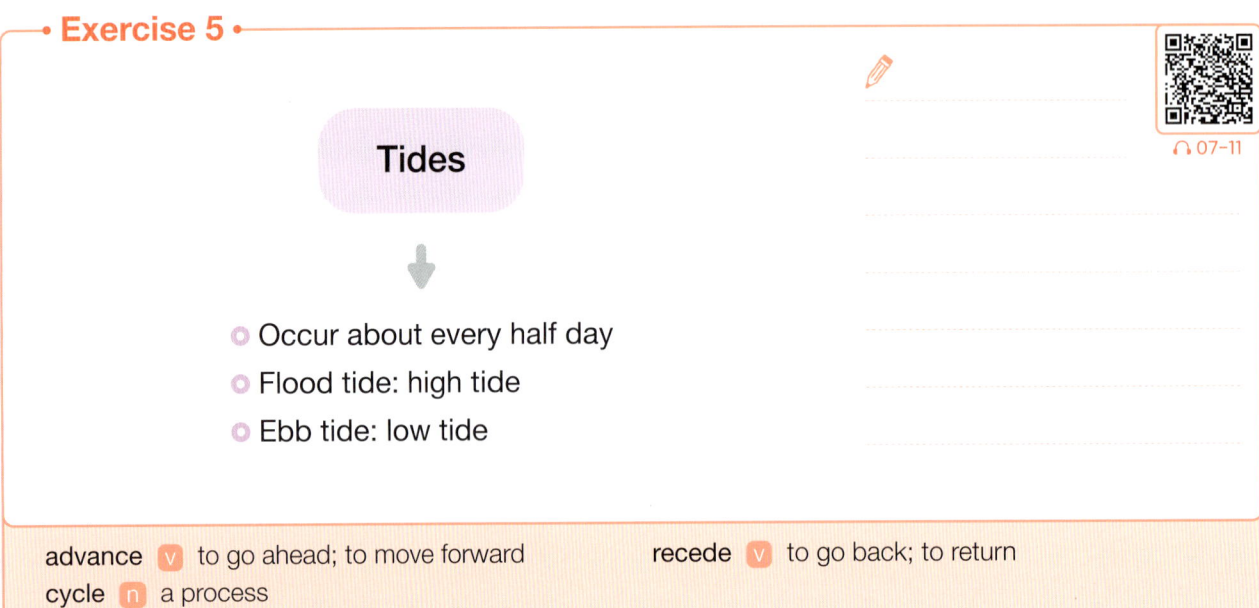

Tides
- Occur about every half day
- Flood tide: high tide
- Ebb tide: low tide

advance v to go ahead; to move forward   **recede** v to go back; to return
cycle n a process

Q1 What does the professor imply about tides?
- Ⓐ They are difficult to predict.
- Ⓑ They change about twice a day.
- Ⓒ They can destroy beaches.
- Ⓓ The sun does not affect them.

Q2 Are the following characteristics of a flood tide or an ebb tide?

	Flood Tide	Ebb Tide
① Water advances up the beach.		
② High tide is a part of it.		
③ Water recedes from the beach.		
④ Low tide is a part of it.		

Listening Skills Distinguishing Consonants

✓ **Check-Up** Listen carefully and circle the words you hear.

1 tide – lied   2 bar – far
3 never – level   4 low – row

116

• Exercise 6 •

The Red and Black Seas

- Red Sea: large amount of salt
- Black Sea: very deep

presume v to believe; to consider
directly adv without any space; immediately
abyssal adj deep in the ocean

Q1 What does the professor imply about the Red Sea?
- Ⓐ It is not certain where its name comes from.
- Ⓑ It will be dry in a century.
- Ⓒ Its water is very good for people's health.
- Ⓓ It gets its salt from nearby mountains.

Q2 Are the following characteristics of the Red Sea or the Black Sea?

	Red Sea	Black Sea
1 Its depth makes it look dark.		
2 It is near northeast Africa.		
3 It is in Southeastern Europe.		
4 It has a high salt content.		

Listening Skills Distinguishing Consonants

✓ **Check-Up** Listen carefully and circle the words you hear.
1 bogus – focus
2 look – rook
3 expels – experts
4 lame – name

• **Exercise 7** •

Rogue Waves and Tsunamis

⬇

○ Rogue waves: unknown beginnings
○ Tsunamis: underwater earthquakes
○ Short vs. long distances

legend n a false story
spontaneously adv suddenly; impulsively
ramble v to travel; to move

Q1 What can be inferred about tsunamis?

Ⓐ They can be very dangerous to people on land.
Ⓑ They destroy ships on the open ocean.
Ⓒ They are much smaller than rogue waves.
Ⓓ They can cause rogue waves to occur.

Q2 Are the following characteristics of rogue waves or tsunamis?

	Rogue Waves	Tsunamis
① They are spontaneous.		
② They do more damage on land than on sea.		
③ They are shorter lived.		
④ They can travel thousands of miles.		

Listening Skills Distinguishing Consonants

 **Check-Up** Listen carefully and circle the words you hear.

1 sought – thought
2 vogue – rogue
3 few – view
4 mires – miles

• **Exercise 8** •

07-17

> **The Whale Shark**
>
> - The largest fish
> - Slow and gentle
> - Eats plankton, not other fish or humans

sluggish adj slow; inactive
miniscule adj tiny; small
immense adj very big; massive; huge

Q1 What does the professor imply about the blue whale?
- Ⓐ It is not as big as the whale shark.
- Ⓑ It does not feed on other fish.
- Ⓒ It only lives in cold waters.
- Ⓓ It is not a fish.

Q2 Are the following characteristics of the blue whale or the whale shark?

	Blue Whale	Whale Shark
① It has very tiny teeth.		
② It is the largest mammal on the Earth.		
③ It is the largest fish on the Earth.		
④ Its maximum length is around fifty feet.		

Listening Skills — Distinguishing Consonants

07-18

 **Check-Up** Listen carefully and then circle the words you hear.

1 plume – blue
2 sing – thing
3 feed – bead
4 now – low

Vocabulary Review

A Circle the words that best complete the sentences.

1. The rocks (rambled / grew) down the side of the mountain.
2. Benson got a (miniscule / dangerous) paper cut.
3. You must go (simply / directly) to the doctor. Hurry!
4. There are many (cycles / rounds) in nature.
5. The iceberg will (drift / meet) in the ocean a long distance.

B Choose the best words to complete the sentences.

1. The volcano is probably going to _____ soon.
   - A break off
   - B erupt
   - C hit
   - D encounter

2. It is hard for many animals to _____ in the desert.
   - A exist
   - B real
   - C send
   - D tire

3. The hikers _____ the mountain in record time.
   - A climbing
   - B fall
   - C freeze
   - D went up

4. Even though it is dark, the mountain is still _____.
   - A hard
   - B high
   - C visible
   - D hidden

5. Amanda has a fever, and the _____ of her skin is hot.
   - A pore
   - B fat
   - C surface
   - D wave

C Choose the words with the closest meanings to the highlighted words.

1 Whales are huge animals that live in the ocean.
  - Ⓐ enormous
  - Ⓑ unique
  - Ⓒ common
  - Ⓓ friendly

2 The cause of the accident is still under investigation.
  - Ⓐ crash
  - Ⓑ solution
  - Ⓒ reason
  - Ⓓ place

3 All of her relatives will visit for Thanksgiving dinner.
  - Ⓐ family
  - Ⓑ sisters
  - Ⓒ friends
  - Ⓓ enemies

4 The tourists were in great peril on the cruise ship.
  - Ⓐ happiness
  - Ⓑ excitement
  - Ⓒ fear
  - Ⓓ danger

5 After the flood, the river water began to recede.
  - Ⓐ rush
  - Ⓑ return
  - Ⓒ increase
  - Ⓓ swallow

D Complete the sentences by filling in the blanks with the best words from the list. Change the forms of the words if necessary. Use each word only once.

> presume   legend   sluggish   multitude   spontaneously

1 Experts are not sure if the _____ is true or not.
2 Sometimes a cold can make you feel _____.
3 The kids found a _____ of shells on the sandy beach.
4 The fireman found the fire started _____.
5 The professor _____ the student would retake the class.

Chapter ❼   121

Practice Test

1-4 Listen to part of a lecture in an oceanography class.

Oceanography

1. What is the main topic of the lecture?
   - Ⓐ The equator
   - Ⓑ The major oceans
   - Ⓒ Cape Horn
   - Ⓓ Seawater

2. Are the following characteristics of the Atlantic Ocean or the Pacific Ocean?
   Click in the correct box for each sentence.

	Atlantic Ocean	Pacific Ocean
1 It is the largest ocean in the world.		
2 It contains twenty percent of the world's seawater.		
3 It is deeper than the other.		
4 It touches the coast of Portugal.		

3. Why does the professor mention Cape Horn?
   - Ⓐ To show where the Atlantic and Pacific oceans meet
   - Ⓑ To describe the size of the equator
   - Ⓒ To explain why the Atlantic Ocean is shallow
   - Ⓓ To note the terrible weather in that area

4. What does the professor imply when he says this: "Oceans are the warmest near the equator."
   - Ⓐ The Pacific Ocean is warmer than the Atlantic.
   - Ⓑ Many volcanoes are located near the equator.
   - Ⓒ It is not very sunny around the equator.
   - Ⓓ Water is cooler away from the equator.

CHAPTER 08

Endangered Animals
(Listening for Numbers)

CHAPTER 8 Endangered Animals (Listening for Numbers)

Understanding TOEFL Question Types & Listening Skills

1 Question Types — Making Inferences Questions

Making Inferences questions are based on the facts in the listening passage. In many cases, the professor may imply something without directly stating it.

- **Example Making Inferences Questions**
  - What does the professor imply about X?
  - What can be inferred about X?
  - What does the professor imply when he says this: (replay)

- **Useful Tips for Your Success**
  - Pay attention to what the professor implies.
  - The answer will usually use vocabulary not mentioned in the passage.

Sample Question

Polar Bears

- The biggest meat eaters on land
- Good at swimming

carnivore *n* a meat eater
superior *adj* expert; better than another thing

Q What does the professor imply about polar bears?

Ⓐ Fish is an important part of their diet.
Ⓑ Some bears are larger than them.
Ⓒ They cannot swim very well.
Ⓓ Female bears are larger than males.

2 Listening Skills — Listening for Numbers

We often hear numbers in lectures. A pause is especially important when you are listening to numbers in measurements, years, and other examples. Notice how spaces and punctuation are used to group the numbers.

Check-Up

▶ Listen and fill in the blanks with suitable numbers.

1. It weighs between _____ and _____ pounds.
2. A standing male might be _____ feet tall.
3. Some polar bears can swim for _____ miles at one time.

Chapter 8   127

• **Exercise 1** •

The Alligator

⬇

○ Has a long life
○ Relies on large teeth and jaws

🎧 08-03

lifetime n the time that someone or something lives
deviation n a difference; a separation

Q1 What can be inferred about alligators?

Ⓐ They only eat meat.
Ⓑ They do not live in fresh water.
Ⓒ They rely on their jaws to survive.
Ⓓ They are larger than crocodiles.

Q2 What does the professor imply about crocodiles?

Ⓐ Their teeth are visible when their jaws are shut.
Ⓑ They have more teeth than alligators.
Ⓒ They live shorter lives than alligators.
Ⓓ They have two big front teeth.

Listening Skills Listening for Numbers

🎧 08-04

✓ **Check-Up** Listen and fill in the blanks with suitable numbers.

1 Males average a bit more at around _____ feet.
2 Inside are between _____ and _____ large teeth.
3 The average alligator goes through _____ or even _____ teeth in one lifetime.

• Exercise 2 •

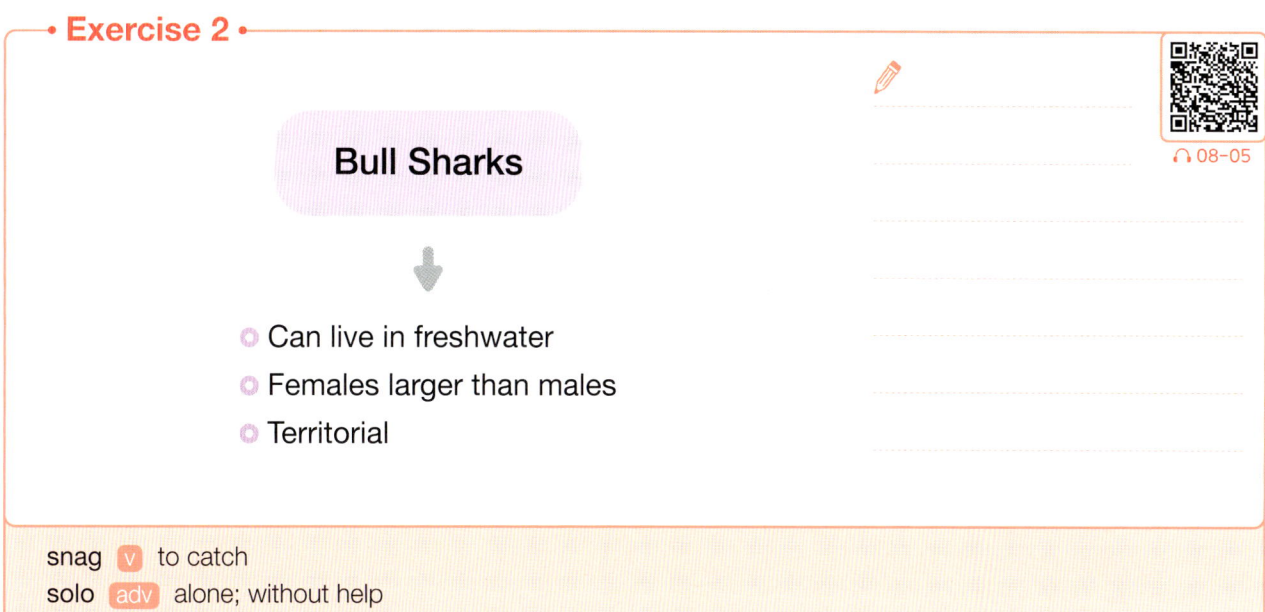

Bull Sharks

- Can live in freshwater
- Females larger than males
- Territorial

08-05

snag **v** to catch
solo **adv** alone; without help

Q1 What does the professor imply about bull sharks?
- Ⓐ They do not mind fresh water.
- Ⓑ They only live in salt water.
- Ⓒ Males can be larger than females.
- Ⓓ They are not very dangerous.

Q2 What can be inferred about bull sharks?
- Ⓐ They always hunt for food alone.
- Ⓑ They might hunt in groups.
- Ⓒ They vary their hunting techniques.
- Ⓓ They migrate to different hunting grounds.

Listening Skills Listening for Numbers

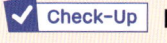 Listen and fill in the blanks with suitable numbers.

1 Males can grow to be about _____ feet long.
2 They can weigh as much as _____ pounds.
3 They can reach _____ feet in length.

08-06

Exercise 3

The Bald Eagle

- A predatory bird
- Great size
- Huge nests

national adj representative
enormous adj large; huge

Q1 What does the professor imply about bald eagles?

- Ⓐ They do not live in South America.
- Ⓑ They are only found in the United States.
- Ⓒ They are the smallest of all the eagles.
- Ⓓ They do not hunt other birds.

Q2 What does the professor imply when he says this: "Amazing!"

- Ⓐ The small size of the bald eagle surprises him.
- Ⓑ The speed of the bald eagle is shocking.
- Ⓒ He cannot believe the size of a bald eagle's nest.
- Ⓓ He thinks the wingspan of the bald eagle is impressive.

Listening Skills — Listening for Numbers

Check-Up Listen and fill in the blanks with suitable numbers.

1. The length of its body is usually between _____ and _____ centimeters.
2. Its wingspan is normally between _____ and _____ centimeters.
3. It usually weighs about _____ to _____ kilograms.

• **Exercise 4** •

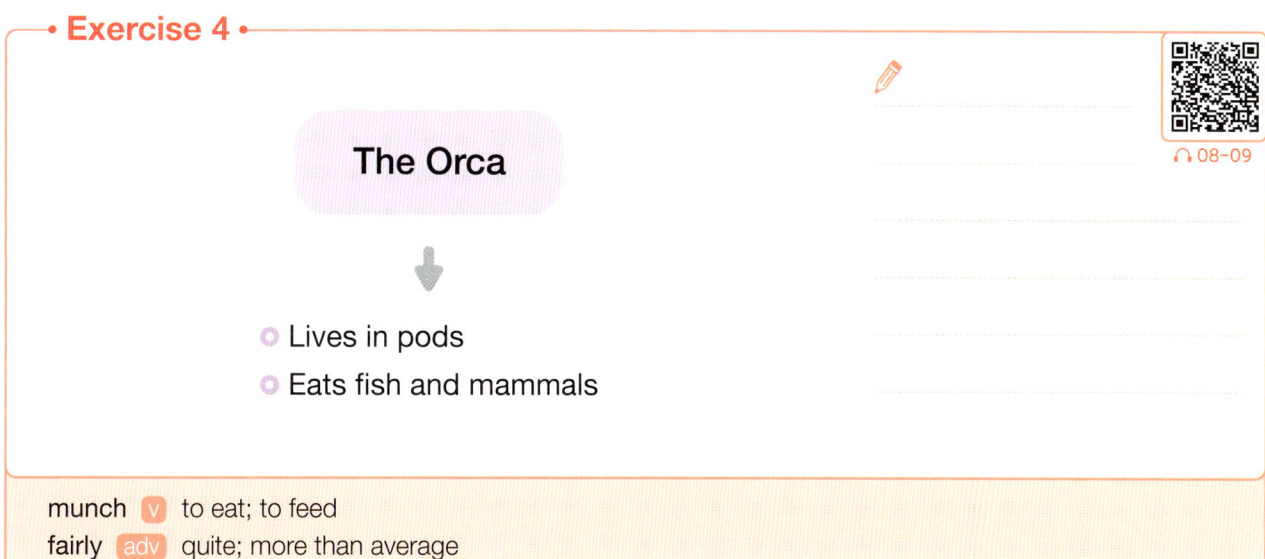

munch v	to eat; to feed
fairly adv	quite; more than average

Q1 What does the professor imply about the orca?

- Ⓐ It only feeds on fish.
- Ⓑ It feeds on different animals.
- Ⓒ It only lives near Japan.
- Ⓓ It does not live very long.

Q2 What can be inferred about the orca?

- Ⓐ It can live for more than fifty years.
- Ⓑ It prefers to eat seals over fish.
- Ⓒ It rarely reaches twenty feet in length.
- Ⓓ It has one or two calves in a lifetime.

Listening Skills Listening for Numbers

✓ **Check-Up** Listen and fill in the blanks with suitable numbers.

1 The largest orca ever recorded weighed _____ pounds.
2 At birth, they can weigh more than _____ pounds.
3 It lives to be about _____ years old.

• **Exercise 5** •

Komodo Dragons

- Reptile predators
- Live isolated lives
- Losing habitat; numbers reducing

keen adj sharp; intense
adroit adj clever; skilled
intimidate v to threaten; to terrorize

Q1 What does the professor imply about Komodo dragons?

  Ⓐ They once lived on many continents.
  Ⓑ They rely heavily on their sense of smell.
  Ⓒ They are threatened because of hunting.
  Ⓓ They never attack human beings.

Q2 What can be inferred about Komodo dragons?

  Ⓐ They cannot see very well.
  Ⓑ They only eat plants.
  Ⓒ They prefer fishing to hunting.
  Ⓓ They are quiet hunters.

Listening Skills Listening for Numbers

✓ **Check-Up** Listen and fill in the blanks with suitable numbers.

1 They can smell prey up to nearly _____ miles away.
2 Some can run about _____ miles per hour.
3 Western scientists first saw Komodo dragons in _____.

• Exercise 6 •

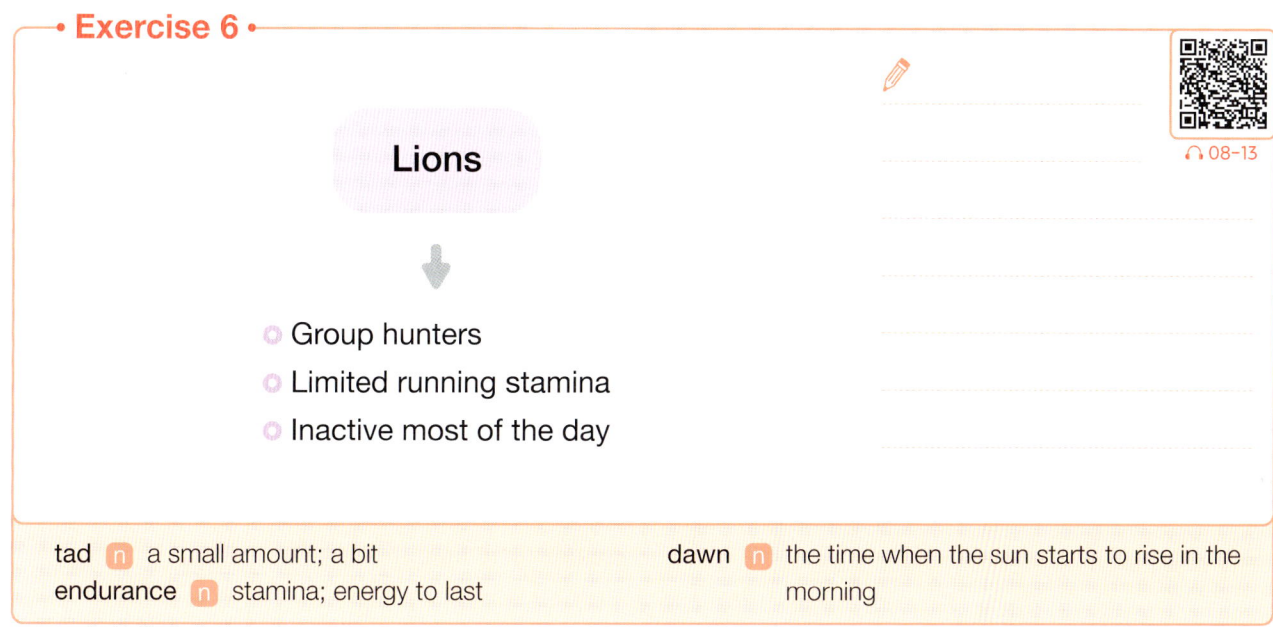

tad n a small amount; a bit	dawn n the time when the sun starts to rise in the morning
endurance n stamina; energy to last	

Q1 What does the professor imply about lions?

Ⓐ Full-grown lions can weigh less than tigers.
Ⓑ They only like to hunt by themselves.
Ⓒ They prefer to hunt small prey.
Ⓓ They occasionally attack tigers.

Q2 What can be inferred when the professor says this: "We call this cooperative hunting."

Ⓐ Lions do not work well in groups.
Ⓑ Female lions do all of the hunting.
Ⓒ Lions usually outrun their prey.
Ⓓ Lions work together to get food.

Listening Skills Listening for Numbers

✓ Check-Up Listen and fill in the blanks with suitable numbers.

1 Lions typically grow to be about _____ kilograms.
2 They are not active for about _____ hours a day.
3 Then they spend nearly _____ minutes a day eating.

Chapter 8   133

Exercise 7

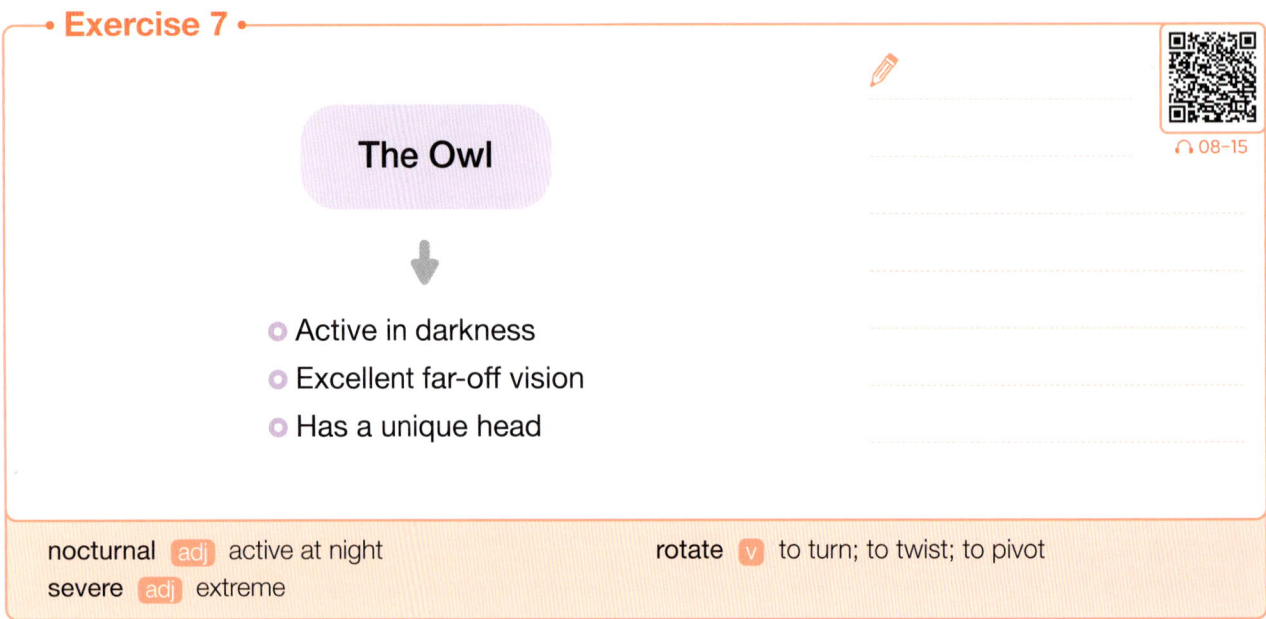

The Owl
- Active in darkness
- Excellent far-off vision
- Has a unique head

nocturnal [adj] active at night
severe [adj] extreme
rotate [v] to turn; to twist; to pivot

Q1 What does the professor imply when he says this: "This means that it hunts mainly at night."

    Ⓐ The owl prefers to hunt during the day.
    Ⓑ The owl may hunt during the day.
    Ⓒ The owl only hunts in darkness.
    Ⓓ The owl cannot see well at night.

Q2 What can be inferred about the owl?

    Ⓐ It has deadly claws.
    Ⓑ It cannot see things up close.
    Ⓒ It has bright feathers.
    Ⓓ It cannot look behind its body.

Listening Skills Listening for Numbers

✓ **Check-Up** Listen and fill in the blanks with suitable numbers.

1 There are more than _____ species of owls.
2 It is able to turn its head _____ degrees.
3 It simply quietly rotates its head more than _____ degrees.

• **Exercise 8** •

The Rhino

- May have one horn or two
- Peaceful creature
- Can attack if scared

peaceful adj not violent
scared adj afraid

extremely adv very; highly

Q1 What does the professor imply about the rhino?
- Ⓐ It is most commonly found in Africa.
- Ⓑ It is often hunted by people.
- Ⓒ It kills and eats other animals.
- Ⓓ It prefers to live near water.

Q2 What can be inferred about the rhino?
- Ⓐ It kills more people than lions do.
- Ⓑ It is the world's largest land creature.
- Ⓒ It is scared of large animals.
- Ⓓ It is not normally dangerous.

Listening Skills | **Listening for Numbers**

✓ **Check-Up** Listen and fill in the blanks with suitable numbers.

1 As a result, there are only around _____ rhinos in the wild today.
2 Some can weigh up to _____ kilograms.
3 They can also run more than _____ kilometers an hour.

Vocabulary Review

A Circle the words that best complete the sentences.

1 Sheep are usually quiet and (peaceful / dangerous) animals.
2 The thunderstorm yesterday was very (endangered / severe).
3 Shaun likes to watch the sun rise at (dawn / night).
4 Players on opposite teams like to (intimidate / help) others.
5 Bears have an extremely (keen / visible) sense of smell.

B Choose the best words to complete the sentences.

1 Marathon runners need to have excellent _____.

  A attempt
  B strong
  C endurance
  D speeding

2 Squirrels like to _____ on nuts.

  A save
  B follow
  C munch
  D chews

3 The shark they saw in the ocean was _____.

  A death
  B attack
  C land
  D enormous

4 Kelley was nervous during his first _____ flight.

  A solo
  B similar
  C repetition
  D above

5 The pro football player is very _____ on the field.

  A rich
  B adroit
  C relation
  D command

C Choose the words with the closest meanings to the highlighted words.

1. Brenda was a tad short of making the team.
   - A bit
   - B first
   - C lot
   - D brief

2. Some predators are nocturnal hunters.
   - A day
   - B sneaky
   - C excellent
   - D night

3. Coaches like to rotate players to keep them fresh.
   - A support
   - B change
   - C yell at
   - D approve

4. It is important to be careful around lions and other big cats.
   - A cautious
   - B scared
   - C strong
   - D quiet

5. Emanuel snagged his new sweater on the desk.
   - A purchased
   - B saw
   - C caught
   - D placed

D Complete the sentences by filling in the blanks with the best words from the list. Change the forms of the words if necessary. Use each word only once.

> attack   superior   national   fairly   dangerous

1. Lots of animals in the jungle are very _____.
2. This sound system is of _____ quality compared to that one.
3. The _____ presidential election will take place next year.
4. Rene has a(n) _____ good idea for her research project.
5. Some animals _____ others when they are scared.

Chapter 8   137

Practice Test

1-4 Listen to part of a lecture in a biology class.

1 What is the main topic of the lecture?

    A The habitats of red and gray foxes
    B The hunting techniques of foxes
    C Why foxes are in danger
    D Differences between red and gray foxes

2 How does the professor organize the discussion?

    A By comparing continents
    B By contrasting two species
    C By relating a personal story
    D By focusing on past events

3 Are the following characteristics of gray or red foxes?
   Click in the correct box for each sentence.

	Gray Foxes	Red Foxes
1 They are more aggressive.		
2 They can climb trees.		
3 They like hilly habitats.		
4 They are more comfortable with humans.		

4 What is true about gray foxes?

    A They live in Europe.
    B They have trouble escaping predators.
    C They are the largest kind of fox.
    D They live in swampy areas.

Actual Test

Actual Test 1

Questions 1-4 Listen to part of a conversation between a student and a professor.

09-01

1 Why did the student visit the professor?
   Ⓐ To ask about a homework assignment
   Ⓑ To apologize for missing a class
   Ⓒ To discuss her recent performance
   Ⓓ To go over her recent presentation

2 What does the student give the professor?
   Ⓐ Her test paper
   Ⓑ A homework assignment
   Ⓒ A doctor's note
   Ⓓ An essay

3 What is the professor's attitude toward the student?
   Ⓐ He is very critical of her performance.
   Ⓑ He is understanding of her situation.
   Ⓒ He believes she should drop the class.
   Ⓓ He encourages her to do better.

4 Why does the student say this: "I guess I misunderstood the directions."
   Ⓐ To ask the professor to give her another chance
   Ⓑ To encourage the professor to let her try again
   Ⓒ To explain why she did poorly on an exam
   Ⓓ To complain about the grade that she received

Questions 5-9 Listen to part of a lecture in a meteorology class.

Meteorology

5 What aspect of severe weather does the professor mainly discuss?
- Ⓐ The seasons when it takes place
- Ⓑ The type of damage it can do
- Ⓒ The reasons that is happens
- Ⓓ The places it usually occurs

6 Why does the professor mention last night's storm?
- Ⓐ To complain about weather predictions
- Ⓑ To describe hurricanes
- Ⓒ To introduce the topic to the class
- Ⓓ To say her house was damaged

7 According to the professor, what do hailstorms often do?
- Ⓐ Hurt people
- Ⓑ Destroy building
- Ⓒ Damage cars
- Ⓓ Knock down trees

8 Are the following examples of general severe weather or localized severe weather? Click in the correct box for each sentence.

	General Severe Weather	Localized Severe Weather
1 Tornadoes		
2 Typhoons		
3 Hailstorms		
4 Blizzards		

9 What will the professor probably do next?
- Ⓐ Ask some questions
- Ⓑ Continue to lecture
- Ⓒ Give the students a quiz
- Ⓓ End the class

Actual Test 2

Questions 1-4 Listen to part of a conversation between a student and a librarian.

09-03

1 What is the student's problem?
   - Ⓐ He does not like his topic.
   - Ⓑ He cannot use the library's computer system.
   - Ⓒ He cannot find some books he needs.
   - Ⓓ He does not have much time.

2 What can be inferred about the student?
   - Ⓐ He is frustrated.
   - Ⓑ He is scared.
   - Ⓒ He is excited.
   - Ⓓ He is nervous.

3 What will the librarian probably do next?
   - Ⓐ Give the student a new library card
   - Ⓑ Describe the interlibrary loan program
   - Ⓒ Check out a book for the student
   - Ⓓ Look for a book on the bookshelves

4 What does the student imply when he says this: "My paper isn't due until two months from now."
   - Ⓐ He does not have much time to finish.
   - Ⓑ He will recall the books that are checked out.
   - Ⓒ He always starts doing projects early.
   - Ⓓ He has many other work assignments to do.

Actual Test 2

Questions 5-9 Listen to part of a lecture in an anthropology class.

Anthropology

5 What is the lecture mainly about?
- Ⓐ The homes of Neanderthals
- Ⓑ The hunting methods of Neanderthals
- Ⓒ The lifestyles of Neanderthals
- Ⓓ The characteristics of Neanderthals

6 According to the professor, when did Neanderthals die out?
- Ⓐ Around 400,000 years ago
- Ⓑ Around 50,000 years ago
- Ⓒ Around 40,000 years ago
- Ⓓ Around 1,856 years ago

7 The professor mentions Neanderthals. Are the following sentences true or false?
Click in the correct box for each sentence.

	True	False
1 They only lived in Europe.		
2 They lived in cold and warm places.		
3 They ate meat and plants.		
4 They could be around 1.75 meters tall.		

8 Why does the professor mention Neanderthal's large brains?
- Ⓐ To prove that Neanderthals could speak
- Ⓑ To say Neanderthals were smarter than humans
- Ⓒ To compare them with humans' brains
- Ⓓ To describe some problems with them

9 What does the professor mean when he says this: "It's likely the two fought, and Neanderthals were the losers."
- Ⓐ Modern humans made Neanderthals go extinct.
- Ⓑ Neanderthals were very good at fighting.
- Ⓒ Nobody knows what happened to the Neanderthals.
- Ⓓ Modern humans live everywhere on the Earth today.

Actual Test 3

Questions 1-4 Listen to part of a conversation between a student and a professor.

1   Why did the student visit the professor?
   - Ⓐ To talk about a paper
   - Ⓑ To get some lecture notes
   - Ⓒ To go over her presentation
   - Ⓓ To request some study tips

2   What can be inferred about the professor?
   - Ⓐ He has class in a few minutes.
   - Ⓑ He is a difficult grader.
   - Ⓒ He does not know the student.
   - Ⓓ He teaches biology.

3   What will the student probably do next?
   - Ⓐ Attend her next class
   - Ⓑ Ask another question
   - Ⓒ Go to the library
   - Ⓓ Return to her home

4   What can be inferred about the student when she says: "We have?"
   - Ⓐ She brought her research material with her.
   - Ⓑ She is surprised by the professor's comment.
   - Ⓒ She is ready to submit her final paper.
   - Ⓓ She is pleased with the professor's decision.

Actual Test 3

Questions 5-9 Listen to part of a lecture in a biology class.

5 What aspect of marsupials does the professor mainly discuss?

- Ⓐ Where they usually live
- Ⓑ What kind of food they like to eat
- Ⓒ How they protect themselves
- Ⓓ How they are different from mammals

6 According to the professor, where do most marsupials live?
Click on 2 answers.

- Ⓐ In North America
- Ⓑ In Australia
- Ⓒ In Africa
- Ⓓ In South America

7 Are the following characteristics of mammals or marsupials?
Click in the correct box for each sentence.

	Mammals	Marsupials
1 Have less teeth than the other		
2 Carry their babies in a pouch		
3 Have a low metabolic rate		
4 Give birth to well-developed young		

8 How does the professor organize the information about marsupials?

- Ⓐ By comparing and contrasting it with mammals
- Ⓑ By discussing it in alphabetical order
- Ⓒ By talking about it in chronological order
- Ⓓ By talking about land animals first and then ocean animals

9 What can be inferred about the professor when she says this: "Marsupial is spelled M-A-R-S-U-P-I-A-L, by the way."

- Ⓐ She will test the students on the information.
- Ⓑ She thinks the students did not hear her.
- Ⓒ She believes it is a difficult word to spell.
- Ⓓ She wants the students to say the word out loud.

Appendix

Dictation Exercises

Dictation Exercises

Chapter 1

Sample Question

M Professor: Actually, class, _____ the Eiffel Tower _____ on it _____. _____ for the World's Fair _____. It was _____ until 1930. But _____ wanted to _____ after a while. _____, too. Can you believe it? Many people thought _____. Of course, _____. Today, _____ visit it _____.

Exercise 1

W Professor: The Egyptians _____ around the year _____. Now, think about this for a moment . . . These magnificent structures were _____ on the Earth for around _____. _____ in Egyptian culture. They were _____. That's right. Egyptian pharaohs _____ many, many years _____ the pyramids to be their _____. _____, there is often _____ _____, or _____. _____ the pharaoh's mummified body. For example, the Pyramid at Giza has _____. _____, or room, is right in _____ _____. It's _____, too.

156

The engineers _____. They built _____

_____. For thousands of years, _____ the

pharaohs' _____ _____.

Exercise 2

W Professor: _____ were great _____.

They made _____. In fact, many of their buildings _____

_____ today. Go to Athens and other Greek cities today. You will see

_____ and _____

_____ in many places.

Greek architecture is _____.

A column is a _____, _____, _____ structure. It often provides

_____. The Greeks had

_____. They are

Doric, Ionic, and Corinthian.

Doric columns were very _____. They were

_____, too. Ionic columns had _____. They had

_____ as well. Corinthian columns

had _____. _____

_____, and the Romans _____. Let's look

at some picture of them now.

Exercise 3

M Professor: _____ the Great Wall of China _____

_____ today. The Chinese _____

_____ their empire. For example, it _____

the Mongols, their great rival. The Chinese _____

_____ around _____ century B.C.

At first, the Chinese _____, _____, and even

Dictation Exercises 157

_____ and _____ to build the wall. The stones were _____

_____. Some were _____ and

_____. However, over time, the Chinese developed _____.

Later, they used _____. Bricks also

made the wall _____. Actually, the bricks were small

and easy _____. This helped the

Chinese build _____. Even today,

the Great Wall of China is the _____ on the Earth. It

_____ 4,000 miles.

Exercise 4

M Professor: Gothic architecture _____ in France in _____

_____. Now, I would like to discuss _____

_____. Could somebody turn the lights off, please . . .? Thank you.

Now, _____ of Notre Dame

Cathedral in Paris. It is _____ of Gothic architecture.

The first thing you'll notice are its _____

_____ at the top. You should also _____

_____ of the church. This is the facade. It _____

_____. Beautiful, isn't it, class?

Now, this _____ is _____ of Notre Dame.

Look at the _____. Look at all the stained-glass

windows. Look at how the light _____. These are _____

_____ of Gothic architecture. Don't you think it's marvelous?

Exercise 5

W Professor: _____ Frank Lloyd Wright was a _____. Let

me explain. He didn't just take out a pencil and paper and design something. No, _____

_____ at all.

_____, he formed his work _____

_____, from nature. Let me give you an example. Fallingwater is one of _____ _____. _____ today near Pittsburgh, Pennsylvania. Wright actually built the house _____ _____. I'm sure some of you have seen pictures of it. _____ Wright's _____. Anyway, the point is that Wright _____ _____ to build something. He used them by _____ _____. He also used _____ _____, not artificial, _____. At Fallingwater, rock and stone are _____ _____. Take a look at this picture of Fallingwater . . . Beautiful, huh? It _____ it is growing right _____ _____ and _____ _____. Any comments?

Exercise 6

M Professor: The Leaning Tower of Pisa is _____ _____ in the world. Today, I think it _____ _____. That's a lot. It looks like it _____ at any minute. But it hasn't. It has stood _____ _____ for more than 800 years. Please take note, class. It is _____ of a cathedral. It _____. It _____ _____ because it leans to one side. Now, uh, _____ on it _____. Soon after, the tower began to lean _____. Why? Well, first, the architects were _____. They did not _____ _____ a _____ foundation. Second, the location _____. The tower was built _____ _____. So poor planning _____ _____. Even today, it _____ more and more. But reinforcements have made it _____ and _____.

Exercise 7

M Professor: The Taj Mahal _____ is an _____. It is a domed structure made _____. In the seventeenth century, an _____ built it _____ after her death. It was _____, class. Around one thousand elephants _____ to the worksite. Interestingly, _____ make up the Taj Mahal. _____, they laid almost _____ precious stones. These _____ on the Asian continent. For example, the turquoise _____ Tibet. The sapphires came from Sri Lanka. And the magnificent crystal came _____. In this way, the Taj Mahal is _____. It is _____ the most beautiful _____ available in Asia. Now, let's _____ this video I made of the Taj Mahal last year.

Exercise 8

W Professor: _____ to architecture is the skyscraper. They came about in the _____ New York and Chicago. For the first time, architects used _____ to _____. Before steel, concrete was _____ of choice. However, steel allowed architects _____ structures. _____ was the Home Insurance Building in Chicago. It was only _____ but was _____ to have a steel frame.

Now, the reason skyscrapers came about was _____ _____ in larger cities. _____ the need for _____, architects had to develop _____ _____. Skyscrapers were their _____. Probably _____ _____ ever is the Empire State Building in New York City. It _____ in 1931. For _____ _____, it held the title of _____ _____.

Practice Test

M Professor: The Romans were _____. And as most of you probably know, gladiator contests were _____ _____ during Roman times. The Romans needed large venues, _____ _____ and _____ _____. Therefore, they _____ and _____ the amphitheater. Amphitheaters are _____-_____. _____ amphitheaters were _____ _____ on two sides of a circular ground. Basically, they were like _____ _____ that _____, and this gave spectators _____. However, wooden amphitheaters were _____. For one thing, they were _____. They were set up for a contest and _____ _____. People _____ doing that. The wood was a danger _____ _____ and _____, too. Therefore, _____ more _____ came about.

The Romans _____ permanent amphitheaters _____ such as marble or limestone. _____

_____ in Rome around 70 A.D. was the famous Colosseum. In addition, _____ _____, just about _____ - _____ city had an amphitheater. Like the Colosseum, we can _____ _____ today. _____ they are still standing _____ and _____ were.

Chapter 2

Sample Question

W Professor: Oh, hello, Ryan. Have you _____ _____ yet?

M Student: No. _____ _____, Professor Stearns.

W: Really? What _____ _____?

M: Well, I love _____.

W: Then _____ _____ major in art?

M: Well, I also _____. I _____!

W: I see. I _____, Ryan.

M: Sure.

W: Why don't you do _____ _____?

M: Do you mean _____? I _____.

Exercise 1

W Student: Professor Goodman, _____ _____, please?

M Professor: Sure, Christine. How are you?

W: I _____ in class.

M: You do? _____?

W: I am _____.
I try to _____ you say, but I can't.

M: Just _____.
_____ I say.

W: I do that. But I still _____.

M: Hmm. How about _____
_____?

W: I _____ in the class. _____
_____.

M: Okay. Then _____
_____ by using your smartphone?

W: You _____ students _____
_____?

M: Sure. _____ don't like it. But I am fine _____
_____.

W: That's _____. Thanks so much, sir.

Exercise 2

M Student: Hello, Professor Thomas.

W Professor: Good morning, Eric. Congratulations on _____
_____ for me.

M: Ah, yeah. Thanks a lot. I _____
an A+.

W: You _____. In fact, it was
_____ in the class.

M: Wow. Thanks

W: So _____
_____?

M: Actually, I'm here to _____.

W: What about it?

M: Well, I _____ writing it. And I

_____, too.

W: That's good.

M: I think I _____

_____ archaeology. What do you think?

W: You're _____. You could do it.

M: Wonderful. Do you have _____

_____ now?

W: Of course. _____ to know?

Exercise 3

M Professor: _____

_____ for a moment, Isabella?

W Student: Sure. _____?

M: Preston _____ that you're _____

_____.

W: Did he? I told him _____.

I wanted to tell you.

M: So it's true. Well, _____?

W: Oh, don't worry, Professor Rogers. I just _____.

M: So you will be back?

W: That's right. I'm just going to _____

_____.

M: So you'll _____?

W: Yes, sir. I'm _____ for a while.

M: Actually, that's a good idea.

W: Yeah. It will give me _____

_____ my future.

M: That's a wonderful idea. I _____ you come back

soon. You're one of _____.

164

W: It's _____

_____. Thank you.

Exercise 4

M Professor: Welcome, Susan. Please _____.

W Student: Hi, Professor Harper. That was a good class today.

M: Thanks. I'm _____. I always

_____ that topic.

W: So what do you need _____?

M: I've _____ for you.

W: Really?

M: I need to _____.

W: For what?

M: You don't know yet? You _____

to _____.

W: No way. Are you serious?

M: I _____ about something like this.

W: I _____. This is amazing.

M: You'll _____ in Scotland this summer. All of your

expenses will be _____.

W: I _____. Thank you very much.

M: You're welcome, Susan.

Exercise 5

W Professor: Are you _____

_____, Hugh?

M Student: Yes, ma'am. Did you get my email?

W: No. I _____.

Why?

M: I _____.

Dictation Exercises 165

W: Do you need _____ _____?

M: Well, that _____, but no.

W: Okay. Then . . .

M: Actually, I _____ tomorrow.

W: Really? And the reason is . . .?

M: I have _____ tomorrow afternoon.

W: I see. _____ is it?

M: It's an internship _____. It's _____ for me.

W: _____. In that case, I _____ a problem _____ the lecture.

M: Thanks so much. I _____.

W: Just _____ you _____ from someone.

M: My roommate _____. I'll _____.

W: Great. Good luck at the interview. I _____ the job.

Exercise 6

M Professor: You need _____ _____? Is that correct?

W Student: Actually, I _____.

M: Do you want me to _____?

W: Well, I have _____. I want to know, well, _____ . . .

M: Okay. _____ then.

W: _____

Hemingway. I _____ _____ as an ambulance driver in the war.

M: I see. And the other?

W: _____ Hemingway's novel *The Old Man and the Sea*. I _____ man versus nature . . .

M: Well, they are _____. Which is _____ _____ you?

W: I _____ and _____. That's _____.

M: Well, how about _____?

W: Hmm . . . I _____.

M: Yeah. Perhaps the ambulance driver and the old man are _____ . . .

W: _____, Professor Brooks. I know my topic now. Thanks so much.

M: It's _____.

Exercise 7

M Student: Are you going home, Professor Lewis?

W Professor: Yes, Brandon. But _____. What's up?

M: I need to _____ to you.

W: That _____, Brandon.

M: I know. I'm really sorry.

W: _____ everyone in class?

M: You said that you _____ _____.

W: That's right. I'm sorry. I can't do it. It would _____.

🎧 02-15

M: Well, I had to try. I just _____ last week.

W: _____?

M: Well, someone _____. Then, _____ in my family.

W: _____. Look, Brandon . . .

M: Yes?

W: You're a good student. So I'm going to _____ . . .

M: How so?

W: Well, I _____ the paper. However, your next paper _____. So _____ you get on it _____ that you get _____.

M: That's wonderful. Thank you for _____.

Exercise 8

W Student: Hello. Are you Dr. Lewis?

M Professor: Yes. _____ Lori Wilkins. Please come in . . .

W: Thank you.

M: You _____ you want to _____.

W: Yes, sir.

M: Well, it's _____ in the semester, _____?

W: Yes. I just want to _____. I don't want to get a grade or anything.

M: _____?

W: I want to take _____ next year.

I thought this would be _____.

M: Well, you are correct. It would _____

_____. But there's a problem. According to the university rules, you _____

_____ the classes _____ _____. I'm sorry, but I

_____ _____ in on my class.

W: Oh, that's too bad. I was afraid _____.

M: However, _____? I'll give you a syllabus. I'll tell

you _____ _____ _____. That way, you can

_____ and _____.

_____?

W: That's great. I _____.

Practice Test

M Student: Hello. _____

_____?

W Fitness Center Employee: Oh, hi. We're open _____

_____.

M: That's great. Every day?

W: Yep. Every day.

M: Okay. Well, I want to _____. _____

_____ to do?

W: You're _____, right?

M: Yes, I am.

W: _____, I

_____.

M: _____.

W: Thanks. Would you like me to _____

_____ of the facilities?

M: Sure.

W: _____

_____ of the fitness center. We're here.

Dictation Exercises 169

M: Okay.

W: _____ the locker rooms. _____

_____ the aerobics area. And _____

_____ the weight training area.

M: It _____ to me.

W: _____ ?

M: Just one. Can I get a locker?

W: _____ really quickly . . . Yes, there are

_____ . There's _____

_____ though. Well, it isn't really a charge. You _____

_____ twenty dollars.

M: No problem. Here you go.

W: Great. Just _____ , and you are _____ .

Chapter 3

Sample Question

W Professor: _____ Old English.

It was _____ of the English language. We're talking

_____ about _____

_____ . This, of course, was in England. But Old

English _____ on the island.

People _____ Old English _____

_____ . You see, there were _____

in England. In each, people used _____ or

_____ of Old English.

03-01

170

Exercise 1

M Professor: William Caxton _____ _____ the spread of the English language. That's C-A-X-T-O-N. He's in your textbook. But you should have him in your notes, too.

Caxton was _____ _____. He was _____ _____ to _____ to England. This was around the mid- to late _____. He _____ in, I believe, 1475 or 1476.

He was also _____. He _____ _____ English. This was _____. It _____ _____ books and knowledge.

Caxton _____ —the rich and the poor— _____ _____. He published his books _____ _____ of English. After that, the language _____ _____.

Exercise 2

W Professor: William Shakespeare _____, of course, _____ _____ the English language. Many _____ and _____ we still use today _____ Shakespeare. He also _____ that we _____ _____ today. He _____ _____ too. Basically, he _____ English _____ _____. Pretty amazing, isn't it?

Oh, some students often _____: _____ Shakespeare _____ so many clichés? A cliché is _____. For example, let me see . . . " _____ and _____" is a cliché. " _____ " is another. Well, Shakespeare was actually _____ _____. People after Shakespeare

_____. _____ _____, they _____ they became clichés.

Exercise 3

M Professor: There were _____ Old English. These were the Scandinavian influence and the Latin language. The Scandinavians, _____, the Danes, _____ _____ the British Isles. Oh, _____ the Norwegians. This all _____. They _____ with them. We call this language Old Norse. It was _____ the Anglo-Saxon language. They were both Germanic languages.

Now, _____ Latin. The Romans were perhaps _____ on the planet _____. They brought with them _____ and _____. They also brought Latin and specialized names for _____ and _____. These words _____ to become _____ _____ and _____.

Exercise 4

W Professor: American English _____ _____ from British English. This started as soon as _____ _____ North America. _____ for you. _____ _____ at Jamestown in 1607 and the early Puritan settlements in New England. _____ Native American Indians, who already used pidgin, or _____, _____. In addition, other European languages _____ American soil. This

_____ began to _____ American English. _____ of English _____ in America. For example, Americans in the North and the South have _____ _____ of _____. They even have _____. Sometimes these dialects _____ _____ Americans to _____ _____. Really. It's true.

Exercise 5

M Professor: The *Oxford English Dictionary*, or the *OED*, is _____. It is _____. The *OED* project _____ in the _____ - _____. _____ is quite interesting. Of course, its creators wanted to _____ _____. They even _____ _____ in words. So this was—and still is— _____. The *OED* includes _____ definitions of _____ _____. _____ it is _____ _____. For example, slang is _____ _____ the *OED* as sophisticated, intellectual terms. There's _____ the *OED*. You might think it has a, well, _____. It's _____. It _____ worldwide English usage, _____ British or American English. Today, the *OED* has _____. And it's _____ _____.

Exercise 6

W Professor: There were _____ important influences on _____. Early on _____, the language had _____. That is, many books _____ spelling, grammar, and pronunciation. Two men _____. In England, Samuel Johnson helped _____ one of the _____. It established _____ of _____. Later, in the United States, Noah Webster _____. I'm sure all of you _____ Webster. _____, World War I and World War II _____. Think about it. Many people from _____ came together _____. English _____ between speakers of different languages. In a way, it helped _____ with one another. _____, it helped establish _____ of English. _____, during the _____, _____ and _____ contributed to the creation of _____ of English.

Exercise 7

M Professor: Let's _____ a little. _____ Britain. Think about the British colonies . . . Yes, British colonialism. The British Empire. It had a major influence _____ throughout the world. Generally, this was _____ and _____. However, the American colonies also _____, _____ especially _____

_____ _____ the rise of the independent United States. I'm sorry. Let me _____ _____ _____ the topic. _____

_____ countries and territories that England colonized, _____ the English language _____. _____

at one point, England had colonized or had a major influence _____ _____ - _____ of the land _____

_____. That's quite a lot, isn't it?

At that time, Britain _____ and _____. _____

_____. This is _____

_____. _____, such as India and Singapore, excellent English ability _____

and _____.

_____ of the British Empire: _____

_____.

Exercise 8

M Professor: _____ about the English language.

_____ it has around _____

_____. Tho _____ _____ knows about

_____. _____ only use

around _____ they know.

Now, uh, English has _____ than most languages.

Why is this? Well, the English language often _____

_____. We call these loanwords. _____

_____. An English speaker _____

_____. But _____ for that thing _____

_____. So the person _____

_____ from another language. _____, that word

_____.

Here's an example: Ballet. That's a loanword _____. But

_____. Sushi is _____

🎧 03-17

Dictation Exercises 175

_____. It's _____. But it _____ in the English language _____ people _____ raw fish that people eat. Scholars believe that _____ of all English words _____. Impressive, isn't it?

Practice Test

W Professor: The reason *Beowulf* is _____ it's _____ in the English language. There is only _____—a written text—and it is _____. Today, _____ the British Library. But _____ the author or authors wrote *Beowulf* well before the eleventh century. _____ even believe it _____ around _____. So _____? Well, _____, and we'll probably _____. Actually, *Beowulf* probably _____ just _____. What I mean is the story was most likely _____. This means that _____ over and over again and _____ to the following generations. That is, _____ on by word _____. Sometime, somewhere, certain individuals began to _____. Eventually, _____. Is everyone with me . . .? Great.

I should also mention that *Beowulf* continues _____ today. It is _____ of _____ versus _____. In many ways, it is _____

_____ _____ in the English language.

Chapter 4

Sample Question

M Welcome Center Employee: You look _____.

_____?

W Student: Yes, um . . . no . . . Well, I'm not sure. Is this _____

_____?

M: No. This is _____. Are you

_____?

W: No. I'm a _____. I need _____

_____.

M: Your transcript? _____ the Registrar's office.

W: Okay. _____ the Registrar's office?

M: _____ Keller Hall is?

W: Of course. I _____ Keller.

M: Okay. It's the building _____.

Exercise 1

W Bursar's Office Employee: Next.

M Student: Hello. I think I'm next. I need to _____, please.

W: _____, please . . .

M: 2-4-1-7-7-8-0-1. My _____ is Savage. S-A-V . . .

W: It's okay. I just need _____. Okay. _____

_____?

M: _____?

W: Actually, there are _____

Dictation Exercises 177

_____. You can use _____ or

_____ _____.

M: So no personal checks, huh? All right. Then _____

_____ today?

W: No. You can pay _____ and _____

_____.

M: _____, please?

W: Let's see here. _____ of class . . . That's 2,465.29 dollars for this

semester.

M: Then I guess I'll just _____

today.

Exercise 2

M Registrar's Office Employee: So you want to, um, _____

_____?

W Student: Excuse me? I'm sorry . . . ?

M: _____?

W: _____, I want to _____. I'm

overloaded.

M: Oh, okay. _____ do you want to _____?

W: My _____. It's _____. We have

homework every day.

M: Okay. No problem. I can _____.

W: I _____, right?

M: I'm not sure about that. Let me see. Well, you get _____

_____.

W: That's great. I thought _____.

M: But . . .

W: Uh-oh. _____?

M: You will _____ next semester, _____

_____.

178

W: That's fine. I _____ .

M: Okay. Then, um, congratulations. _____ for you.

W: Well, _____

. . . Thanks so much!

Exercise 3

M Student: Good afternoon. _____
_____, please?

W Math Department Office Employee: Sure. _____
_____?

M: I'm _____ Professor Matzek. I'm a student in _____
_____.

W: His office is in _____.

M: I _____, I _____
_____ a couple of times.

W: Hmm . . . That's strange. He _____
_____ having office hours _____.

M: That's right. I _____ _____
_____ about my class. So that's _____
_____.

W: Oh, wait a minute. I just _____.

M: What's that?

W: This morning, he told me that he _____
_____ today.

M: Oh, _____.

W: Please _____ tomorrow morning. I know _____
_____ in his office _____.

Exercise 4

W Student: Excuse me. Is this _____ _____ ?

M Financial Aid Office Employee: Yes. Are you _____, or are you still _____ _____ ?

W: High school? Gosh. Do I look that young?

M: Well, no, not really. I just _____ that question.

W: Oh, I see. Anyway, I'm _____.

M: Are you _____ now?

W: Yes. I have _____. But it only _____ my _____ and _____.

M: I see. Are _____ ?

W: Yes. I have a 4.0 GPA.

M: Then you _____ the Bertram scholarship. It _____.

W: Are _____? Of getting it, I mean.

M: I think so. Just _____ and _____ by next Friday.

W: Great. Thanks for your help.

Exercise 5

M Dining Services Employee: Good afternoon. _____ _____ ?

W Student: Hello. Are you Mr. Reynolds? I was told _____ _____.

M: Yes, I'm James Reynolds.

W: That's great. Um, does the school dining services _____ _____ _____ ?

M: Yes, _____. _____ do you have?

W: Well, I'm _____. And we'd like to _____ _____.

M: So you want to _____?

W: Exactly.

M: Sure. We have _____. They _____ simple sandwiches and drinks _____ a full banquet.

W: Sandwiches will probably _____.

M: You're _____?

W: That's right.

M: Okay. I've got a brochure right here . . . Uh, _____. Take a look at it, and _____ _____.

W: Do I need to _____? The event _____ _____.

M: Just _____ you have the event.

W: _____. Thanks for letting me know.

Exercise 6

W Cafeteria Assistant: Meal card, please.

M Student: Okay, I think I have it . . . _____.

W: Thank you. Oh, you only have _____ on this card.

M: Really? Thanks for _____. Can you _____ _____?

W: Sure. You can only add them _____ or _____.

M: I'll _____.

W: Fine. _____ your card again?

Dictation Exercises 181

M: Sure. Here you are . . .

W: Thank you. _____ _____ 128 dollars.

M: Let's _____. I _____ right now.

W: Okay. Can I see your card _____?

M: Sure, sorry.

W: Thanks. So _____ _____ sixty-four dollars.

M: Here's twenty, forty, sixty and one, two, three, four . . . Sixty-four.

W: Thank you very much. Can I help you _____?

M: Actually, yes. Can I use my card _____?

W: Of course.

M: Thanks for everything.

W: My pleasure.

Exercise 7

M Teaching Assistant: Hi. Are you here to _____ _____ _____?

W Student: Um, yes, I guess so.

M: You _____.

W: Well, I _____, but you know.

M: Anyway, first, I _____ your student ID.

W: Quick question. _____ do I _____?

M: _____. You take the test _____.

W: A computer?

M: Sure. _____ are on them. It _____ after you finish.

W: Oh, okay. Here's my ID.

M: Great. You are _____. That's _____. Do you need _____ or _____?

W: Yes, please.

M: _____ _____ _____. And here is your ID. Remember that you can _____ _____

_____.

W: Really?

M: Of course. But most students _____ _____ _____

_____ _____.

W: Two hours? I'll probably need _____.

M: Just try to _____ and _____.

W: Okay. I will.

M: Good luck.

Exercise 8

W Campus Policewoman: Excuse me. I'm sorry, but you _____

_____.

M Student: Really? Why not?

W: You _____ _____ _____ for campus.

M: _____ _____ a sticker for _____

_____?

W: Yes. This lot _____ _____ with parking stickers.

M: Oh, I see. I'm sorry about that, officer.

W: Don't worry about it. Many people _____

_____.

M: Then _____ _____? I have class

_____.

W: There is a lot _____. You _____

_____ for that one.

M: Wow! Thanks for _____.

W: It's _____. But try it anyway.

M: Okay.

W: _____, park _____ _____.

M: We can _____, too?

W: Of course. Well, on _____ a game day.

M: You're _____. Thanks.

W: _____. I hope you _____ _____.

Practice Test

W Student: Hello. Can you _____, please?

M Bookstore Employee: That's _____ _____.

W: Wonderful. I'm _____, but I don't know _____.

M: Okay. Do you know _____?

W: No idea.

M: _____?

W: It's for Chemistry 204.

M: Let me see. The computer says there are _____ Chemistry 204 classes. And the professors are using _____.

W: Right. My professor's name is Zephyr. Dr. Zephyr.

M: Perfect. You're _____ _Organic Chemistry_. _____ Alan Lewis.

W: Wonderful. Can you _____?

M: _____ . . . It's 89.45 dollars.

W: Wow. That's _____, isn't it?

M: No, chemistry books are _____ . . . Uh-oh.

W: _____ do you _____ uh-oh?

M: I mean that the book is _____.

W: You can't be serious.

M: I am. It's _____ right now. If you want, _____ _____ for you today.

W: Really? Then when can I get it? I have _____ _____ to do for a quiz _____ _____.

M: You will get the book _____ _____ _____.

W: Okay, I think I _____ _____ _____. I'll _____ and _____ _____ next Monday.

Chapter 5

Sample Question

M Student: Good morning, Professor Goodman. You _____ _____ me?

W Professor: Yes, Judd. Please _____ _____ and _____ _____.

M: I hope it is _____ _____ _____.

W: Oh, no. Actually, you _____ _____.

M: That's wonderful.

W: I _____ _____ _____. _____ you _____ about _____ _____?

M: Grad school? You must _____ _____.

W: Really. I think you _____ _____.

🎧 05-01

Exercise 1

M Professor: Heather, do you _____ _____?

W Student: Sure, Professor Greene. I _____ today.

M: Great. How is _____ _____?

🎧 05-03

W: Quite well. Is _____?

M: Well, yes and no.

W: I see. Well, _____ _____ first.

M: I wouldn't say it's bad news. It's just that _____ are having _____ _____ _____ in class.

W: Well, _____ is intricate. But your lectures are great, Professor.

M: Thank you for _____ _____, Heather.

W: Is there _____ to help?

M: Actually, yes. I was hoping _____ _____. You know, by _____ _____ _____.

W: I _____ this semester. But I think I can _____ _____.

M: That's wonderful. Just meet with them _____ or _____ _____. _____ they have. Do _____.

Exercise 2

W Professor: Hi, Sean. Please have a seat. I want to _____ _____ about something.

M Student: Hi, Professor Lambert. _____?

W: I want to _____.

M: Really? Um, _____?

W: Do you _____ on John F. Kennedy?

M: Sure.

W: Well, the university _____ _____ to the new freshman class.

M: Really?

W: Yes. It's _____. There were _____

_____.

I _____, and it _____. Isn't that wonderful?

M: Um, well, I guess so. I mean, I'm ecstatic about it, but . . .

W: But what?

M: I'm _____ in front of _____ _____.

W: Oh, you'll do fine. We'll _____.

M: That _____, ma'am. But I _____.

W: We have three weeks. Don't worry.

Exercise 3

W Student: Professor Harrow. Professor Harrow.

M Professor: Yes? Um, _____?

W: I'm in _____, sir. I'm Regan Holloway.

M: Oh, Regan. I _____. What can I do for you?

W: Can you _____ _____? I _____ I _____ . . .

M: Paper? Um . . . You know that it's _____ _____, right?

W: Well, I like to _____.

M: A head start? Well, _____. That's _____ these days.

W: Can you _____ now?

M: Well, I'm _____. Can you _____ at 3:00 PM?

W: Of course. _____. Thanks so much.

M: Great. I'll _____ then.

Exercise 4

W Professor: Marty, could I _____ for a moment, please?

M Student: Sure, Professor Watson. What can I do for you?

W: Are you _____ for the summer?

M: Yes, I am. I _____ so far though.

W: Well, I just _____ Professor Dobson that he needs _____.

M: Oh, yeah?

W: Yes. He's _____ on the Italian Renaissance. You _____, right?

M: I _____ for six years when I was younger.

W: Wonderful. Well, he needs _____ and _____ some _____. What do you think?

M: Is it a full-time position?

W: I _____. But you'd _____ Professor Dobson _____. Shall I _____ with him?

M: I _____. Thanks for thinking of me, Professor Watson.

Exercise 5

M Student: So, Professor Blaire, _____ the presentation I wrote? I'm _____ this Friday.

W Professor: _____ here is fine.

M: Great.

W: But . . .

188

M: Uh, oh. But what?

W: Well, you _____ _____ the topic I gave you. You _____ _____ the directions precisely.

M: Oh, sorry. I just _____ I liked better, so I thought I would _____ about it.

W: _____.

M: Why not?

W: You have to _____, Jason. I gave you that topic _____. Your presentation _____.

M: Are you sure I _____?

W: This is _____.

M: Okay, but, uh . . . Today is Tuesday. Friday is just _____.

W: Right.

M: _____ prepare my presentation by then?

W: If you _____ on the right topic, you _____, would you?

M: Er, yes . . . _____ _____.

W: Good luck.

Exercise 6

W Professor: Hello, Timothy. I _____ from my secretary. What can I do for you?

M Student: Professor Perry. We're _____. _____ my grade _____?

W: Let me see . . . Timothy Fabian . . . Well, it _____ _____.

M: Really? _____ "pretty good" _____?

W: You have _____.

Dictation Exercises 189

M: A high B? But I need an A _____.

W: An A, huh?

M: Yes.

W: Well, you have _____ _____. Try to _____.
That's _____.

M: I know. But the school _____ my grades next week.

W: I see. Well, _____ . . . You could _____ _____. Your average is about an eighty-eight.

M: Really? _____.

W: _____ - _____ _____ by Wednesday.

M: What's the topic?

W: Something on, um, _____?

M: _____ _____.

W: I _____ though. But I will _____ _____.

M: Thanks, Professor Perry.

Exercise 7

M Professor: Are you _____ _____, Amber?

W Student: Actually, I'm _____.

M: I have class _____.

W: _____.

M: Okay. _____?

W: I think _____ in your classroom yesterday. I _____ _____ at 2:00 PM yesterday.

M: Did you? Did you _____?

W: No, it's _____.

M: Well, I have the key. I can check really quickly _____

_____.

W: _____ you have time?

M: Oh, don't worry about that. Okay. _____ and _____.

_____ it is still there.

W: It is. I can _____ the book _____. It's _____

_____.

_____. It's an expensive book.

M: Amber, can you _____?

W: Sure.

M: I have to run. Can you _____ and

_____ tomorrow? I have to

_____.

W: Sure thing. Go ahead. I'll _____.

Exercise 8

M Professor: Did you _____?

W Student: Yes. It was _____.

M: I'm glad. Can you _____?

W: Uh, sure.

M: Can you help me _____

_____? I _____ to my office.

W: No problem. Some of these are _____, aren't they?

M: They sure are. I bought this one _____. I was _____

_____.

W: And you _____

_____?

M: Sure. I _____ I buy.

W: Wow. Your office _____ .

M: Yes, _____ . My home is _____ .

W: I usually _____ . That is, after the class is over.

M: Yes. Most students _____ . I understand it. You _____ .

W: That's right.

M: Do you _____ ?

W: No, I don't. I _____ . I actually have _____ in my apartment.

Practice Test

W Professor: Good morning, Stewart. Thanks for coming in.

M Student: Good morning, Professor Maddux.

W: I have _____ . What are your _____ ?

M: I'm _____ . Why?

W: You know I'm _____ , right?

M: Yes.

W: I want to _____ for undergrads. You know, to _____ , especially new ones, _____ common questions, _____ phone numbers, and _____ .

M: That's a great idea.

W: Well, I hope you can _____ .

M: Me?

W: Sure. _____ ?

M: Oh, I would love to _____ .

W: _____ I want to start the project this summer. _____ I asked if you are going _____.

M: I see.

W: I want to _____ every day. _____, the website _____ for _____.

M: I've got it. Well, _____ _____ about summer.

W: I _____. _____ think about it. Of course, I'll _____, Stewart.

M: Thanks. I'll definitely _____.

Chapter 6

Sample Question

W Professor: We call it the circulatory system. It _____ the _____ and _____. There are _____ of _____. They are arteries and veins. _____, the _____ from the heart _____. These _____ in them. They are _____. Then, the _____ to it _____. This blood looks _____ as it _____.

06-01

Exercise 1

M Professor: Let's _____ _____ in our bodies, class. Sound good? Okay. Now, um, there are _____: cardiac, skeletal, and smooth.

06-03

Dictation Exercises 193

Everyone, look at the screen . . . Okay . . . _____, look at this image. This is a view of _____. It is _____. _____. It's also an involuntary muscle. This means that _____. Humans _____ _____ by thinking. Now, the _____ image . . . Okay, next are _____. These are a kind of _____. These are the muscles we use _____ _____. They are, _____, in our _____ and _____. They are _____.

Next, the _____ image. The last ones are _____. They are _____, like cardiac muscles. They are found, for example, _____ _____.

Exercise 2

W Professor: The _____ in the human body have _____ _____. Some, _____, such as the backbone or spinal column, _____. They _____ us _____ _____ and _____. _____ of bones is _____. Bones like your ribs in the ribcage _____. Actually, the ribs are kind of like armor, uh, like _____. _____, _____ the spinal cord. The spinal cord allows _____ the rest of your body.

The brain is _____ _____ in the body. _____ _____ this sensitive organ _____ dangerous _____ and _____. _____, the bones are _____. _____ is bone marrow. This substance _____ and _____ in people's bodies.

194

Exercise 3

M Professor: The _____ _____ is actually _____ _____ _____. Well, it's really like a large muscle pump. Um, hang on a second. It is _____ _____ _____ _____. The _____ _____ of the heart _____ _____ from the rest of the body and _____ _____ _____ _____. The left side _____ _____ _____. It _____ _____ _____ and _____ _____ _____ to the rest of the body.

Now, let's go a little deeper. _____ the heart are _____. They're like little rooms in the heart. There are _____ _____. The name of the _____ is atria. They _____ _____ _____ the body and the lungs. The _____ _____ are ventricles. They _____ _____ the lungs and the rest of the body. Everyone got it . . .? Great.

Exercise 4

W Professor: _____ _____ that slice of pizza _____ _____ _____. Or that fried chicken. Whatever. _____ _____ to it? Yes, I'm talking about _____ _____. You know, the digestive system. _____, saliva, um, spit, begins to _____ _____ in your mouth. As a result, it _____ and _____ to swallow. _____, the food _____ _____, or esophagus. This is the tube _____ _____. Small muscles help _____ _____ to your stomach. _____, the esophagus serves _____ _____. _____ food _____ into your windpipe, the breathing tube _____.

That's _____, huh? _____, the food _____ _____. The stomach _____ the food and _____ _____ into a liquid substance.

Exercise 5

M Professor: _____ the immune system now. This is _____ _____. _____ basically _____ germs, viruses, bacteria, and other harmful organisms. It tries to _____ _____. If they get in the body, it attempts _____ _____.

_____, the immune system has _____ _____. The _____ is the _____ of it. It _____ pathogens— you know, germs and other harmful things— _____ _____. There's also mucus _____ and _____. If pathogens get past the skin, _____ can _____ them and _____ them.

_____ pathogens get inside the body? Well, _____ try to _____ them. These cells _____ in your body. They fight infections, diseases, sicknesses, and other problems. Some white blood cells also _____ _____, _____. So if you get a virus _____, the immune system _____ _____. They then _____ and _____ _____.

Exercise 6

W Professor: _____ a full set of teeth. _____, by the time babies are six to twelve months old, _____ _____. At the _____

06-13

_____, most children have _____ _____ _____. We call these primary, or baby, teeth. Ultimately, children have _____. _____, they are _____ _____.
As kids turn five or six years old, their primary teeth _____ _____. Well, they don't just fall out. _____ _____ in the gums begin to _____ _____ _____. We call adult teeth _____ _____. By the age of twelve or thirteen, most kids have _____ _____ _____ _____.

There are twenty-eight in all. That's _____ _____ the first set. But this _____ _____ _____ tooth development. _____, perhaps between the ages of eighteen and twenty-one, some young adults _____ _____ _____. Notice, class, that I said some. _____ _____ wisdom teeth.

Exercise 7

M Professor: The _____ is _____ _____ in the body. Really. It _____ _____ _____ together. The skin also _____ us and _____ us _____ _____ _____. And it _____ us the _____ _____ _____.
Okay. There are _____ to our skin. Let's start with _____ _____. _____ _____ is the epidermis. Actually, it _____ _____ dead skin cells. They are _____ and _____. _____ _____ of weeks, they _____ _____. More dead skin cells _____ _____. _____ the dermis. It _____ _____ and _____ _____. _____ allows us _____ _____ like hot water and cool breezes. The sweat glands are _____

Dictation Exercises   197

_____, We _____
_____ in the skin. These openings _____
_____ pores. _____ helps us _____ on hot days.
_____ is _____. It
_____. It is also _____
_____.

Exercise 8

W Professor: _____, human beings _____
_____. One is _____. This is the _____
_____. We _____
_____. _____, some people _____. We
_____. Another sense is _____. Take
this word down in your notes, class: audition. The experts _____
_____. It could be on your test. Hint, hint . . .
Now, we hear _____. People with
the _____ are _____. Everyone with
me . . .? Great. Next is _____. The
nose is the _____ for _____. Some experts believe the sense
of smell is _____.
We have _____ to discuss. One is _____
_____. _____ we use
for taste is the _____. _____, we have _____
_____. It _____ for
feeling and sensation. And, yes, the _____ is the _____ we
use _____.

Practice Test

M Professor: _____ tendons or ligaments, we _____. Together with muscles, they _____ us the _____ _____, _____, _____ things, _____ things, and _____ just about any _____. _____, let's discuss tendons. These are connective tissues that _____ or _____. Tendons are fairly _____ and very _____ and _____. However, sometimes we can _____, and this can _____. A common tendon injury _____. We call this tendon the Achilles tendon. It _____ the calf, which is a _____-_____. The Achilles is _____ in the human body. Now, let me discuss ligaments. _____ tendons, they are _____, but unlike tendons, they _____. So ligaments basically _____ in our bodies. Let me _____ you _____. Um, well, your _____ are _____ of where ligaments _____ of in arms. Your _____ are _____. Moreover, ligaments are elastic. That is, they can _____, but _____ if they _____.

Chapter 7

Sample Question

W Professor: The Great Barrier Reef _____. The _____ in the world is _____. Some experts think it _____

Dictation Exercises **199**

_____. Remember, everyone, that coral reefs are _____ _____. They _____ _____ in the ocean. And _____ _____ are the _____ _____ of this sad situation. The reef _____ _____. Some fish _____ _____ when the _____ _____.

Exercise 1

M Professor: We all know about _____. You probably saw _____ _____ about the one that just _____ _____ _____. Well, volcanoes do _____ _____. There are also _____ volcanoes. Now, uh, here's _____ _____ about underwater volcanoes. When they _____, the lava _____ _____. This usually makes the lava _____ _____ and _____. _____ _____, the volcano _____ _____. The lava _____ _____. So the volcano _____ _____ under the water. If it _____ _____, the volcano will _____. This _____ _____ _____. There are _____ around the world. There are many islands _____ _____. They are all _____ _____. A new island just _____ _____ _____. Let me show you some pictures.

Exercise 2

W Professor: _____ _____ on the Earth _____ _____ is the Marianas Trench. We can find it _____ near

200

Guam. _____ is nearly seven miles deep. And it's _____, so it's _____.
Think of it like this. Mount Everest is _____ in the world. The Marianas Trench is _____ _____, making it _____ Mount Everest. _____ is it _____? It _____ _____ plate tectonics. Continental plates and oceanic plates are always _____ or _____. The oceanic plate near the trench is _____, so it is _____ _____. _____, the continental plate in the area is _____. Their actions _____ the Marianas Trench.

Exercise 3

W Professor: There are many types of _____. But there are _____ of corals, too. Deep corals _____ _____ like their shallow relatives. There are _____ of _____ _____. They are _____, _____, and _____ _____. Please make note of them, class. Okay. Stony corals are _____ _____ and _____. They can _____ _____. soft corals. They are _____. Pinks and reds are _____ _____. They come _____ shapes and sizes. _____ of them is the sea fan. It's _____ and _____. It's _____, actually. _____ are black corals. They are often _____ or _____ with a _____. Many of them can _____ _____.

Dictation Exercises 201

Exercise 4

M Professor: This is a _____ of _____. Icebergs are basically _____ chunks of _____ can be quite _____. Some can be _____. They might be _____, too. And here's something interesting. _____ of an iceberg is actually _____. Most of its bulk is _____. _____ icebergs are _____. Throughout history, _____ have _____ and _____. The *Titanic* is _____, of course.

Most icebergs _____. They break off _____. Then, they _____ the water. Some of them _____. These icebergs often _____ and _____. Others _____ for years and years.

Exercise 5

W Professor: _____ are simply the _____ and _____ of the _____. The _____ of _____ creates tides. Tides _____ about _____ or so. There are basically _____: flood and ebb tides. _____? Okay. Think about a time _____. Say you were _____. After around thirty minutes or so, you probably noticed _____.

202

_____ to your sandcastle. This was _____ _____. The water was _____ and _____ the beach. Is everyone with me . . .? Now, at a certain time, the water _____ _____ as it could. That was _____. Then, _____, and the tide began to recede. That means it _____ the beach. We call this _____. _____, the _____ of the ocean _____. We call this _____. Then, the cycle _____.

Exercise 6

M Professor: I want to _____ today: the Red Sea and the Black Sea. _____ the Red Sea. Everyone, _____ in your book on page 244. Now, find the Red Sea . . . It's _____ Saudi Arabia _____ Africa. It has _____ of all the oceans on the Earth. Some experts presume its name _____ located nearby. _____ the Black Sea. See if you can find it in your text. _____ directly north of Turkey in Southeastern Europe. It has _____ the Red Sea. _____, the Black Sea is very abyssal. This makes _____. Some experts believe _____ the Black Sea. Are there any questions so far, class?

07-13

Exercise 7

W Professor: We _____ _____ rogue waves were just _____. In other words, we thought that _____ _____. However, modern research proves they _____ _____. We also call them _____. They are giant waves that _____ _____. That is, they form _____ _____. Now, _____ the better-known tsunamis. It's clear that _____ _____ tsunamis. But rogue waves seem to _____. They can _____ on the ocean surface. They are like _____ _____. Tsunamis, _____ _____, _____ _____ on the surface like rogue waves. They _____ and do their damage _____. Is everyone clear on this . . .? Perfect.

Oh, _____ between rogue waves and tsunamis. Rogue waves simply _____. Sometimes they _____ _____ or so. However, tsunamis often _____ _____ and _____ before striking land.

Exercise 8

M Professor: _____ the blue whale is _____ on the Earth. We also know that _____. But _____ _____? _____ on the Earth . . .? Nobody . . .? Actually, it _____ as the blue whale. It is _____. The whale shark _____ _____ though.

204

It is pretty sluggish _____. It can

_____ _____ around _____

in length. It also has _____, unlike many man-eating sharks. Whale

sharks _____

_____. Well, they might eat some tiny ones _____

_____. But they usually feed on _____ and _____. They're basically

_____, _____. _____

_____, unlike some species of sharks, they're _____. They

are even _____ at times. Isn't that amazing, class?

Well, I think it is.

Practice Test

M Professor: The Pacific and Atlantic oceans are _____

_____ in the world. However, the Pacific is about _____

_____. It _____

_____ of the world's seawater. The Atlantic holds

just _____. _____

between the two is that _____ is _____

_____ the Atlantic.

Moving on, the Atlantic _____

the east coast of the Americas _____ the west coast of Europe and Africa. Everyone,

please _____

_____ on page ninety-seven in your text. Do you see it . . .? Very good.

_____, please note _____

_____

_____ of the world. It _____

_____. We call this _____. It _____ the

Earth _____. Oceans are _____

_____. The equator also _____ the

_____ and _____ oceans. Now,

_____ the west

Dictation Exercises 205

coast of the Americas _____ the east coast of Asia. Of course, these _____

_____ have to _____, don't they?

Off _____

_____ at Cape Horn, they _____ as one.

Chapter 8

Sample Question

W Professor: The _____ is _____ of all

bears. Actually, it's _____ on the

planet. Carnivores are _____. It

650 _____ 1,350 pounds. Big, huh? In addition, _____

_____ is between eight and ten feet. But that's when it's _____

_____.

_____ might be thirteen feet tall. It's also _____

_____ and _____. Some polar bears can

_____ at one time.

🎧 08-01

Exercise 1

M Professor: _____ might be scary, but they are _____.

Some species _____ or even

_____. The _____ of _____

_____ is about 8.2 feet. _____ a bit more at around 11.2

feet. They also have _____, _____.

_____ between seventy-four and eighty _____. New teeth

_____ during their lives. Some alligator experts believe

the average alligator _____ or even _____

_____ in one lifetime. That's a lot of teeth.

I _____ something to you. Alligators have

_____ that you can't see if their

🎧 08-03

jaws are closed. These teeth _____, _____. There are _____ between _____ and _____. Let me discuss them . . .

Exercise 2

W Professor: Bull sharks are perhaps some of _____. They like to _____. They are even _____. Sometimes they even _____. A few years ago, _____ a bull shark more than 2,000 miles _____.

_____ be about 6.8 feet long. They can _____ 196 pounds. However, _____ get _____! They can _____ 11.7 feet _____ and _____ nearly 700 pounds. Now that's _____.

And how about _____? Well, they are usually—but not always—_____. They _____ just about _____—_____! Bull sharks are _____ _____, too. This means that they _____ _____. They'll _____ that crosses _____.

Exercise 3

M Professor: There are _____. These are predatory birds. One you probably know of is _____. It lives _____. Actually, it is _____ of the United States. Anyway, the bald eagle is _____. The _____ is usually _____ seventy-two _____ ninety-five centimeters. That's _____ _____

_____. Its _____ is normally _____ 167 _____ 223

centimeters. Yeah, that's _____. Oh, and it usually _____

about 3.7 to 6.4 kilograms.

And how about _____ _____? Well, the bald eagle _____

_____ of any North American bird. These nests are

enormous! They can be _____

_____. _____ even 2.4 to 2.7 meters _____.

_____, a single nest can _____ _____

_____. Amazing!

Exercise 4

M Professor: Let's move on to _____, which

_____ an orca. Some populations, or pods,

_____. _____,

some populations _____ such as seals. It really

_____ and

_____.

The orca is _____ with _____

_____, or underside. Males can be almost _____

_____. Many orcas _____

_____ 12,000 pounds. _____ ever

_____ 17,636 pounds. It _____

_____ the coast of Japan. _____ are big.

Just so you know, we _____. At birth, they can weigh

_____.

An orca _____,

too. On average, it lives to be _____

_____. However, _____ can live to be _____ or even

_____.

208

Exercise 5

W Professor: Komodo dragons are very _____ _____.
Today, they are _____ only _____
_____ in Indonesia. Komodo dragons are _____. This means that they are
_____.
They are _____. They _____
_____ and then, at the last minute, _____ and
_____. They also have an _____ —I mean keen— _____
_____. They can _____ prey up to nearly _____
_____. They are _____
_____, too. Some can _____ about _____
_____.
Western scientists _____ Komodo dragons _____
_____. Today, scientists _____ there are between _____ and
_____ Komodo dragons _____
_____. They are _____ considered a _____ _____.
_____ and _____ are _____ _____
_____ they are in danger of extinction.
Now, are they _____? Sure, they intimidate people. And if you _____
_____ to one, it might _____. So it's _____
_____ from
them.

Exercise 6

W Professor: _____ typically _____ about
272 kilograms. They are _____
after the tiger. The average weight of the tiger is _____
_____.
Lions _____. We call this _____
_____. They like to _____. They

_____ such as wildebeests, zebras, and buffaloes. They _____ and _____ their prey. Then, _____. They must be _____ before they attack. Sure, they can _____. _____ are close to _____ _____ per hour. However, they _____ the best _____. _____ they must be _____ _____ to their prey. _____ _____, kind of like pet cats, lions are _____ _____. They are _____ for about _____ _____. _____ is their most _____ time. And most of their _____ happens _____ _____. They also _____ about _____ a day _____ and then nearly _____ a day _____.

Exercise 7

M Professor: _____ is the owl. There are _____ of owls. It's a _____. This means that it _____ _____. It is also a nocturnal predator. This means that it _____ _____. You can _____ owls _____ on the planet. That is, _____ like Antarctica. Now, _____ help the owl _____ a very _____. One is its _____. It can _____ - _____ very clearly. It _____ _____ things _____ though. _____ is its _____. It _____ _____ its head _____. This means it can _____ _____. It simply quietly _____

_____ more than _____ - _____.

Oh, there's _____. _____ helps it _____ in with the _____. This lets it _____. You could say it has _____ in the wild.

Exercise 8

W Professor: This is the rhinoceros. People often just _____ _____. There are _____ on the planet today. They live _____, _____, and _____. Most people recognize rhinos _____. Some types have _____ _____.

Sadly, the rhino is _____ _____ today. Many people _____ them _____. They believe _____ can be _____ from the _____. _____, there are _____ _____ in the wild today. _____, rhinos are _____. However, they _____. You see, rhinos _____. And they _____. When they are _____, they _____. And they're _____. Some can _____ 2,500 kilograms. They can also _____ _____ an hour. So you _____ _____ rhinos. They can be _____ if you _____. They have even been _____.

Practice Test

M Professor: I want to _____ today. They _____ mainly _____, but we can also _____ them _____. Well, they're _____ of South America. They are one of _____ in the Americas. Now, there's _____ about gray foxes. You see, they have the unique _____. Most other foxes _____ or _____. The _____ they climb trees are _____ and _____ _____. They also usually live _____ _____ with a lot of brush, but they also live _____ _____. Now, I want to move on to _____. They are _____ _____. In general, red foxes are _____ _____. The two types tend to _____, but _____ _____ tend to be more _____. They are _____ _____, _____ like to live in _____, and we can find them _____ and _____. _____, _____, unlike gray foxes, are able to _____.

Actual Test

Actual Test 1 Conversation

W Student: Good afternoon, Professor Tomlinson. _____ _____ now?

M Professor: Well, I was _____. But

I'm _____ _____ _____ _____. What can I do for you, Cindy?

W: Thanks so much, sir. I _____ _____. This _____ _____ _____ _____.

M: Sure.

W: So, uh, I'm here _____ _____ _____.

M: That's _____ _____ _____.

W: You know, uh, _____ _____ was _____ _____ _____ _____ I had expected. I'm _____ _____ my score was _____ _____.

M: Did you _____ _____ _____ with you?

W: Yes, _____ _____ _____ here . . . Uh, here you are . . .

M: Thanks. _____ _____ _____ . . . Ah, okay. I remember now.

W: Yes?

M: Well, this was _____ _____ _____. You were supposed to _____ _____ _____ to the questions. But you _____ _____ _____ _____ instead.

W: Oh, I see.

M: Take a look at _____ _____. Most students wrote _____ _____ _____ _____ for their answers. But you wrote _____ _____ _____. That's _____ _____ _____. You _____ _____ for two other questions.

W: I guess _____ _____ _____.

M: Well, try to _____ _____ _____ the next time. I know you _____ _____ _____. But you need to show me that _____ _____ _____ _____.

W: Yes, sir. I'll _____ _____ _____ on the final exam.

M: Great. _____ _____ and _____ _____. Then, I'm sure your test will _____ _____ _____.

Dictation Exercises 213

Actual Test 1 Lecture

W Professor: _____ was intense, wasn't it? _____ , _____ , we got _____ in just two hours. Lots of trees _____ by the wind, too. Today, I want to talk about _____ like _____ _____ . What is severe weather? It's basically _____ _____ that _____ _____ buildings, _____ people, and _____ _____ to daily life. There are _____ severe weather. There are _____ , of course. _____ and _____ are severe weather. _____ blizzards, ice storms, and hailstorms. And _____ _____ tornadoes. They are _____ _____ . We can _____ severe weather _____ . _____ is _____ severe weather. _____ _____ is _____ severe weather. General severe weather happens _____ . _____ hurricanes, typhoons, and blizzards. Localized severe weather is _____ _____ . It includes _____ as well as _____ _____ . _____ are localized weather, too. Severe weather can be _____ . A single typhoon or hurricane _____ . It may _____ many more and _____ buildings _____ _____ and _____ . Tornadoes can _____ _____ . _____ because of one tornado. _____ a tremendous amount of _____ , especially to _____ . Fortunately, _____ severe weather. So people can _____ . Their property _____ , but they will be okay. Let me _____ of how

214

_____ recently.

Actual Test 2

Actual Test 2 Conversation

W Librarian: Excuse me. You seem like _____ _____. _____ with something?

M Student: Oh, hello. You're _____?

W: That's right.

M: Great. I've got a problem.

W: You _____ _____?

M: It's _____. There are several books _____. But they're either _____ _____ or _____ _____.

W: _____?

M: It's _____ in France _____ _____. It's for _____.

W: Hmm . . . _____ _____ we have too many books _____.

M: I have _____ I want. I checked the _____. Of the ten books I need, the library _____ _____. _____ at all.

W: What about _____?

M: Three are _____. One is _____ _____ available, but I _____ _____ on the shelves.

W: _____. Which is _____ _____?

M: It's _____ on the list . . . The book

_____ _____ Claude Desmond.

W: I'm _____. But I'll _____ we need to find it.

M: Thanks. Now, uh, what about _____?

W: You have _____. _____, you can _____ that are checked out. That means they _____ _____. Then, you can _____ _____.

M: My paper _____ _____ from now.

W: Great. So you'll be _____ _____, you can use the interlibrary loan program. That means you can _____ _____.

M: _____ this program. Can you tell me _____, please?

Actual Test 2 Lecture

M Professor: In 1856, _____ _____ in the Neander Valley in Germany. People realized it was _____ _____. _____ the Neanderthal after where it was dug up. Since then, anthropologists _____ Neanderthal skeletons. They have found _____ and _____, too. So we _____ Neanderthals now.

_____, Neanderthals _____ _____. They also lived in _____ of _____ and _____ _____. They _____ around _____. They _____ approximately _____

216

_____. They are considered _____ today.

Neanderthals _____ around 1.50 to 1.75 meters _____. _____ between sixty-four and eighty-two kilograms. They also had _____. We believe their brains _____. We know they _____ _____, so they were definitely able to _____. Ah, yes, they _____. They also ate _____ and _____. Those that _____ _____ and _____, too. Now, uh, as I said, they _____ around _____ _____. Why? _____. They _____ because of _____ _____. They were _____ _____ in frigid temperatures. They _____ because of _____ either. They lived in _____ _____ such as _____ and _____. Some anthropologists believe _____ made them _____. You see, modern humans _____ _____ _____ and _____. They _____ Neanderthals. It's likely _____ _____, and Neanderthals were _____.

Actual Test 3

Actual Test 3 Conversation

W Student: Professor Moore, you _____ now, right?

M Professor: I sure do, Tina. What do you _____ _____?

W: I'm _____ with the _____

_____ .

M: _____ problems?

W: Well, actually, I _____ .

I _____ .

M: All right. I asked everyone _____ we discussed _____ .

W: That's right. We _____ interesting things, but, uh, I just don't know _____ .

M: Why don't you tell me _____ ? I mean, what topics _____ ?

W: Hmm . . . I loved _____ . I also liked the lecture on _____ - _____ .

M: _____ ?

W: Sharks. It was _____ sharks.

M: Okay. _____ you mentioned did you _____ ?

W: Oh . . . that's _____ . _____ deep-sea creatures. I really _____ .

M: That's good. Was there _____ learning about?

W: _____ the lanternfish was _____ . I also _____ the octopus. I _____ shoot ink as a defense mechanism.

M: Hmm . . . I think _____ .

W: We have?

M: Yes. I _____ the defenses deep-sea creatures have. Choose _____ or _____ _____ , _____ they _____ _____ from predators. _____ .

W: Oh, wow. That _____ . Um . . . _____ I should start?

218

M: _____, I'd go to the library.

W: Great idea. _____ my next class starts. Thanks so much for helping, Professor Moore. See you in class tomorrow.

Actual Test 3 Lecture

W Professor: _____
_____ humans, dogs, cows, horses, and dolphins. They are _____-
_____ that have _____
_____. They _____ their young _____
and _____ _____. Mammals can _____
_____, like whales, elephants, and hippos.
Now, uh, there is _____ called
marsupials. Marsupial _____ M-A-R-S-U-P-I-A-L, by the way. There are
_____ of marsupials. Most live in _____
and _____. They _____ the _____, the
_____, and the wombat. Ah, there's _____ marsupial _____
_____. It's the possum.
Marsupials _____ with _____.
_____, they have _____
_____ of mammals I just mentioned. But there are also
_____. For example, _____
_____ well-developed young. When marsupials give
birth, _____
_____. They are _____ and _____
_____ and _____. Obviously, they _____
_____. A marsupial female _____
_____ in her stomach. The babies _____
_____, where they can _____
_____. They _____ in
the pouch.
There are _____. Let me see . . . Marsupials have

_____ regular mammals. _____, they _____ _____ their entire lives. Marsupials have _____ _____ than mammals. And they have lower metabolic rates. Okay. _____ for now. Why don't we _____ _____? When we come back, I'm going to _____ _____ _____ on marsupials.

High Score iBT TOEFL LISTENING For Junior Intermediate
2nd Edition

Publisher Kyudo Chung
Editors Woonhee Park, Sangik Cho
Author William Link
Designers Minji Kim, Kyuok Jeong

First published in February 2008 by Happy House
Second edition first published in June 2023 by Darakwon, Inc.
Darakwon Bldg., 211, Munbal-ro, Paju-si, Gyeonggi-do 10881
Republic of Korea
Tel: 82-2-736-2031 (Ext. 250)
Fax: 82-2-732-2037

Copyright © 2008 Happy House, 2023 Darakwon

All rights reserved. No part of this publication may be reproduced, stored in a retrieval system, or transmitted in any form or by any means, electronic, mechanical, photocopying or otherwise, without the prior consent of the copyright owner. Refund after purchase is possible only according to the company regulations. Contact the above telephone number for any inquiries. Consumer damages caused by loss, damage, etc. can be compensated according to the consumer dispute resolution standards announced by the Korea Fair Trade Commission. An incorrectly collated book will be exchanged.

ISBN 978-89-277-8060-1 14740
       978-89-277-8056-4 14740 (set)

www.darakwon.co.kr

Photo Credits
Shutterstock.com

Components Main Book / Answer Key
8 7 6 5 4 3 2   24 25 26 27 28

High Score iBT TOEFL LISTENING For Junior

2nd Edition

Intermediate

Answer Key

DARAKWON

Intermediate

Answer Key

CHAPTER 1 Architecture

Understanding TOEFL Question Types & Listening Skills
p.14

1 Question Types ▶ Sample Question

Ⓒ

스크립트 🎧 01-01

M Professor: Actually, class, the builders of the Eiffel Tower didn't plan on it being permanent. The French built it for the World's Fair in 1889. It was the world's tallest structure until 1930. But the government wanted to tear it down after a while. Many French citizens wanted to do that, too. Can you believe it? Many people thought it was ugly. Of course, the Eiffel Tower survived. Today, more people visit it than any other monument.

해석

M Professor: 사실은 말이죠, 여러분, 에펠탑을 세운 사람들은 그것을 계속해서 세워 두려고 계획하지는 않았어요. 프랑스 사람들은 1889년 세계 박람회 때문에 에펠탑을 세웠죠. 에펠탑은 1930년까지 세계에서 가장 높은 구조물이었습니다. 하지만 정부는 얼마 후에 에펠탑을 분해하고 싶어했어요. 많은 프랑스 시민들도 그렇게 하길 원했고요. 믿어지나요? 많은 사람들이 에펠탑을 흉물스럽다고 생각했습니다. 물론, 에펠탑은 그 위기를 넘겼습니다. 오늘날 이제는 다른 어떤 기념탑보다 더 많은 사람들이 에펠탑을 방문하고 있습니다.

2 Listening Skills ▶ Check-Up

1 The French built it for the World's Fair.
2 Many French citizens wanted to do that, too.
3 Many people thought it was ugly.
4 Of course, the Eiffel Tower survived.

• Exercise 1 •
p.16

정답 Q1 Ⓓ Q2 Ⓒ

스크립트 🎧 01-03

W Professor: The Egyptians began building pyramids around the year 3000 B.C. Now, think about this for a moment . . . These magnificent structures were the tallest things on the Earth for around several thousand years.
The pyramids served important roles in Egyptian culture. They were tombs for kings. That's right. Egyptian pharaohs spent many, many years building the pyramids to be their final resting places. Inside a pyramid, there is often an elaborate network of chambers, or rooms. The main one houses the pharaoh's mummified body. For example, the Pyramid at Giza has three main chambers. The king's chamber, or room, is right in the center of the pyramid. It's difficult to reach, too. The engineers were clever. They built solid rock blocking systems. For thousands of years, these protected the pharaohs' tombs from thieves.

해석

W Professor: 이집트인들은 기원전 3000년경에 피라미드 건설을 시작하였습니다. 자, 이것에 대해 잠깐 생각해봅시다… 이 어마어마한 구조물은 어림잡아 몇천 년 동안 지구상에서 가장 높은 물체였습니다.
피라미드는 이집트 문화에서 중요한 역할을 담당했습니다. 피라미드는 왕의 무덤이었습니다. 맞아요. 이집트의 파라오는 그들이 마지막으로 쉴 장소가 될 피라미드를 짓는 데 아주 오랜 시간을 들였어요. 피라미드의 안에는 흔히 내실(內室), 그러니까 방들이 정교하게 연결되어 있습니다. 주실(主室)에는 파라오의 미라가 보관되어 있습니다. 예를 들어, 기자(Giza)의 피라미드에는 3개의 주실이 있습니다. 왕의 내실, 즉 왕의 방이 피라미드의 정중앙에 있습니다. 그곳까지 들어가는 것 역시 어렵습니다. 설계자들은 현명했습니다. 그들은 단단한 바위로 차단 시스템을 구축했습니다. 수천 년 동안 이 시스템이 도굴꾼들로부터 파라오의 무덤을 지켰습니다.

Listening Skills

1 They were tombs for kings.
2 Inside a pyramid, there is often an elaborate network of chambers, or rooms.
3 It's difficult to reach, too.
4 These protected the pharaohs' tombs from thieves.

• Exercise 2 •
p.17

정답 Q1 Ⓑ Q2 Ⓓ

스크립트 🎧 01-05

W Professor: The ancient Greeks were great architects. They made impressive buildings. In fact, many of their buildings are still standing today. Go to Athens and other Greek cities today. You will see the remains of temples and other structures in many places.
Greek architecture is known for its columns. A column is a slender, tall, circular structure. It often provides support for a building. The Greeks had three main types of columns. They are Doric, Ionic, and Corinthian.
Doric columns were very simple in style. They were thicker than the others, too. Ionic columns had a base at the bottom. They had decorations at the top as well. Corinthian columns had lots of decorations. They were popular, and the Romans copied them later. Let's look at some pictures of them now.

해석

W Professor: 고대 그리스인들은 뛰어난 건축가였습니다. 그들은 인상적인 건축물들을 만들었죠. 실제로 이들의 건축물 중 다수는 오늘날에도 여전히 남아 있습니다. 아테나와 그리스의 다른 도시들에 지금 가보세요. 여러 곳에서 사원들과 다른 구조물들의 유적을 보게 될 거예요.
그리스 건축은 기둥으로 유명합니다. 기둥은 얇고 긴 원형 구조물입니다. 그것은 보통 건물을 지탱해 주죠. 그리스인들은 세 가지 주된 형태의 기둥을 사용했습니다. 도리아식, 이오니아식, 그리고 코린트식 기둥입니다.
도리아식 기둥은 형태가 매우 단순했어요. 또한 다른 기둥들보다 더 두꺼웠죠. 이오니아식 기둥의 아랫부분에는 받침이 있었어요. 또한 꼭대기에는 장식이 되어 있었죠. 코린트식 기둥에는 장식이 많이 달려 있었습니다. 이 기둥은 인기가 높아서 이후에 로마인들이 이 양식을 따라했습니다. 이제 기둥에 대한 사진들을 몇 장 살펴보도록 할게요.

Listening Skills

1 The ancient Greeks were great architects.
2 Greek architecture is known for its columns.
3 A column is a slender, tall, circular structure.
4 Corinthian columns had lots of decorations.

• **Exercise 3** • p.18

정답 Q1 Ⓓ Q2 Ⓓ
스크립트 🎧 01-07

M Professor: Much of the Great Wall of China still stands today. The Chinese built it to protect their empire. For example, it helped them fight the Mongols, their great rival. The Chinese began to build it around the fifth century B.C.
At first, the Chinese used stone, rock, and even soil and grass to build the wall. The stones were hard to work with. Some were big and heavy. However, over time, the Chinese developed better methods. Later, they used bricks to construct it. Bricks also made the wall stronger and sturdier. Actually, the bricks were small and easy for workers to carry. This helped the Chinese build the wall more quickly. Even today, the Great Wall of China is the longest manmade structure on the Earth. It spans about 4,000 miles.

해석
M Professor: 중국 만리장성의 많은 부분이 오늘날까지 남아 있습니다. 중국인들은 제국을 지키기 위해 만리장성을 세웠습니다. 예를 들어, 만리장성은 강하게 대립하는 사이였던 몽골족과 전쟁을 하는 데 도움이 되었습니다. 중국인들은 기원전 5세기경에 만리장성을 세우기 시작했습니다.
처음에, 중국인들은 만리장성을 짓는 데 돌, 바위, 심지어 흙과 풀까지도 사용했습니다. 돌은 작업하기가 힘들었습니다. 어떤 것들은 크고 무거웠죠. 그러나 시간이 지날수록 중국인들은 더 나은 방법들을 개발했습니다. 나중에 그들은 만리장성을 짓는 데 벽돌을 사용했습니다. 게다가 벽돌 덕분에 만리장성은 더 튼튼하고 강하게 만들어졌습니다. 실제로 벽돌은 크기가 작아서 일꾼들이 나르기가 쉬웠습니다. 이런 방식 덕분에 중국인들은 만리장성을 더 빨리 짓게 되었습니다. 현재까지도 중국의 만리장성은 인간이 만든 세계에서 가장 긴 구조물입니다. 그것은 약 4,000마일에 이릅니다.

Listening Skills

1 The Chinese built it to protect their empire.
2 The stones were hard to work with.
3 Later, they used bricks to construct it.
4 Bricks also made the wall stronger and sturdier.

• **Exercise 4** • p.19

정답 Q1 Ⓑ Q2 Ⓑ
스크립트 🎧 01-09

M Professor: Gothic architecture started in France in the twelfth century. Now, I would like to discuss some of its main features. Could somebody turn the lights off, please . . .? Thank you.
Now, this is an image of Notre Dame Cathedral in Paris. It is a classic example of Gothic architecture. The first thing you'll notice are its two towers with pointed spires at the top. You should also notice the huge front of the church. This is the facade. It contains a large rose window. Beautiful, isn't it, class? Now, this next image is the inside of Notre Dame. Look at the massive open space. Look at all the stained-glass windows. Look at how the light filters through. These are other important qualities of Gothic architecture. Don't you think it's marvelous?

해석
M Professor: 고딕 양식은 12세기에 프랑스에서 시작되었습니다. 이제 고딕 양식의 몇 가지 주요한 특징에 대해 이야기하려고 합니다. 누가 불 좀 꺼 줄래요…? 고마워요.
자, 이것은 파리에 있는 노트르담 대성당의 이미지입니다. 노트르담 대성당은 고딕 양식의 전형적인 예라고 할 수 있습니다. 맨 먼저, 꼭대기에 첨탑을 가진 두 개의 탑이 눈에 띌 것입니다. 또한 성당의 넓은 전면도 눈에 띄죠. 이것이 성당의 정면입니다. 전면에는 장미 문양의 커다란 창문이 있습니다. 아름답지 않나요, 여러분? 자, 다음 이미지는 노트르담 대성당의 내부입니다. 웅장하고 탁 트인 공간을 보세요. 모든 창문이 스테인드 글라스로 되어 있는 것을 보세요. 빛이 어떻게 새어 들어오는지 보세요. 이러한 것들이 고딕 양식의 또 다른 중요한 특징들이라고 할 수 있습니다. 멋지지 않나요?

Listening Skills

1 It is a classic example of Gothic architecture.
2 This is the facade.
3 Look at the massive open space.
4 Look at how the light filters through.

• **Exercise 5** • p.20

정답 Q1 Ⓑ Q2 Ⓐ
스크립트 🎧 01-11

W Professor: American architect Frank Lloyd Wright was a genius. Let me explain. He didn't just take out a pencil and paper and design something. No, that wasn't his style at all. Instead, he formed his work based on its surroundings, from nature. Let me give you an example. Fallingwater is one of his most famous homes. It still stands today near Pittsburgh, Pennsylvania. Wright actually built the house on top of a waterfall. I'm sure some of you have seen pictures of it. Many consider it Wright's masterpiece.
Anyway, the point is that Wright didn't destroy the surroundings to build something. He used them by blending them with his design. He also used mostly organic, not artificial, material. At Fallingwater, rock and stone are the main materials. Take a look at this picture of Fallingwater . . . Beautiful, huh? It looks like it is growing right out of the forest and the river. Any comments?

해석

W Professor: 미국의 건축가 프랭크 로이드 라이트는 천재였습니다. 설명을 하자면요. 그는 단순히 연필과 종이를 꺼내 어떤 것을 디자인하지 않았습니다. 전혀요, 그것은 그의 방식이 전혀 아니었죠.
대신에, 그는 주변 환경에 기반해서, 그러니까 자연에서 작품을 구성했습니다. 예를 들어 드릴게요. 팔링워터는 그의 가장 유명한 집 중 하나입니다. 그것은 펜실베이니아주, 피츠버그 근방에 오늘날까지 남아 있습니다. 라이트는 그 집을 정말로 폭포 꼭대기 위에 지었습니다. 여러분들 중에는 그 집의 사진을 본 사람이 있을 것입니다. 많은 사람들이 그것을 라이트의 걸작품이라고 여깁니다.
어쨌든, 중요한 것은 라이트가 어떤 것을 지으면서도 주변 환경을 전혀 파괴하지 않았다는 데 있습니다. 그는 환경을 자신의 디자인과 잘 섞이게 하는 방식으로 주변 환경을 이용했습니다. 그는 또한 주로 인공이 아닌, 천연 자재를 사용했습니다. 팔링워터는 바위와 돌이 주요 자재입니다. 이 팔링워터의 사진을 보세요… 아름답죠, 그렇죠? 그것은 마치 숲과 강에서 바로 이어져 자라는 것처럼 보입니다. 다른 의견 있나요?

Listening Skills

1 He formed his work based on its surroundings, from nature.
2 Fallingwater is one of his most famous homes.
3 Many consider it Wright's masterpiece.
4 It looks like it is growing right out of the forest and the river.

• Exercise 6 •  p.21

정답 Q1 ⓒ Q2 Ⓐ
스크립트 ∩ 01-13

M Professor: The Leaning Tower of Pisa is one of the most dramatic structures in the world. Today, I think it leans more than six degrees. That's a lot. It looks like it might fall over at any minute. But it hasn't. It has stood in a similar position for more than 800 years.
Please take note, class. It is the bell tower of a cathedral. It does not stand alone. It also became famous because it leans to one side.
Now, uh, construction on it began in 1173. Soon after, the tower began to lean to one side. Why? Well, first, the architects were not experienced. They did not design or build a strong enough foundation. Second, the location wasn't the best. The tower was built on very soft ground. So poor planning caused the tower to sink. Even today, it continues to lean more and more. But reinforcements have made it stronger and safer.

해석

M Professor: 피사의 사탑은 세계에서 가장 인상적인 건축물 중 하나입니다. 오늘날까지도 그것은 6도 이상 기울어져 있다고 알고 있습니다. 상당히 기울어진 것입니다. 그 탑은 언제고 무너져버릴 것처럼 보이죠. 하지만 아직까지 그렇지는 않습니다. 그것은 800년 넘게 비슷한 자세로 서 있습니다.
필기하세요, 여러분. 피사의 사탑은 대성당의 종탑입니다. 그것은 홀로 서 있지 않습니다. 그것은 또한 한 쪽이 기울어져 있기 때문에 유명해졌습니다.
이제, 아, 그것은 1173년에 축조가 시작되었습니다. 얼마 지나지 않아 탑이 한 쪽으로 기울기 시작했습니다. 왜일까요? 음, 첫째로, 건축가들이 숙련되지 않았습니다. 그들은 기초를 충분히 튼튼하게 디자인하여 세우지 않았습니다. 둘째로, 위치가 좋지 않았습니다. 그 탑은 지반이 매우 약한 땅 위에 세워졌습니다. 그러니까, 빈약한 계획으로 인해 탑이 가라앉게 된 것입니다. 오늘날까지도 탑은 계속해서 점점 더 기울고 있습니다. 그러나 보강을 해서 그것을 더 튼튼하고 안전하게 만들고 있습니다.

Listening Skills

1 It looks like it might fall over at any minute.
2 It does not stand alone.
3 The location wasn't the best.
4 Even today, it continues to lean more and more.

• Exercise 7 •  p.22

정답 Q1 Ⓑ Q2 ⓒ
스크립트 ∩ 01-15

M Professor: The Taj Mahal in India is an extraordinary building. It is a domed structure made mainly of white marble. In the seventeenth century, an Indian emperor built it for his wife after her death. It was a very difficult task, class.
Around one thousand elephants brought all the materials to the worksite. Interestingly, materials from all over Asia make up the Taj Mahal. Inside the white marble, they laid almost thirty different kinds of precious stones. These came from different regions on the Asian continent. For example, the turquoise came from Tibet. The sapphires came from Sri Lanka. And the magnificent crystal came from China. In this way, the Taj Mahal is a very diverse structure. It is a collection of the most beautiful natural materials available in Asia. Now, let's take a look at this video I made of the Taj Mahal last year.

해석

M Professor: 인도의 타지마할은 아주 특별한 건축물입니다. 그것은 주로 흰 대리석으로 이루어진 돔 구조의 건축물입니다. 17세기에 인도의 한 황제는 아내가 죽은 후 그녀를 기리기 위해 타지마할을 지었습니다. 그것은 매우 어려운 작업이었답니다, 여러분.
1000여 마리의 코끼리들이 모든 자재를 작업장으로 옮겼습니다. 흥미롭게도, 아시아 전역에서 공수한 자재들이 타지마할을 구성합니다. 흰 대리석 안을 거의 서른 가지의 다양하고 귀한 보석들로 장식했습니다. 이 보석들은 아시아 대륙의 여러 지역에서 가져온 것이었습니다. 예를 들어, 터키석은 티벳에서 가져왔습니다. 사파이어는 스리랑카에서 가져온 것입니다. 그리고 아름다운 크리스탈은 중국에서 가져왔습니다. 이런 방식 때문에, 타지마할은 매우 다채로운 건축물입니다. 타지마할은 아시아에서 구할 수 있는 가장 아름다운 천연 재료들의 총집합이라고 할 수 있습니다. 이제 작년에 제가 찍어온 이 타지마할에 관한 동영상을 보도록 합시다.

Listening Skills

1 It was a very difficult task, class.
2 The turquoise came from Tibet.
3 The Taj Mahal is a very diverse structure.
4 It is a collection of the most beautiful natural materials available in Asia.

• Exercise 8 • p.23

정답 Q1 Ⓑ Q2 Ⓒ

스크립트 🎧 01-17

W Professor: One of the greatest American contributions to architecture is the skyscraper. They came about in the late nineteenth century in cities like New York and Chicago.
For the first time, architects used steel frames to support buildings. Before steel, concrete was the building material of choice. However, steel allowed architects to design much taller structures. The very first skyscraper was the Home Insurance Building in Chicago. It was only ten stories tall but was the first building to have a steel frame.
Now, the reason skyscrapers came about was the lack of land in larger cities. To satisfy the need for space, architects had to develop new ways of building upward. Skyscrapers were their solution. Probably the most famous skyscraper ever is the Empire State Building in New York City. It was completed in 1931. For the next thirty years, it held the title of the world's tallest building.

해석

W Professor: 미국이 건축에 기여한 가장 큰 업적 중 하나는 마천루입니다. 초고층빌딩들은 뉴욕과 시카고와 같은 도시에서 19세기 후반경에 등장했습니다.
최초로, 건축가들이 철골 구조를 건물을 지지하는 데 사용했습니다. 철골이 등장하기 전에는 콘크리트가 건축 자재로 선택되었습니다. 그러나 철골을 사용하여 건축가들은 훨씬 더 높은 건축물을 디자인할 수 있게 되었습니다. 맨 처음 세워진 마천루는 시카고의 홈 인슈어런스 빌딩이었습니다. 그 건물은 10층 높이밖에 되지 않았지만 철골 구조를 가진 최초의 건물이었습니다.
자, 마천루가 들어서게 된 이유는 대도시에 땅이 부족했기 때문이었습니다. 공간에 대한 수요를 충족시키기 위해, 건축가들은 건물을 세우는 새로운 방식을 개발해야 했습니다. 마천루가 그들의 해답이 되었던 거죠. 아마도 지금까지 가장 유명한 마천루는 뉴욕시의 엠파이어 스테이트 빌딩일 것입니다. 그 빌딩은 1931년에 완공되었습니다. 그 후로 30년 동안 그것은 세계에서 가장 높은 건물이라는 수식어를 달고 있었습니다.

Listening Skills

1 Architects used steel frames to support buildings.
2 Steel allowed architects to design much taller structures.
3 Skyscrapers were their solution.
4 It was completed in 1931.

Vocabulary Review p.24

A 1 tomb
   2 columns
   3 soil
   4 organic
   5 leaning

B 1 Ⓑ 2 Ⓐ 3 Ⓓ 4 Ⓒ 5 Ⓐ

C 1 Ⓒ 2 Ⓓ 3 Ⓐ 4 Ⓑ 5 Ⓐ

D 1 decorations
   2 diverse
   3 permanent
   4 surroundings
   5 sturdy

Practice Test p.26

1 Ⓓ 2 Ⓑ 3 Ⓐ 4 Ⓐ

스크립트 🎧 01-19

M Professor: The Romans were huge sports fans. And as most of you probably know, gladiator contests were the most popular events during Roman times.
The Romans needed large venues, places to have these contests and to seat all the people. Therefore, they developed and designed the amphitheater. Amphitheaters are open-air stadiums. The earliest amphitheaters were wooden seating structures on two sides of a circular ground. Basically, they were like two theaters that faced each other, and this gave spectators the best views.
However, wooden amphitheaters were not perfect. For one thing, they were not permanent. They were set up for a contest and then taken down. People got tired of doing that. The wood was a danger to catch on fire and to burn down, too. Therefore, a need for more permanent amphitheaters came about.
The Romans built the first permanent amphitheaters out of stone such as marble or limestone. The first one built in Rome around 70 A.D. was the famous Colosseum. In addition, during the Roman Empire, just about every decent-sized city had an amphitheater. Like the Colosseum, we can still see many of them today. The fact that they are still standing shows how great Roman builders and designers were.

해석

M Professor: 로마인들은 엄청난 스포츠 팬이었습니다. 그리고 여러분 대부분이 알지도 모르지만, 검투사 경기는 로마 시대에 최고로 인기 있는 행사였습니다.
로마인들은 이 경기를 치르고 사람들이 모두 앉을 만큼 큰 장소인 경기장이 필요했습니다. 그래서 그들은 원형 경기장을 개발하고 디자인했습니다. 원형 경기장은 야외 경기장입니다. 초기의 원형 경기장은 둥근 모양의 땅 양쪽에 나무로 만든 좌석이 있는 구조였습니다. 기본적으로 그것은 서로를 마주볼 수 있는 두 개의 극장과 같은 것으로, 이 점은 관람객들에게 최상의 시야를 제공했습니다.
그러나 나무로 만들어진 원형 경기장은 완벽하지 않았습니다. 우선 그것은 영구적이지 않았습니다. 그것은 경기를 위해 지어졌다가 철거되었습니다. 사람들은 이렇게 하는 데 지쳐버렸습니다. 또한 목조는 화재와 전소의 위험이 있었습니다. 그래서 더 영구적인 원형 경기장에 대한 필요성이 제기되었습니다.
로마인들은 대리석이나 석암과 같은 돌로 최초의 영구적인 원형 경기장을 지었습니다. 서기 70년경에 로마에 지어진 최초의 원형 경기장은 그 유명한 콜로세움이었습니다. 게다가 로마 제정 당시에는, 모든 중소 도시마다 원형 경기장이 있었습니다. 콜로세움과 마찬가지로 그것들 중 많은 것을 오늘날까지도 볼 수 있습니다. 그 경기장들이 지금까지 그대로 남아 있다는 사실은 로마의 건축가와 디자이너들이 얼마나 훌륭했는지를 보여줍니다.

CHAPTER 2 Office Hours

Understanding TOEFL Question Types & Listening Skills
p.30

1 Question Types ▶ Sample Question

Ⓑ

스크립트 🎧 02-01

W Professor: Oh, hello, Ryan. Have you decided on your major yet?
M Student: No. Not yet, Professor Stearns.
W: Really? What seems to be the problem?
M: Well, I love studying art.
W: Then why don't you major in art?
M: Well, I also enjoy literature. I find it fascinating!
W: I see. I have an idea, Ryan.
M: Sure. What is it?
W: Why don't you do a double major?
M: Do you mean have two majors? I didn't know I could do that.

해석

W Professor: 아, 잘 있었죠, 라이언. 전공을 이제 정했나요?
M Student: 아뇨. 아직 정하지 못했어요, 스턴스 교수님.
W: 그래요? 무슨 문제라도 있나요?
M: 음, 전 미술을 공부하고 싶어요.
W: 그렇다면 미술을 전공하면 될 텐데요?
M: 음, 전 문학도 좋아해요. 문학은 저에게 매력적이거든요!
W: 그렇군요. 나에게 좋은 생각이 있어요, 라이언.
M: 역시 교수님이세요. 그게 뭐죠?
W: 복수 전공을 하면 어때요?
M: 전공을 두 가지 하라는 말씀이시죠? 그렇게 할 생각은 못했네요.

2 Listening Skills ▶ Check-Up

1 decide on
2 find it
3 have an
4 didn't know

• Exercise 1 •
p.32

정답 Q1 Ⓓ   Q2 Ⓑ
스크립트 🎧 02-03

W Student: Professor Goodman, can I talk to you, please?
M Professor: Sure, Christine. How are you?
W: I have a small problem in class.
M: You do? What's the matter?
W: I am not good at taking notes. I try to write down everything you say, but I can't.
M: Just focus on the important points. Don't write everything I say.

W: I do that. But I still can't write fast enough.
M: Hmm. How about borrowing notes from a friend?
W: I don't know anyone in the class. That won't work.
M: Okay. Then why don't you record my lecture by using your smartphone?
W: You allow students to record your lectures?
M: Sure. Some professors don't like it. But I am fine with students recording.
W: That's a great idea. Thanks so much, sir.

해석
W Student: 굿맨 교수님, 잠깐 이야기를 나눌 수 있을까요?
M Professor: 물론이에요, 크리스틴. 어떻게 지내나요?
W: 수업에서 작은 문제를 하나 겪고 있어요.
M: 그래요? 무슨 문제인가요?
W: 제가 필기를 잘 못하거든요. 교수님의 말씀을 다 받아 적으려고 노력하는데, 그럴 수가 없어요.
M: 중요한 부분들에만 집중해요. 내가 말하는 것을 다 적지 말고요.
W: 그렇게 하고 있어요. 하지만 그래도 필기를 빨리 할 수가 없어요.
M: 흠. 친구의 필기를 빌리는 건 어떨까요?
W: 수업을 듣는 사람 중에 아는 사람이 없어요. 그래서 그건 불가능해요.
M: 그렇군요. 그러면 내 강의를 스마트폰을 사용해서 녹음하는 건 어떤가요?
W: 학생들이 교수님의 강의를 녹음하는 걸 허용하시나요?
M: 물론이죠. 몇몇 교수님들께서는 좋아하지 않으시지만요. 하지만 나는 학생들이 녹음해도 괜찮아요.
W: 정말 좋은 생각이네요. 정말 감사합니다, 교수님.

Listening Skills
1 write down
2 fast enough
3 borrowing notes
4 great idea

• **Exercise 2** • p.33

정답 Q1 Ⓓ Q2 Ⓑ
스크립트 🎧 02-05
M Student: Hello, Professor Thomas.
W Professor: Good morning, Eric. Congratulations on the paper you wrote for me.
M: Ah, yeah. Thanks a lot. I was happy to get an A+.
W: You did an outstanding job. In fact, it was the best report in the class.
M: Wow. Thanks.
W: So what can I do for you?
M: Actually, I'm here to discuss the paper.
W: What about it?
M: Well, I had lots of fun writing it. And I learned very much, too.
W: That's good.
M: I think I might like to major in archaeology. What do you think?
W: You're only a sophomore. You could do it.

M: Wonderful. Do you have some time to talk about it now?
W: Of course. What do you want to know?

해석
M Student: 안녕하세요, 토마스 교수님.
W Professor: 좋은 아침이에요, 에릭. 작성한 보고서에 대해서는 축하를 하고 싶군요.
M: 아, 네. 정말 감사합니다. 제가 A+를 받다니 기뻤어요.
W: 훌륭하게 해냈더군요. 사실, 수업에서 가장 훌륭한 보고서였어요.
M: 와, 감사합니다.
W: 그런데 무엇을 도와주면 되죠?
M: 실은 보고서에 대해 상의하고 싶은 게 있어서 왔어요.
W: 어떤 점에서요?
M: 음, 보고서를 쓰면서 꽤 즐거웠거든요. 그리고 많이 배우기도 했고요.
W: 잘됐군요.
M: 제가 고고학을 전공해도 좋을 것 같아서요. 어떻게 생각하세요?
W: 아직 2학년이잖아요. 할 수 있을 거예요.
M: 정말 다행이에요. 지금 그것에 대해서 잠시 이야기할 시간을 내주실 수 있나요?
W: 물론이죠. 무엇이 알고 싶나요?

Listening Skills
1 congratulations on
2 best report
3 major in
4 some time

• **Exercise 3** • p.34

정답 Q1 Ⓐ Q2 Ⓑ
스크립트 🎧 02-07
M Professor: Can I talk to you for a moment, Isabella?
W Student: Sure. What's up?
M: Preston mentioned to me that you're quitting school.
W: Did he? I told him not to say anything. I wanted to tell you.
M: So it's true. Well, is everything okay?
W: Oh, don't worry, Professor Rogers. I just need a break.
M: So you will be back?
W: That's right. I'm just going to take one semester off.
M: So you'll return in the fall?
W: Yes, sir. I'm planning on traveling for a while.
M: Actually, that's a good idea.
W: Yeah. It will give me some time to think about my future.
M: That's a wonderful idea. I do hope that you come back soon. You're one of my best students.
W: It's so kind of you to say that. Thank you.

해석
M Professor: 잠시 이야기 좀 나눌 수 있나요, 이사벨라?
W Student: 그럼요. 무슨 일이세요?
M: 프레스톤이 그러던데 자네가 학교를 그만둘 거라고 하더군요.
W: 프레스톤이요? 제가 말하지 말아 달라고 얘기했는데. 제가 교수님께 직접 말씀드리고 싶었거든요.

M: 그럼 사실인가 보군요. 음, 괜찮은 건가요?
W: 아, 걱정 마세요, 로저스 교수님. 그냥 휴식이 좀 필요해서요.
M: 그러면 다시 복학할 건가요?
W: 그렇게 하려고요. 한 학기만 휴학을 할 예정이에요.
M: 그렇다면 가을 학기에 복학하겠네요?
W: 네, 교수님. 잠시 여행을 갈 계획이에요.
M: 그렇다면, 좋은 생각이군요.
W: 네. 제 미래에 대해 생각할 시간을 가져야 할 것 같아요.
M: 좋은 생각이네요. 곧 다시 돌아오면 정말 좋겠어요. 자네는 정말 훌륭한 학생 중 한 명이에요.
W: 그렇게 말씀해 주시다니 정말 자상하세요. 감사합니다.

Listening Skills

1 told him
2 be back
3 planning on
4 that's a

• Exercise 4 • p.35

정답 Q1 ⓒ Q2 ⓒ
스크립트  02-09

M Professor: Welcome, Susan. Please have a seat.
W Student: Hi, Professor Harper. That was a good class today.
M: Thanks. I'm glad you enjoyed it. I always enjoy lecturing on that topic.
W: So what do you need to see me for?
M: I've got some good news for you.
W: Really?
M: I need to congratulate you.
W: For what?
M: You don't know yet? You have won a scholarship to study abroad.
W: No way. Are you serious?
M: I wouldn't joke about something like this.
W: I must be dreaming. This is amazing.
M: You'll get to study in Scotland this summer. All of your expenses will be completely paid for.
W: I can't believe it. Thank you very much.
M: You're welcome, Susan.

해석

M Professor: 어서 와요, 수잔. 자리에 앉아요.
W Student: 안녕하세요, 하퍼 교수님. 오늘 강의 정말 좋았습니다.
M: 고마워요. 좋았다니 기쁘네요. 그런 주제에 대해 강의하는 건 항상 재미있지요.
W: 그런데 무슨 일로 보자고 하신 거예요?
M: 수잔에게 좋은 소식이 있어요.
W: 정말이요?
M: 축하부터 해야 겠네요.
W: 무슨 일로요?
M: 아직 모르고 있었나요? 수잔이 해외 유학 장학금을 받게 되었어요.

W: 그럴 리가요? 정말인가요?
M: 이런 일로 농담할 리가 있겠어요?
W: 꿈을 꾸고 있는 거 같아요. 정말 놀랍네요.
M: 이번 여름에 스코틀랜드에서 공부하게 될 거예요. 모든 비용이 지불될 거예요.
W: 믿을 수가 없어요. 정말 감사합니다.
M: 천만에요, 수잔.

Listening Skills

1 good class
2 got some
3 get to
4 can't believe

• Exercise 5 • p.36

정답 Q1 ⓓ Q2 ⓒ
스크립트  02-11

W Professor: Are you on your way to class, Hugh?
M Student: Yes, ma'am. Did you get my email?
W: No. I haven't checked my email yet. Why?
M: I have a small problem.
W: Do you need more time for your essay?
M: Well, that would be nice, but no.
W: Okay. Then . . .
M: Actually, I can't attend your lecture tomorrow.
W: Really? And the reason is . . .?
M: I have an important job interview tomorrow afternoon.
W: I see. What kind of job is it?
M: It's an internship at the local newspaper. It's the perfect position for me.
W: It sounds like it. In that case, I don't see a problem with you missing the lecture.
M: Thanks so much. I appreciate it.
W: Just make sure that you get the class notes from someone.
M: My roommate is taking the class. I'll talk to him.
W: Great. Good luck at the interview. I hope you get the job.

해석

W Professor: 수업 들어가는 길인가요, 휴?
M Student: 네, 교수님. 제 이메일 받으셨나요?
W: 아뇨. 아직 이메일을 확인하지 못했어요. 왜죠?
M: 약간의 문제가 생겨서요.
W: 에세이 쓰는 데 시간이 더 필요한가요?
M: 음, 그러면 좋죠. 그런데 아니에요.
W: 알겠어요. 그러면…
M: 사실, 제가 내일 교수님 수업에 출석할 수가 없어서요.
W: 그래요? 그러면 이유가…?
M: 내일 오후에 중요한 입사 면접이 있어요.
W: 그렇군요. 어떤 종류의 일인가요?
M: 지역 신문사의 인턴사원직이에요. 저에게는 완벽한 자리거든요.
W: 그런 것 같네요. 그런 경우에, 수업에 빠지는 건 문제가 되지 않아요.

M: 정말 감사합니다. 진심으로 감사드려요.
W: 다만 다른 사람이 수업 내용을 필기한 것을 꼭 확인하도록 하세요.
M: 제 룸메이트가 그 수업을 듣거든요. 그 친구한테 말해둘게요.
W: 좋네요. 면접 잘해요. 꼭 입사하길 바랄게요.

Listening Skills

1 have a
2 would be
3 sounds like
4 hope you

• Exercise 6 • p.37

정답 Q1 Ⓑ   Q2 Ⓒ

스크립트 02-13

M Professor: You need help with researching your essay? Is that correct?
W Student: Actually, I can't decide on a topic.
M: Do you want me to suggest one?
W: Well, I have two ideas. I want to know, well, your thoughts . . .
M: Okay. Let me hear them then.
W: The first one is on Hemingway. I could write about his early years as an ambulance driver in the war.
M: I see. And the other?
W: The second is on Hemingway's novel *The Old Man and the Sea*. I could write something about man versus nature . . .
M: Well, they are both excellent ideas. Which is more interesting to you?
W: I like them both and can't decide. That's why I'm here.
M: Well, how about connecting the two?
W: Hmm . . . I hadn't thought about that.
M: Yeah. Perhaps the ambulance driver and the old man are similar in some ways . . .
W: It just hit me, Professor Brooks. I know my topic now. Thanks so much.
M: It's my pleasure.

해석

M Professor: 에세이 조사에 도움이 필요하다는 거죠? 맞나요?
W Student: 사실, 주제를 정하지 못하겠어요.
M: 내가 주제를 제안해 줄 원하는 건가요?
W: 음, 두 가지 주제가 있긴 한데요. 교수님 생각은 어떠신지, 음, 알고 싶어서요…
M: 좋아요. 그렇다면 어떤 건지 들어보죠.
W: 첫 번째 주제는 헤밍웨이예요. 그가 전쟁 중에 야전병원 수송차 운전병으로서 활동했던 초창기 시절에 대해 쓸 수 있을 것 같아요.
M: 알겠어요. 다른 하나는요?
W: 두 번째는 헤밍웨이의 소설인 *노인과 바다*에 대한 거예요. 인간 대 자연과 같은 주제에 대해 쓸 수 있을 것 같은데요…
M: 음, 둘 다 좋은 아이디어네요. 어떤 것에 더 흥미가 가나요?
W: 저는 둘 다 좋아서 결정을 못하겠어요. 그래서 교수님께 온 것이고요.
M: 음, 그렇다면 그 둘을 연관시켜 보면 어떨까요?

W: 음… 그건 생각해 보지 못했네요.
M: 그래요. 아마도 야전병원 수송차 운전병과 노인 간에는 어떤 면에서 공통점이 있을 거예요…
W: 바로 그거네요, 브룩스 교수님. 이제야 주제를 알겠어요. 정말 감사합니다.
M: 천만에요.

Listening Skills

1 help with
2 hear them
3 is on
4 hit me

• Exercise 7 • p.38

정답 Q1 Ⓐ   Q2 Ⓒ

스크립트 02-15

M Student: Are you going home, Professor Lewis?
W Professor: Yes, Brandon. But I have a minute. What's up?
M: I need to turn in my research paper to you.
W: That was due last week, Brandon.
M: I know. I'm really sorry.
W: What did I tell everyone in class?
M: You said that you won't accept any late papers.
W: That's right. I'm sorry. I can't do it. It would not be fair to other students.
M: Well, I had to try. I just had a terrible week last week.
W: What happened?
M: Well, someone stole my car. Then, there was an illness in my family.
W: I'm sorry to hear that. Look, Brandon . . .
M: Yes?
W: You're a good student. So I'm going to give you a bit of a break . . .
M: How so?
W: Well, I still can't accept the paper. However, your next paper will be counted twice. So whatever grade you get on it will be the grade that you get for this assignment.
M: That's wonderful. Thank you for being so generous.

해석

M Student: 집에 가시는 길이세요, 루이스 교수님?
W Professor: 그래요, 브랜든. 하지만 시간은 좀 있어요. 무슨 일이죠?
M: 제 조사 보고서를 제출하려고요.
W: 그건 기한이 지난주였어요, 브랜든.
M: 알고 있습니다. 정말 죄송합니다.
W: 수업시간에 내가 여러분에게 뭐라고 했죠?
M: 기한이 지나면 보고서를 받지 않는다고 하셨어요.
W: 맞아요. 미안해요. 받을 수 없어요. 다른 학생에게는 공평하지 않으니까요.
M: 음, 제가 더 노력했어야 하는데. 지난주는 저에게 너무 힘들었던 주였거든요.
W: 무슨 일이 있었죠?
M: 그게, 누군가 제 차를 훔쳐갔어요. 그리고 가족 중에 아픈 사람이 생겼어요.

W: 그건 유감이에요. 이렇게 합시다, 브랜든…
M: 네?
W: 자네는 훌륭한 학생이에요. 그래서 일종의 기회를 줄까 해요…
M: 어떻게요?
W: 음, 그 보고서는 받을 수 없어요. 하지만 다음 보고서 때 점수를 두 배로 줄게요. 어떤 점수를 받는지, 그게 이번 과제에 대해 자네가 받는 점수가 될 거예요.
M: 정말 좋아요. 이해해 주셔서 감사합니다.

Listening Skills

1 turn in
2 had to
3 can't accept
4 next paper

• Exercise 8 • p.39

정답 Q1 Ⓒ Q2 Ⓐ

스크립트 02-17

W Student: Hello. Are you Dr. Lewis?
M Professor: Yes. You must be Lori Wilkins. Please come in . . .
W: Thank you.
M: You said on the phone you want to join my class.
W: Yes, sir.
M: Well, it's kind of late in the semester, isn't it?
W: Yes. I just want to sit in on your lectures. I don't want to get a grade or anything.
M: Any reason why?
W: I want to take your marine biology class next year. I thought this would be good practice.
M: Well, you are correct. It would prepare you quite well. But there's a problem. According to the university rules, you must pay for the classes you attend. I'm sorry, but I can't let you sit in on my class.
W: Oh, that's too bad. I was afraid this might happen.
M: However, how about this? I'll give you a syllabus. I'll tell you which books to buy. That way, you can study and prepare on your own. Does that sound good?
W: That's great. I appreciate it.

해석

W Student: 안녕하세요. 루이스 교수님이신가요?
M Professor: 그래요. 로리 윌킨스 양이지요? 들어와요…
W: 감사합니다.
M: 전화로 내 수업에 참여하고 싶다고 말했죠.
W: 네, 교수님.
M: 음, 학기 중이라 좀 늦은 것 같은데요, 그렇지 않나요?
W: 맞아요. 전 그저 교수님 강의를 청강하고 싶어서요. 학점을 따거나 그럴 생각은 아닙니다.
M: 어떤 이유가 있나요?
W: 저는 내년에 교수님의 해양 생물학 강의를 듣고 싶거든요. 제 생각에 이번 강의가 좋은 연습이 될 것 같습니다.

M: 음, 그렇긴 하네요. 아마도 자네에게 좋은 준비가 되겠지요. 하지만 문제가 있어요. 교칙에 따르면, 학생들은 듣는 수업에 대해 반드시 수업료를 내야 해요. 미안하지만, 내 수업을 청강할 수는 없어요.
W: 아, 어쩔 수 없네요. 이렇게 될까 봐 걱정하긴 했어요.
M: 그렇지만 이렇게 하면 어떨까요? 강의 계획서를 줄게요. 어떤 책을 사야 할지도 알려주고요. 그러면, 혼자서 공부하고 준비할 수 있을 거예요. 그건 괜찮지요?
W: 정말 좋네요. 정말 감사합니다.

Listening Skills

1 must be
2 sit in
3 don't want
4 tell you

Vocabulary Review p.40

A 1 join
   2 fair
   3 research
   4 Essays
   5 major in

B 1 Ⓑ   2 Ⓒ   3 Ⓓ   4 Ⓐ   5 Ⓑ

C 1 Ⓑ   2 Ⓒ   3 Ⓐ   4 Ⓒ   5 Ⓓ

D 1 outstanding
   2 notes
   3 moment
   4 sophomore
   5 allow

Practice Test p.42

1 Ⓑ   2 Ⓓ   3 Ⓒ

스크립트 02-19

M Student: Hello. How late are you open?
W Fitness Center Employee: Oh, hi. We're open until eleven at night.
M: That's great. Every day?
W: Yep. Every day.
M: Okay. Well, I want to start exercising here. What do I need to do?
W: You're a student here, right?
M: Yes, I am.
W: First, I need to see your student ID.
M: Here you go.
W: Thanks. Would you like me to give you a short tour of the facilities?

M: Sure.
W: Take a look at this map of the fitness center. We're here.
M: Okay.
W: Over here are the locker rooms. Here is the aerobics area. And over on this side is the weight training area.
M: It looks pretty simple to me.
W: Do you have any questions?
M: Just one. Can I get a locker?
W: Let me check really quickly . . . Yes, there are a few available. There's an extra charge though. Well, it isn't really a charge. You must put down a deposit of twenty dollars.
M: No problem. Here you go.
W: Great. Just sign here, and you are all set.

해석

M Student: 안녕하세요. 언제까지 문을 여나요?
W Fitness Center Employee: 아, 안녕하세요. 저희는 밤 11시까지 열어요.
M: 좋네요. 매일 그런가요?
W: 맞아요. 매일이요.
M: 알겠어요. 음, 여기서 운동을 시작하고 싶은데요. 필요한 게 있을까요?
W: 여기 학생 맞으시죠?
M: 네, 맞아요.
W: 그럼 우선 학생증을 좀 보여주세요.
M: 여기 있습니다.
W: 감사합니다. 간단히 시설을 안내해 드릴까요?
M: 좋습니다.
W: 이 피트니스 센터의 안내도를 보세요. 우리가 있는 곳은 여기예요.
M: 네.
W: 이쪽에 있는 것이 탈의실이고요. 여기가 에어로빅실이에요. 그리고 이쪽에 있는 것이 웨이트 트레이닝 구역이지요.
M: 알아보기 쉽네요.
W: 질문 있으신가요?
M: 한 가지 있어요. 사물함을 쓸 수 있나요?
W: 빨리 확인해 볼게요… 네, 몇 개가 남아 있네요. 그런데 약간의 추가 요금이 있어요. 음, 실제로 청구되는 건 아니고요. 보증금으로 20달러를 내야 해요.
M: 문제 없습니다. 여기 있어요.
W: 좋습니다. 여기 서명하시면 다 된 겁니다.

CHAPTER 3 The History of English

Understanding TOEFL Question Types & Listening Skills
p.46

1 Question Types ▶ Sample Question
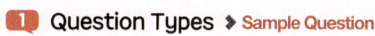

스크립트 03-01

W Professor: Let me talk about Old English. It was an early form of the English language. We're talking from about the fifth century to the twelfth century. This, of course, was in England. But Old English wasn't the same everywhere on the island. People spoke Old English according to their region. You see, there were four main kingdoms in England. In each, people used a different form or dialect of Old English.

해석

W Professor: 고대 영어에 대해 이야기해 보겠습니다. 고대 영어는 영어의 초기 형태였습니다. 우리는 약 5세기부터 12세기까지의 영어에 대해서 이야기해 볼 것입니다. 물론, 이것은 잉글랜드에 존재했습니다. 그러나 고대 영어가 잉글랜드 섬 모든 곳에서 똑같이 사용된 것은 아니었습니다. 지역에 따라 다른 고대 영어가 사용되었어요. 알다시피, 잉글랜드에는 4개의 주요 왕국이 있었습니다. 각각의 왕국에서 사람들은 고대 영어의 각기 다른 형태 즉, 방언을 사용했습니다.

2 Listening Skills ▶ Check-Up
1 It was an early form of the English language.
2 This was in England.
3 People spoke Old English according to their region.
4 There were four main kingdoms in England.

• Exercise 1 •
p.48

정답 Q1 ⓓ   Q2 ⓑ
스크립트 03-03

M Professor: William Caxton had a major influence on the spread of the English language. That's C-A-X-T-O-N. He's in your textbook. But you should have him in your notes, too.
Caxton was a printer. He was the first person to introduce the printing press to England. This was around the mid- to late fourteenth century. He published the first English book in, I believe, 1475 or 1476.
He was also a translator. He translated books into English. This was very important. It allowed more people access to books and knowledge. Caxton wanted everyone—the rich and the poor—to read. He published his books in a more standard style of English. After that, the language began to grow more quickly.

해석

M Professor: 윌리엄 캑스턴은 영어의 확산에 주요한 영향을 끼친 사람이었습니다. 철자가 C-A-X-T-O-N입니다. 교재에 나와요. 하지만 그에 대해 필

기도 해 놓으세요.

캑스턴은 인쇄업자였습니다. 그는 영국에 최초로 인쇄기를 소개한 사람이었어요. 이때가 14세기 중후반쯤이었습니다. 그는, 제가 알기로는 1475년 또는 1476년에 영어로 된 책을 처음으로 출간했습니다.

그는 또한 번역가였습니다. 그는 책을 영어로 번역했지요. 이것은 아주 중요했습니다. 그 때문에 더 많은 사람들이 책과 지식에 접근할 수 있었습니다. 캑스턴은 모든 사람—즉, 부자나 가난한 사람이나—책을 읽기를 원했습니다. 그는 자신의 책을 좀 더 표준 영어에 가까운 스타일로 출간했습니다. 그 후로, 영어는 더 빠르게 발전하기 시작했습니다.

Listening Skills

1 He's in your textbook.
2 He was also a translator.
3 This was very important.
4 The language began to grow more quickly.

• Exercise 2 • p.49

정답 Q1 Ⓑ   Q2 Ⓒ
스크립트 🎧 03-05

W Professor: William Shakespeare had, of course, a major influence on the English language. Many idioms and expressions we still use today come from Shakespeare. He also created new words that we continue to use today. He borrowed words from other languages too. Basically, he helped make English a more colorful language. Pretty amazing, isn't it?

Oh, some students often ask me this question: Why does Shakespeare use so many clichés? A cliché is an overused expression. For example, let me see . . . "Flesh and blood" is a cliché. "Vanish into thin air" is another. Well, Shakespeare was actually the first to use these expressions. People after Shakespeare borrowed these terms. Over time, they were used so much that they became clichés.

해석

W Professor: 윌리엄 셰익스피어는 물론, 영어라는 언어에 주요한 영향을 끼쳤습니다. 오늘날까지도 우리가 사용하고 있는 관용구와 표현들은 셰익스피어에서 유래한 것이 많습니다. 그는 또한 우리가 오늘날에도 계속 사용하는 단어들을 새로이 만들기도 했습니다. 그는 다른 언어에서도 단어들을 차용했습니다. 기본적으로 그는 영어를 좀 더 다채로운 언어로 만드는 데 기여한 것이지요. 정말 놀랍지 않나요?

아, 어떤 학생들이 종종 저에게 이런 질문을 합니다: "왜 셰익스피어는 그렇게나 많은 클리셰들을 사용할까요?"라고요. 클리셰란 과도하게 사용되는 진부한 표현을 말합니다. 예를 들어 보자면… 혈육(Flesh and blood)"은 클리셰입니다. "자취를 감추다(Vanish into thin air)"도 또 다른 클리셰입니다. 음, 셰익스피어는 사실 이러한 표현들을 최초로 사용한 사람이었습니다. 셰익스피어 이후의 사람들이 이러한 용어들을 차용한 것이죠. 시간이 지나면서, 이러한 표현들이 너무 많이 사용되면서 클리셰가 되어버린 것입니다.

Listening Skills

1 He also created new words that we continue to use today.
2 Pretty amazing, isn't it?
3 "Flesh and blood" is a cliché.
4 People after Shakespeare borrowed these terms.

• Exercise 3 • p.50

정답 Q1 Ⓐ   Q2 Ⓒ
스크립트 🎧 03-07

M Professor: There were two major influences on Old English. These were the Scandinavian influence and the Latin language. The Scandinavians, for example, the Danes, began invading the British Isles. Oh, so did the Norwegians. This all started around the eighth century. They brought their native language with them. We call this language Old Norse. It was very similar to the Anglo-Saxon language. They were both Germanic languages. Now, let me move on to Latin. The Romans were perhaps the highest culture on the planet at the time. They brought with them advanced knowledge and tools. They also brought Latin and specialized names for their advanced thinking and abilities. These words allowed English later to become more specialized and specific.

해석

M Professor: 고대 영어에 주요한 영향을 미친 두 가지가 있었습니다. 스칸디나비아어의 영향과 라틴어였습니다.

스칸디나비아인들, 예를 들자면, 덴마크인들이 영국의 섬들을 침략하기 시작했습니다. 아, 그리고 노르웨이인들도요. 이 모든 일이 8세기쯤 시작되었습니다. 그들은 자신의 모국어를 들여왔습니다. 우리는 이 언어를 고대 노르웨이어라고 부릅니다. 그 언어는 앵글로색슨어(고대 영어)와 매우 비슷했습니다. 둘 다 게르만어파입니다.

이번엔 라틴어로 가볼까요. 아마도 로마인들은 그 당시 지구상에서 가장 수준 높은 문화를 가지고 있었을 것입니다. 그들은 선진 지식과 기술을 가지고 왔습니다. 그들은 또한 라틴어, 그리고 진보적인 사상과 역량을 지칭하는 전문용어들도 들여왔습니다. 이러한 단어들 덕분에 영어가 이후 더 전문적이고 세분화될 수 있었습니다.

Listening Skills

1 These were the Scandinavian influence and the Latin language.
2 They brought their native language with them.
3 They were both Germanic languages.
4 These words allowed English later to become more specialized and specific.

• Exercise 4 • p.51

정답 Q1 Ⓑ   Q2 Ⓐ
스크립트 🎧 03-09

W Professor: American English began to separate itself from British English. This started as soon as the early explorers set foot in North America.

Let me outline it for you. First were the early settlements at Jamestown in 1607 and the early Puritan settlements in New

England. The settlers met Native American Indians, who already used pidgin, or broken, English. In addition, other European languages took hold on American soil. This mixture of languages began to shape American English.

Different dialects of English began to develop in America. For example, Americans in the North and the South have very different ways of pronouncing words. They even have different vocabularies. Sometimes these dialects make it difficult for Americans to understand one another. Really. It's true.

해석
W Professor: 미국 영어는 영국 영어에서 자체적으로 분리되기 시작했습니다. 이것은 초기 탐험가들이 북아메리카에 상륙했을 때부터 시작되었습니다. 큰 틀을 이야기해 드리겠습니다. 최초의 초기 이주는 1607년에 제임스타운에서 있었고, 뉴잉글랜드에 청교도인들의 초기 이주가 이루어졌습니다. 이민자들은 아메리칸 인디언 원주민들을 만났는데, 그들은 이미 피진어 즉, 서툰 영어를 사용하고 있었습니다. 게다가 유럽의 다른 언어들이 아메리카 땅에 자리잡고 있었습니다. 이렇게 다양한 언어의 혼합이 미국 영어를 형성하기 시작했습니다.

다양한 영어 방언들이 미국에서 발생하기 시작했습니다. 예를 들어, 북부와 남부 미국인들은 단어를 발음하는 방식이 매우 다릅니다. 심지어 그들은 아예 다른 단어를 쓰기도 합니다. 때로 이러한 방언 때문에 미국인들은 서로를 이해하기가 어려울 때가 있습니다. 정말로 그렇습니다.

Listening Skills

1 Let me outline it for you.
2 Other European languages took hold on American soil.
3 Different dialects of English began to develop in America.
4 It's true.

• **Exercise 5** • p.52

정답 Q1 Ⓓ Q2 Ⓒ
스크립트

M Professor: The *Oxford English Dictionary,* or the *OED*, is very important. It is the most comprehensive English dictionary.
The *OED* project began in the mid-nineteenth century. Its original purpose is quite interesting. Of course, its creators wanted to make a complete dictionary. They even invited readers to mail in words. So this was—and still is—a very large task.
The *OED* includes not only definitions of common words but also unfamiliar ones. That's why I say it is the most comprehensive dictionary. For example, slang is as much a part of the *OED* as sophisticated, intellectual terms. There's another interesting thing about the *OED*. You might think it has a, well, a British emphasis. It's quite the opposite. It accounts for worldwide English usage, not just British or American English. Today, the *OED* has nearly 620,000 entries. And it's still growing.

해석
M Professor: 옥스포드 영어 사전, 다시 말해 *OED*는 아주 중요합니다. 그것은 가장 종합적인 영어 사전입니다.

OED 프로젝트는 19세기 중반에 시작되었습니다. 그것의 본래 목적은 매우 흥미롭습니다. 물론, 그 사전의 개발자들은 완벽한 사전을 만들고 싶었습니다. 그들은 심지어 독자들에게 단어들로 편지를 보내 달라고 요청하기도 했습니다. 그러니까 이것은—그리고 지금까지도—정말 엄청난 작업이었던 것입니다.
*OED*는 일상적인 단어들뿐 아니라 낯선 단어들에 대한 정의도 포함하고 있습니다. 이것이 제가 그것을 가장 종합적인 사전이라고 말하는 이유입니다. 예를 들어, 속어는 세련되고 지적인 용어만큼이나 *OED*에서 많은 부분을 차지합니다. *OED*에 대한 또 다른 흥미로운 점이 있습니다. 여러분은 그것이 아마도, 음, 영국 영어에 중점을 두었다고 생각할 것입니다. 정확히는 정반대입니다. 그것은 단순히 영국 영어나 미국 영어가 아닌 전 세계적으로 사용되는 영어 어법을 설명합니다. 오늘날 *OED*에는 거의 62만 단어가 수록되어 있습니다. 그리고 그 수는 계속해서 늘어나고 있습니다.

Listening Skills

1 that's ..... That's why I say it is the most comprehensive dictionary.
2 there's ..... There's another interesting thing.
3 it's ..... It's quite the opposite.
4 it's ..... And it's still growing.

• **Exercise 6** • p.53

정답 Q1 Ⓐ Q2 Ⓑ
스크립트 🎧 03-13

W Professor: There were a number of important influences on modern English. Early on during the eighteenth century, the language had no true standard form. That is, many books taught various ways of spelling, grammar, and pronunciation.
Two men helped change this. In England, Samuel Johnson helped create one of the first English dictionaries. It established a standard form of spelling. Later, in the United States, Noah Webster did the same thing. I'm sure all of you are familiar with Webster.
Next, World War I and World War II helped spread the English language. Think about it. Many people from different cultures came together during the wars. English allowed for communication between speakers of different languages. In a way, it helped unite European countries with one another. Furthermore, it helped establish a more standard form of English. Finally, during the twentieth century, radio and television contributed to the creation of the most standardized form of English.

해석
W Professor: 현대 영어에 중요한 영향을 끼친 일들이 많이 있었습니다. 18세기 초반, 영어에는 확실하게 표준화된 형태가 존재하지 않았습니다. 그 말은 철자, 문법, 발음을 여러 다른 방식으로 알려주는 책이 많았던 것입니다.

두 사람이 이것을 바꾸는 데 기여했습니다. 영국에서는 새뮤얼 존슨이라는 사람이 최초의 영어 사전 중 하나로 여겨지는 것을 만드는 데 공헌했습니다. 그 사전은 철자의 표준 형태를 확립하였습니다. 이후에 미국에서는 노아 웹스터가 그와 같은 일을 했습니다. 여러분 모두 웹스터를 익히 알고 있을 거라 생각합니다.

다음으로, 1차 세계 대전과 2차 세계 대전이 영어를 전파하는 데 도움이 되었습니다. 생각해 보세요. 여러 다양한 문화권에서 온 많은 사람들이 전쟁 중에 함께하게 되었습니다. 영어는 다른 언어권에 있는 사람들 사이의 의사소통을 가능하게 만들었습니다. 어떤 면에서, 영어는 유럽권 국가들이 서로 결속하도록 도왔던 것입니다. 더 나아가 그로 인해 좀 더 표준화된 영어 형태가 확립되었습니다. 마침내 20세기에 이르러, 라디오와 텔레비전이 가장 표준화된 영어 형태를 형성하는 데 공헌했습니다.

Listening Skills

1 Two men helped change this.
2 I'm sure all of you are familiar with Webster.
3 It helped unite European countries with one another.
4 Radio and television contributed to the creation of the most standardized form of English.

• Exercise 7 • — p.54

정답 Q1 ⓑ Q2 ⓑ
스크립트 ∩ 03-15

M Professor: Let's go back in history a little. Think about Britain. Think about the British colonies . . . Yes, British colonialism. The British Empire. It had a major influence on the spread of English throughout the world. Generally, this was during the nineteenth century and early in the twentieth.
However, the American colonies also apply in a sense. This is especially true due to the rise of the independent United States. I'm sorry. Let me try to stick to the topic. The more countries and territories that England colonized, the more the English language spread. I believe that at one point, England had colonized or had a major influence over nearly one-quarter of the land on the Earth. That's quite a lot, isn't it?
At that time, Britain represented wealth and power. So did the English language. This is still true today. In many countries, such as India and Singapore, excellent English ability separates the wealthy and the educated from others. It's one legacy of the British Empire: the English language itself.

해석

M Professor: 역사 속으로 좀 더 되돌아가 봅시다. 영국을 생각해 보세요. 영국의 식민지들을 생각해 보세요… 그래요, 영국의 식민주의요. 대영제국말입니다. 대영제국은 전 세계적인 영어의 확산에 중요한 영향을 미쳤습니다. 전반적으로 이것은 19세기와 20세기 초 사이에 일어난 일이었습니다.
그렇지만, 미국의 식민들 또한 어떤 면에서는 적용됩니다. 독립 이후의 미국의 성장 덕분에 이 또한 매우 사실입니다. 죄송합니다. 다시 주제로 돌아가 보겠습니다. 더 많은 나라와 영토들이 영국의 식민 지배를 받을수록 영어는 더 널리 확산되었습니다. 제가 알기로, 어느 시점에는 지구상의 거의 4분의 1이 넘는 땅을 영국이 식민 지배하거나 중요한 영향력을 미치고 있었습니다. 정말 엄청납니다. 그렇지 않나요?
그 당시 영국은 부와 권력을 대표하였습니다. 물론 영어도 그러했습니다. 이점은 지금도 마찬가지입니다. 인도와 싱가포르와 같은 많은 나라에서 뛰어난 영어 능력은 부자와 지식인들을 다른 이들과 구별 짓습니다. 대영제국의 한 가지 유산이란 바로 영어 그 자체라고 할 수 있습니다.

Listening Skills

1 let's ….. Let's go back in history a little.
2 I'm ….. I'm sorry.
3 that's ….. That's quite a lot, isn't it?
4 it's ….. It's one legacy of the British Empire.

• Exercise 8 • — p.55

정답 Q1 ⓓ Q2 ⓑ
스크립트 ∩ 03-17

M Professor: Here's something interesting about the English language. Scholars estimate that it has around one million words. The average person knows about 42,000 words. Yet most people only use around 20,000 of the words they know.
Now, uh, English has many more words than most languages. Why is this? Well, the English language often borrows words from other languages. We call these loanwords. Here's what happens. An English speaker needs to describe something. But no words for that thing exist in English. So the person borrows a word from another language. Over time, that word becomes an English word.
Here's an example: Ballet. That's a loanword from French. But everyone thinks it's English. Sushi is another loanword. It's a Japanese word. But it became a word in the English language because people used it so much to describe raw fish that people eat. Scholars believe that around eighty percent of all English words are loanwords. Impressive, isn't it?

해석

M Professor: 영어에 관해 흥미로운 점을 알려 드리죠. 학자들은 약 1백만 개의 영단어가 있다고 추정합니다. 보통 사람은 약 42,000개의 단어를 알고 있고요. 하지만 대부분의 사람들은 자신이 알고 있는 단어 중 단 20,000개 정도만을 사용합니다.
그렇다면, 아, 영어는 대부분의 언어들에 비해 단어가 훨씬 더 많습니다. 왜 그럴까요? 음, 영어는 종종 다른 언어에서 단어를 차용합니다. 우리는 이를 차용어라고 부르죠. 어떤 일이 일어나는지 알려 드리겠습니다. 영어를 말하는 사람이 무언가를 묘사해야 해요. 하지만 그 사물에 대한 단어가 영어에는 존재하지 않습니다. 그러면 그 사람은 다른 언어에서 단어를 빌려오게 되죠. 시간이 지나면서 그 단어는 영어 단어가 됩니다.
예를 하나 들게요: 발레입니다. 발레는 프랑스어에서 차용한 단어입니다. 하지만 모든 사람들이 그것을 영어라고 생각하죠. 또 다른 차용어로 스시가 있습니다. 그것은 일본어 단어죠. 하지만 사람들이 먹는 익히지 않은 생선을 설명할 때 그 단어를 너무나 많이 사용했기 때문에 스시는 영어의 한 단어가 되었습니다. 학자들은 전체 영어 단어의 80% 정도가 차용어라고 생각합니다. 놀랍지 않나요?

Listening Skills

1 here's ….. Here's what happens.
2 that's ….. That's a loanword from French.
3 it's ….. But everyone thinks it's English.
4 isn't ….. Impressive, isn't it?

Vocabulary Review   p.56

A
1 specialized
2 colorful
3 translator
4 dialects
5 outline

B 1 Ⓑ   2 Ⓐ   3 Ⓒ   4 Ⓑ   5 Ⓒ

C 1 Ⓑ   2 Ⓒ   3 Ⓐ   4 Ⓑ   5 Ⓐ

D
1 comprehensive
2 access
3 standard
4 borrow
5 wealth

Practice Test   p.58

1 Ⓑ   2 Ⓒ   3 Ⓒ   4 Ⓑ

스크립트 🎧 03-19

W Professor: The reason *Beowulf* is important is that it's the first poem in the English language. There is only one surviving manuscript—a written text—and it is from around the eleventh century. Today, that manuscript is in the British Library.
But I should note that the author or authors wrote *Beowulf* well before the eleventh century. Some experts even believe it dates back to around the eighth century. So who wrote this amazing story? Well, that's unclear, and we'll probably never know. Actually, *Beowulf* probably did not have just one author. What I mean is the story was most likely part of the oral tradition. This means that people told the story over and over again and passed it down to the following generations. That is, people passed it on by word of mouth. Sometime, somewhere, certain individuals began to record the story in writing. Eventually, a single text came about. Is everyone with me . . . ? Great.
I should also mention that *Beowulf* continues to be a major influence for writers today. It is a classic story of hero versus monster. In many ways, it is a source of all the other great stories in the English language.

해석

W Professor: 베오울프가 중요한 이유는 그것이 영어로 쓰여진 최초의 시이기 때문입니다. 남아 있는 필사본 원고는 단 한 권만이 있으며 그것은 11세기경부터 전해집니다. 오늘날 그 원고는 영국 국립 도서관에 있습니다.
그러나 저는 저자 혹은 저자들이 족히 11세기 전에 베오울프를 썼다고 말해 두고 싶습니다. 어떤 전문가들은 그것이 8세기경까지도 거슬러 올라간다고 생각합니다. 그렇다면 누가 이 놀라운 이야기를 썼을까요? 음, 그것은 알 수 없고, 우리는 아마도 결코 알 수 없을지도 모릅니다. 사실 베오울프의 작가가 한 명만은 아닐 것으로 추정됩니다. 제 말은 그 이야기가 대부분 구전 중 일부였을 가능성이 크다는 것입니다. 이것은 사람들이 그 이야기를 계속해서 반복하여 이야기했고 그래서 그것이 다음 세대들에 걸쳐 전해졌다는 의미입니다. 즉, 사람들이 그것을 입에서 입으로 전한 것이지요. 어떤 시점, 어떤 곳에서, 특정 사람들이 그 이야기를 글로 기록하기 시작했습니다. 마침내 단 하나의 필사본이 나타나게 된 것이죠. 모두 잘 따라오고 있나요…? 좋습니다.
베오울프는 오늘날까지 작가들에게 계속해서 중요한 영향을 미치고 있다는 점 또한 말하고 싶습니다. 그것은 영웅 대 괴물에 대한 고전적인 이야기입니다. 여러 면에서, 그것은 영어로 쓰인 다른 위대한 모든 이야기들의 원천입니다.

CHAPTER 4 Service Encounters

Understanding TOEFL Question Types & Listening Skills
p.62

1 Question Types ▶ Sample Question

Ⓒ

스크립트 🎧 04-01

M Welcome Center Employee: You look a bit lost. Can I help you?
W Student: Yes, um . . . no . . . Well, I'm not sure. Is this the admissions office?
M: No. This is the welcome center. Are you a new student?
W: No. I'm a junior. I need a copy of my transcript.
M: Your transcript? Then you need the Registrar's office.
W: Okay. Where's the Registrar's office?
M: Do you know where Keller Hall is?
W: Of course. I live in Keller.
M: Okay. It's the building right next to it.

해석

M Welcome Center Employee: 길을 잃은 것 같네요. 도와드릴까요?
W Student: 네, 음… 아니에요… 음, 잘 모르겠네요. 이곳이 입학처인가요?
M: 아니에요. 여기는 안내센터예요. 신입생인가요?
W: 아뇨. 전 3학년이에요. 성적증명서 사본이 필요해서요.
M: 성적증명서요? 그렇다면 학적과로 가야 해요.
W: 그렇군요. 학적과가 어디에 있죠?
M: 켈러동이 어디인지 아시나요?
W: 물론이죠. 저는 켈러동에 살아요.
M: 그렇군요. 학적과는 켈러동의 바로 옆 건물이에요.

2 Listening Skills ▶ Check-Up

1 You look / a bit lost.
2 Are you a / new student?
3 Where's the / Registrar's office?
4 I live in / Keller.

• Exercise 1 •
p.64

정답 Q1 Ⓑ Q2 Ⓒ
스크립트 🎧 04-03

W Bursar's Office Employee: Next.
M Student: Hello. I think I'm next. I need to pay my tuition, please.
W: Student number, please . . .
M: 2-4-1-7-7-8-0-1. My last name is Savage. S-A-V . . .
W: It's okay. I just need your student number. Okay. How do you want to pay?
M: What are my options?
W: Actually, there are two ways you can pay. You can use a credit card or pay cash.
M: So no personal checks, huh? All right. Then do I have to pay all of it today?
W: No. You can pay one installment now and the other in two weeks.
M: What's the total, please?
W: Let's see here. Fifteen hours of class . . . That's 2,465.29 dollars for this semester.
M: Then I guess I'll just pay half of it today.

해석

W Bursar's Office Employee: 다음 분이요.
M Student: 안녕하세요. 제 순서 같네요. 등록금을 내러 왔습니다.
W: 학번을 말씀해 주세요…
M: 2-4-1-7-7-8-0-1이고요. 제 성은 세비지입니다. S-A-V…
W: 괜찮습니다. 학번만 필요해요. 좋아요. 어떻게 납부하기를 원하시나요?
M: 어떤 방법들이 있나요?
W: 실제로 두 가지 방법으로 납부할 수 있어요. 신용카드를 이용하거나 현금으로 납부할 수 있죠.
M: 그러면 수표는 사용할 수 없다는 거네요, 그렇죠? 알겠어요. 그러면 오늘 전액을 납부해야 하나요?
W: 아니에요. 지금 1회분을 내고, 2주 안에 나머지를 내도 됩니다.
M: 전액이 얼마일까요?
W: 확인해 보죠. 15시간 강의니까… 이번 학기는 2,465달러 29센트네요.
M: 그렇다면 오늘은 반만 내야 겠어요.

Listening Skills

1 I need to pay / my tuition, / please.
2 What / are my options?
3 What's the total, / please?
4 Then / I guess / I'll just pay half of it / today.

• Exercise 2 •
p.65

정답 Q1 Ⓒ Q2 Ⓐ
스크립트 🎧 04-05

M Registrar's Office Employee: So you want to, um, tack on a class?
W Student: Excuse me? I'm sorry . . . ?
M: Add a class?
W: No way. I want to drop one. I'm overloaded.
M: Oh, okay. Which class do you want to drop?
W: My chemistry class. It's killing me. We have homework every day.
M: Okay. No problem. I can take care of this.
W: I get a refund, right?
M: I'm not sure about that. Let me see. Well, you get eighty percent of your money back.
W: That's great. I thought I would get less.
M: But . . .
W: Uh-oh. What's the problem?
M: You will get the refund next semester, not now.

16

W: That's fine. I don't need it right now.
M: Okay. Then, um, congratulations. No more chemistry for you.
W: Well, not until my junior year . . . Thanks so much!

해석

M Registrar's Office Employee: 그러니까 음, 강의를 덧붙이겠다는 말이죠?
W Student: 네? 죄송하지만, 다시 말씀해 주시겠어요…?
M: 강의를 추가하시겠어요?
W: 아니에요. 하나를 취소하려고요. 너무 무리가 되어서요.
M: 아, 알겠어요. 어떤 과목을 취소할 건가요?
W: 화학 수업이요. 정말 죽겠어요. 매일 숙제가 있거든요.
M: 알겠어요. 문제 없습니다. 이렇게 처리하도록 하지요.
W: 환불 받는 거 맞나요?
M: 그건 확실하지 않아요. 확인해 볼게요. 음, 80%의 금액을 환불 받겠네요.
W: 좋아요. 더 적게 받을 거라 생각했어요.
M: 그런데…
W: 앗. 무슨 문제라도 있나요?
M: 지금이 아니라 다음 학기에 되돌려 받게 될 거예요.
W: 괜찮습니다. 당장 필요한 건 아니에요.
M: 알겠습니다. 그러면, 음, 축하해요. 화학 수업은 더 이상 안 들어도 되겠네요.
W: 네, 3학년이 될 때까지는요… 정말 감사합니다!

Listening Skills

1 I want to drop / one.
2 I get a refund, / right?
3 I don't need it / right now.
4 No more chemistry / for you.

• Exercise 3 • p.66

정답 Q1 Ⓓ   Q2 Ⓑ
스크립트 🎧 04-07

M Student: Good afternoon. Do you have a moment, please?
W Math Department Office Employee: Sure. What can I do for you?
M: I'm looking for Professor Matzek. I'm a student in one of his classes.
W: His office is in room number 209.
M: I already went there. I knocked on the door a couple of times.
W: Hmm . . . That's strange. He is supposed to be having office hours now.
M: That's right. I need to talk to him about my class. So that's why I came here.
W: Oh, wait a minute. I just remembered something.
M: What's that?
W: This morning, he told me that he had to leave the school at noon today.
M: Oh, that's too bad.
W: Please come back tomorrow morning. I know he will be in his office then.

해석

M Student: 안녕하세요. 잠시 시간이 있으신가요?
W Math Department Office Employee: 그럼요. 무엇을 도와 드릴까요?
M: 저는 마첵 교수님을 찾고 있어요. 교수님 수업 중 하나를 듣고 있는 학생입니다.
W: 교수님 연구실은 209호예요.
M: 이미 그곳에 다녀왔어요. 두어 차례 문도 두드렸고요.
W: 흠… 이상하군요. 지금은 연구실에 계실 시간일 텐데요.
M: 맞아요. 저는 수업에 대해서 교수님과 이야기를 나누어야 해요. 그래서 제가 여기에 왔고요.
W: 아, 잠깐만요. 방금 기억났어요.
M: 뭔데요?
W: 오늘 아침에 교수님께서 오늘 정오에 퇴근해야 한다고 말씀하셨어요.
M: 아, 아쉽네요.
W: 내일 오전에 다시 오세요. 제가 알기로는, 그때는 연구실에 계실 거예요.

Listening Skills

1 I'm looking for / Professor Matzek.
2 I'm a student / in one of his classes.
3 So that's why / I came here.
4 Please come back / tomorrow morning.

• Exercise 4 • p.67

정답 Q1 Ⓒ   Q2 Ⓑ
스크립트 🎧 04-09

W Student: Excuse me. Is this where I can get scholarship information?
M Financial Aid Office Employee: Yes. Are you a current student, or are you still in high school?
W: High school? Gosh. Do I look that young?
M: Well, no, not really. I just have to ask everyone that question.
W: Oh, I see. Anyway, I'm a junior.
M: Are you on a scholarship now?
W: Yes. I have a swimming scholarship. But it only pays for my books and dorm room.
M: I see. Are your grades good?
W: Yes. I have a 4.0 GPA.
M: Then you should apply for the Bertram scholarship. It covers the cost of tuition.
W: Are my chances good? Of getting it, I mean.
M: I think so. Just fill out this form and bring it back to me by next Friday.
W: Great. Thanks for your help.

해석

W Student: 실례합니다. 이곳에서 제가 장학금에 대한 정보를 얻을 수 있나요?
M Financial Aid Office Employee: 맞습니다. 현재 재학생인가요, 아니면 아직 고등학생인가요?
W: 고등학생이요? 이런. 제가 그렇게 어려 보이나요?
M: 음, 아니요, 사실 그런 게 아니라. 저로서는 모든 사람들에게 해야 하는 질문

이라서요.
W: 아, 그렇군요. 어쨌든 전 3학년이에요.
M: 지금 장학금을 받고 있나요?
W: 네. 수영 장학금을 받고 있어요. 하지만 교재비와 기숙사비만 지급되거든요.
M: 알겠어요. 성적은 좋은가요?
W: 네. 평균 4.0이에요.
M: 그렇다면 버트램 장학금을 신청하는 게 좋겠어요. 그 장학금은 수업료를 지원해줍니다.
W: 제가 가능성이 있는 것이지요? 제 말은 장학금을 받을 가능성이요.
M: 그렇다고 생각해요. 이 신청서만 작성해서 다음 주 금요일까지 저에게 갖다 주세요.
W: 좋습니다. 도움 주셔서 감사합니다.

Listening Skills

1 Are you / a current student, / or are you still / in high school?
2 Anyway, / I'm a junior.
3 I have a / swimming scholarship.
4 Just fill out this form / and bring it back to me.

• Exercise 5 •   p.68

정답 Q1 A   Q2 D
스크립트 04-11

M Dining Services Employee: Good afternoon. How may I be of assistance?
W Student: Hello. Are you Mr. Reynolds? I was told I need to speak with you.
M: Yes, I'm James Reynolds.
W: That's great. Um, does the school dining services cater school events?
M: Yes, we do. What kind of event do you have?
W: Well, I'm the president of the history club. And we'd like to welcome all of our new members.
M: So you want to provide them with food?
W: Exactly.
M: Sure. We have several different options. They range from simple sandwiches and drinks to a full banquet.
W: Sandwiches will probably be best.
M: You're on a limited budget?
W: That's right.
M: Okay. I've got a brochure right here . . . Uh, here you are. Take a look at it, and let me know what you want.
W: Do I need to decide now? The event isn't for three weeks.
M: Just tell me one week before you have the event.
W: What a relief. Thanks for letting me know.

해석

M Dining Services Employee: 안녕하세요. 어떻게 도와 드릴까요?
W Student: 안녕하세요. 혹시 레이놀즈 선생님이신가요? 선생님과 이야기를 해야 한다고 들었거든요.
M: 네, 제가 제임스 레이놀즈예요.

W: 좋네요. 음, 구내식당에서 교내 행사에 음식을 제공해 주나요?
M: 네, 맞아요. 어떤 행사가 있나요?
W: 음, 저는 역사 동아리 회장이에요. 그리고 저희는 신입 회원 전체 환영회를 하고 싶어요.
M: 그러면 그들에게 음식을 제공하고 싶은 거네요?
W: 맞아요.
M: 그렇군요. 여러 다른 선택지들이 있습니다. 간단한 샌드위치와 음료부터 만찬까지 다양해요.
W: 샌드위치가 제일 좋을 것 같네요.
M: 예산이 한정되어 있군요?
W: 맞아요.
M: 좋아요. 여기에 안내 책자를 뒀는데… 아, 여기 있어요. 살펴 보시고 원하는 것을 알려 주세요.
W: 지금 결정해야 하나요? 행사는 3주 후에 있거든요.
M: 행사 일주일 전에만 알려 주세요.
W: 다행이군요. 알려 주셔서 감사합니다.

Listening Skills

1 How may I / be of assistance?
2 What kind of event / do you have?
3 Sandwiches will / probably be best.
4 The event isn't / for three weeks.

• Exercise 6 •   p.69

정답 Q1 B   Q2 A
스크립트 04-13

W Cafeteria Assistant: Meal card, please.
M Student: Okay, I think I have it . . . Here you go.
W: Thank you. Oh, you only have one meal left on this card.
M: Really? Thanks for telling me. Can you add more for me?
W: Sure. You can only add them by the week or month. Not single days.
M: I'll go for two more weeks.
W: Fine. Can I see your card again?
M: Sure. Here you are . . .
W: Thank you. The total is 128 dollars.
M: Let's make it one week. I don't have that much right now.
W: Okay. Can I see your card one more time?
M: Sure, sorry.
W: Thanks. So that will be sixty-four dollars.
M: Here's twenty, forty, sixty and one, two, three, four . . . Sixty-four.
W: Thank you very much. Can I help you with anything else?
M: Actually, yes. Can I use my card for another student?
W: Of course.
M: Thanks for everything.
W: My pleasure.

해석

W Cafeteria Assistant: 식사 카드를 주세요.
M Student: 네, 가지고 있는데… 여기 있어요.

W: 감사합니다. 아, 이 카드에 식사권이 한 번밖에 남지 않았네요.
M: 그래요? 말씀해 주셔서 감사합니다. 더 추가해주실 수 있나요?
W: 물론이지요. 주나 월 단위로만 추가할 수 있어요. 날짜별로는 안되고요.
M: 2주를 더 추가할게요.
W: 좋아요. 식사 카드를 다시 주시겠어요?
M: 네. 여기 있습니다…
W: 감사합니다. 총 128달러입니다.
M: 한 주만 해야겠어요. 지금은 그만큼의 돈이 없네요.
W: 알겠어요. 식사 카드를 다시 한 번 확인해도 될까요?
M: 그럼요. 죄송합니다.
W: 감사합니다. 그러면 64달러입니다.
M: 20, 40, 60달러하고, 1, 2, 3, 4… 여기 64달러입니다.
W: 감사합니다. 또 필요한 건 없으세요?
M: 사실, 있어요. 혹시 제 식권을 다른 사람이 사용해도 되나요?
W: 물론입니다.
M: 모두 감사합니다.
W: 천만에요.

Listening Skills

1 You only have one meal left / on this card.
2 So / that will be / sixty-four dollars.
3 Can I help you / with anything else?
4 Thanks for / everything.

• Exercise 7 •   p.70

정답 Q1 Ⓒ   Q2 Ⓐ
스크립트 🎧 04-15

M Teaching Assistant: Hi. Are you here to take the final exam?
W Student: Um, yes, I guess so.
M: You don't sound too confident.
W: Well, I crammed all night, but you know.
M: Anyway, first, I need to see your student ID.
W: Quick question. When do I get my score?
M: Right after you finish. You take the test on a computer.
W: A computer?
M: Sure. All freshmen math tests are on them. It gives you your score after you finish.
W: Oh, okay. Here's my ID.
M: Great. You are in room number two. That's over there on the left. Do you need pencils or paper?
W: Yes, please.
M: Here you go. And here is your ID. Remember that you can take as long as you like.
W: Really?
M: Of course. But most students only require about two hours.
W: Two hours? I'll probably need four.
M: Just try to relax and do your best.
W: Okay. I will.
M: Good luck.

해석
M Teaching Assistant: 안녕하세요. 기말 시험을 치르러 왔나요?
W Student: 음, 맞아요, 그런 것 같아요.
M: 자신이 없어 보이네요.
W: 음, 밤새 벼락치기를 했거든요, 아시겠지만요.
M: 어쨌든, 먼저 학생증을 보여 주세요.
W: 질문 짧게만요. 제 점수는 언제 알 수 있나요?
M: 끝나자마자요. 컴퓨터로 시험을 보거든요.
W: 컴퓨터요?
M: 맞아요. 모든 신입생 수학 시험은 컴퓨터로 보죠. 끝나면 점수를 받아요.
W: 아, 그렇군요. 여기 학생증이요.
M: 좋습니다. 2번 방이네요. 그 방은 저쪽 왼쪽에 있어요. 연필이나 종이가 필요한가요?
W: 네, 주세요.
M: 여기 있습니다. 그리고 여기 학생증이요. 원하는 시간만큼 시험을 치를 수 있다는 것을 기억해 두세요.
W: 정말요?
M: 물론이죠. 하지만 대부분의 학생들이 2시간 정도면 충분해요.
W: 2시간이요? 아마도 전 4시간은 필요할 거예요.
M: 긴장을 푸시고 최선을 다하세요.
W: 네. 그럴게요.
M: 행운을 빌어요.

Listening Skills

1 When do I get / my score?
2 All freshmen math tests / are on them.
3 You are in room / number two.
4 But most students / only require about two hours.

• Exercise 8 •   p.71

정답 Q1 Ⓒ   Q2 Ⓑ
스크립트 🎧 04-17

W Campus Policewoman: Excuse me. I'm sorry, but you can't park here.
M Student: Really? Why not?
W: You don't have a parking sticker for campus.
M: Do I need a sticker for this parking lot?
W: Yes. This lot is reserved for students with parking stickers.
M: Oh, I see. I'm sorry about that, officer.
W: Don't worry about it. Many people make the same mistake.
M: Then where can I park? I have class in fifteen minutes.
W: There is a lot behind the library. You don't need a sticker for that one.
M: Wow! Thanks for the tip.
W: It's usually full. But try it anyway.
M: Okay.
W: If it's full, park at the football stadium.
M: We can park there, too?
W: Of course. Well, on any day but a game day.
M: You're so helpful. Thanks.
W: My pleasure. I hope you find a parking place.

해석

W Campus Policewoman: 실례합니다. 죄송하지만, 학생은 여기에 주차할 수 없어요.
M Student: 정말요? 왜 안되죠?
W: 학생은 학내 주차 스티커가 없네요.
M: 이 주차구역에는 스티커가 필요한가요?
W: 네. 이 주차구역은 주차 스티커가 있는 학생들에게 배정되어 있어요.
M: 아, 그렇군요. 죄송합니다, 경찰관님.
W: 걱정 마세요. 많은 분들이 같은 실수를 하거든요.
M: 그러면 어디에 주차할 수 있을까요? 저는 15분 후에 수업이 있어요.
W: 도서관 뒤에 주차구역이 있습니다. 그곳은 주차 스티커가 필요 없어요.
M: 와! 정보 감사합니다.
W: 보통 꽉 차긴 해요. 그래도 일단 가 보세요.
M: 알겠습니다.
W: 만약 꽉 차 있다면, 축구장에 주차하세요.
M: 거기에도 주차할 수 있나요?
W: 물론이에요. 음, 경기가 없는 날이면 언제든지요.
M: 정말 많은 도움을 주시네요. 감사합니다.
W: 천만에요. 주차 공간을 찾길 바랄게요.

Listening Skills

1 I'm sorry, / but you can't park here.
2 Do I need a sticker / for this parking lot?
3 There is a lot / behind the library.
4 Well, / on any day / but a game day.

Vocabulary Review   p.72

A
1 tips
2 confident
3 go for
4 knock
5 current

B 1 Ⓐ 2 Ⓓ 3 Ⓑ 4 Ⓐ 5 Ⓓ

C 1 Ⓑ 2 Ⓐ 3 Ⓐ 4 Ⓑ 5 Ⓒ

D
1 transcripts
2 budget
3 game day
4 personal checks
5 installments

Practice Test   p.74

1 Ⓐ 2 Ⓑ 3 Ⓒ

스크립트 04-19

W Student: Hello. Can you help me out, please?
M Bookstore Employee: That's what I'm here for.
W: Wonderful. I'm looking for a textbook, but I don't know the title.
M: Okay. Do you know the author's name?
W: No idea.
M: The class name?
W: It's for Chemistry 204.
M: Let me see. The computer says there are twenty different Chemistry 204 classes. And the professors are using three different texts.
W: Right. My professor's name is Zephyr. Dr. Zephyr.
M: Perfect. You're looking for *Organic Chemistry*. The author is Alan Lewis.
W: Wonderful. Can you tell me the price?
M: Hold on a minute . . . It's 89.45 dollars.
W: Wow. That's a bit steep, isn't it?
M: No, chemistry books are always pricey . . . Uh-oh.
W: What do you mean by uh-oh?
M: I mean that the book is out of stock.
W: You can't be serious.
M: I am. It's not in stock right now. If you want, we can order it for you today.
W: Really? Then when can I get it? I have a lot of reading to do for a quiz in two weeks.
M: You will get the book no later than next Monday.
W: Okay, I think I don't really have any options. I'll come and pick it up next Monday.

해석

W Student: 안녕하세요. 저를 좀 도와주실 수 있나요?
M Bookstore Employee: 제가 있는 이유가 바로 그겁니다.
W: 좋네요. 교재를 찾고 있는데, 제목을 몰라서요.
M: 알겠어요. 저자의 이름은 아나요?
W: 모르겠어요.
M: 수업 이름은요?
W: 화학과 204 강의예요.
M: 어디 봅시다. 컴퓨터에서는 20가지 다른 화학과 204 강의가 있다고 하네요. 그리고 교수님들이 3가지 다른 교재를 사용하고 계시고요.
W: 맞아요. 제 교수님 성함은 제피어예요, 제피어 박사님이요.
M: 좋아요. 학생은 유기화학 교재를 찾고 있군요. 저자는 앨런 루이스고요.
W: 맞아요. 가격이 얼마일까요?
M: 잠시만요… 89달러 45센트예요.
W: 와. 꽤 비싸네요, 그렇지 않나요?
M: 그렇죠. 화학 책들은 항상 비싸요… 이런.
W: 이런이라뇨?
M: 제 말은 그 책이 지금 품절이라서요.
W: 설마요.
M: 정말이에요. 그 책은 지금 재고가 없어요. 원하면, 오늘 그 책을 주문해줄 수 있어요.
W: 정말요? 그러면 언제 책을 받을 수 있을까요? 2주 후에 있을 퀴즈 때문에 읽을 게 많거든요.
M: 적어도 다음 주 월요일에는 책을 받을 거예요.
W: 알겠습니다, 다른 방법이 별로 없는 것 같네요. 다음 주 월요일에 와서 가져갈게요.

CHAPTER 5 Office Hours

Understanding TOEFL Question Types & Listening Skills
p.78

1 Question Types ▶ Sample Question

Ⓑ

스크립트 🎧 05-01

M Student: Good morning, Professor Goodman. You wanted to see me?
W Professor: Yes, Judd. Please come in and have a seat.
M: I hope it is not about the midterm exam.
W: Oh, no. Actually, you aced it.
M: That's wonderful.
W: I have a question. Have you thought about graduate school?
M: Grad school? You must be joshing.
W: Really. I think you should go for it.

해석

M Student: 안녕하세요, 굿맨 교수님. 저를 보자고 하셨나요?
W Professor: 그래요, 저드. 들어와서 앉아요.
M: 중간고사에 대한 건 아니면 좋겠네요.
W: 아, 아니에요. 사실 자네는 아주 잘했죠.
M: 좋네요.
W: 질문이 하나 있어요. 대학원에 대해 생각해 본 적이 있나요?
M: 대학원이요? 농담이시죠?
W: 정말이에요. 나는 자네가 대학원에 진학하는 게 좋을 것 같아요.

2 Listening Skills ▶ Check-Up

Student: I hope it is not about the midterm exam.
Professor: Oh, no. Actually, you aced it.
Student: That's wonderful.
Professor: I have a question.

• Exercise 1 •
p.80

정답 Q1 Ⓑ Q2 Ⓐ

스크립트 🎧 05-03

M Professor: Heather, do you have a second?
W Student: Sure, Professor Greene. I don't have class today.
M: Great. How is your semester going?
W: Quite well. Is there a problem?
M: Well, yes and no.
W: I see. Well, let's hear the bad news first.
M: I wouldn't say it's bad news. It's just that a few students are having a hard time in class.
W: Well, the subject matter is intricate. But your lectures are great, Professor.
M: Thank you for the compliment, Heather.
W: Is there anything I can do to help?
M: Actually, yes. I was hoping you could tutor them. You know, by leading a study group.
W: I have a full plate this semester. But I think I can find the time.
M: That's wonderful. Just meet with them once or twice a week. Answer any questions they have. Do things like that.

해석

M Professor: 헤더, 시간이 좀 있나요?
W Student: 그럼요, 그린 교수님. 오늘은 수업이 없어요.
M: 잘 됐군요. 이번 학기는 좀 어떤가요?
W: 아주 좋아요. 무슨 문제가 있나요?
M: 음, 그렇기도 하고 아니기도 해요.
W: 그렇군요. 그러면, 나쁜 소식을 먼저 들을게요.
M: 나쁜 소식이라고 말할 수는 없을 것 같아요. 몇몇 학생들이 수업시간에 힘들어하고 있다는 정도죠.
W: 음, 주제가 까다롭긴 해요. 하지만 교수님 강의는 훌륭해요, 교수님.
M: 좋게 말해줘서 고마워요, 헤더.
W: 제가 도울 일이 있을까요?
M: 사실, 그래요. 나는 자네가 그 학생들을 가르쳐주면 좋겠어요. 알겠지만, 스터디 그룹을 이끄는 거지요.
W: 제가 이번 학기에는 할 일이 산더미라서요. 하지만 시간을 낼 수는 있을 것 같아요.
M: 좋네요. 일주일에 한두 번 그 학생들을 만나기만 하면 돼요. 질문에 대답을 해주고 그런 것들을 해줘요.

Listening Skills

Professor: Great. How is your semester going?
Student: Quite well. Is there a problem?
Professor: Well, yes and no.
Student: I see.

• Exercise 2 •
p.81

정답 Q1 Ⓐ Q2 Ⓒ

스크립트 🎧 05-05

W Professor: Hi, Sean. Please have a seat. I want to noodle with you about something.
M Student: Hi, Professor Lambert. What's going on?
W: I want to congratulate you personally.
M: Really? Um, did I do something?
W: Do you remember your paper on John F. Kennedy?
M: Sure.
W: Well, the university wants you to read it to the new freshman class.
M: Really?
W: Yes. It's a great honor. There were hundreds of papers to choose from. I entered yours, and it was picked. Isn't that wonderful?
M: Um, well, I guess so. I mean, I'm ecstatic about it, but . . .
W: But what?
M: I'm not very good in front of big audiences.
W: Oh, you'll do fine. We'll practice it together.
M: That makes me feel better, ma'am. But I still feel nervous.

W: We have three weeks. Don't worry.

해석

W Professor: 샨, 션. 자리에 앉아요. 자네와 상의하고 싶은 일이 있어요.
M Student: 안녕하세요, 램버트 교수님. 무슨 일이죠?
W: 개인적으로 축하해 주고 싶어요.
M: 정말요? 음, 제가 무슨 일을 했나요?
W: 존 F. 케네디에 대해 자네가 쓴 논문을 기억하죠?
M: 그럼요.
W: 음, 학교에서 자네가 신입생들 수업시간에 그 논문을 읽어 주기를 원해요.
M: 정말요?
W: 그래요. 정말 자랑스러운 일이지요. 그중 골라야 할 논문들이 수백 개였어요. 내가 자네의 것을 올렸고, 그것이 선정되었어요. 정말 멋지지 않나요?
M: 음, 그게, 그런 것 같네요. 제 말은, 정말 기쁘긴 한데요, 하지만…
W: 하지만 뭐죠?
M: 전 많은 대중 앞에 서는 걸 그렇게 잘하지는 않아요.
W: 아, 잘해낼 수 있을 거예요. 함께 연습해 보도록 하죠.
M: 그러면 좀 나은 것 같아요, 교수님. 하지만 아직도 긴장되는 걸요.
W: 아직 3주가 남았어요. 걱정하지 말아요.

Listening Skills

Student: I mean, I'm ecstatic about it, but . . .
Professor: But what?
Student: I'm not very good in front of big audiences.
Professor: Oh, you'll do fine.

• **Exercise 3** • p.82

정답 Q1 ⓒ   Q2 ⓒ
스크립트 ∩ 05-07

W Student: Professor Harrow. Professor Harrow.
M Professor: Yes? Um, do I know you?
W: I'm in your biology class, sir. I'm Regan Holloway.
M: Oh, Regan. I didn't recognize you. What can I do for you?
W: Can you take a look at my paper? I need your advice. I can't decide if . . .
M: Paper? Um . . . You know that it's not due until next month, right?
W: Well, I like to get a head start.
M: A head start? Well, good for you. That's not too customary these days.
W: Can you look at it now?
M: Well, I'm on my way to a lecture. Can you come to my office at 3:00 PM?
W: Of course. I'll be there. Thanks so much.
M: Great. I'll see you at three then.

해석

W Student: 해로우 교수님. 해로우 교수님.
M Professor: 네? 음, 나를 아나요?
W: 저는 교수님의 생물학 수업을 듣고 있습니다, 교수님. 전 레건 할로웨이라고 합니다.
M: 아, 레건. 못 알아봤어요. 무엇을 도와줄까요?

W: 제 논문을 한 번 봐 주시겠어요? 저는 교수님의 조언이 필요해요. 어떻게 해야 할지 결정을 못하겠어서…
M: 논문이요? 음… 알다시피, 그건 기한이 다음 달인데요, 맞죠?
W: 음, 저는 미리 준비하는 게 좋아서요.
M: 미리 준비한다고요? 음, 훌륭하네요. 요즘엔 자주 있는 경우는 아닌데요.
W: 지금 봐 주실 수 있나요?
M: 음, 내가 강의에 들어가는 길이라서요. 오후 3시에 내 연구실로 오겠어요?
W: 물론이에요. 거기로 갈게요. 정말 감사합니다.
M: 좋아요. 그럼 3시에 보도록 하죠.

Listening Skills

Student: Can you look at it now?
Professor: Can you come to my office at 3:00 PM?
Student: I'll be there. Thanks so much.
Professor: I'll see you at three then.

• **Exercise 4** • p.83

정답 Q1 ⓒ   Q2 ⓓ
스크립트 ∩ 05-09

W Professor: Marty, could I speak with you for a moment, please?
M Student: Sure, Professor Watson. What can I do for you?
W: Are you still looking for a job for the summer?
M: Yes, I am. I haven't had any luck so far though.
W: Well, I just heard from Professor Dobson that he needs a research assistant.
M: Oh, yeah?
W: Yes. He's doing some research on the Italian Renaissance. You speak Italian, right?
M: I lived there for six years when I was younger.
W: Wonderful. Well, he needs someone to read and translate some old texts. What do you think?
M: Is it a full-time position?
W: I believe so. But you'd need to speak with Professor Dobson to be sure. Shall I set up a meeting with him?
M: I would love that. Thanks for thinking of me, Professor Watson.

해석

W Professor: 마티, 잠깐 이야기를 나눌 수 있을까요?
M Student: 물론이죠, 왓슨 교수님. 무슨 일을 도와드릴까요?
W: 아직도 여름에 할 일자리를 구하고 있나요?
M: 네, 맞아요. 지금까지는 운이 없었지만요.
W: 음, 돕슨 교수님이 연구 조수가 필요하다는 말을 방금 들었어요.
M: 아, 그렇군요?
W: 그래요. 그분은 이탈리아 르네상스에 관한 연구를 하고 계세요. 자네는 이탈리아어를 할 줄 알잖아요, 그렇죠?
M: 어렸을 때 6년 동안 그곳에서 살긴 했어요.
W: 잘 되었네요. 음, 그분은 오래된 문서들을 읽고 번역할 사람을 필요로 하세요. 어떻게 생각하나요?
M: 풀타임으로 해야 하는 일인가요?
W: 그런 것으로 알고 있어요. 하지만 돕슨 교수님과 이야기를 해서 확인해야

할 거예요. 그분과 만나게 마련해 줄까요?
M: 그렇게 해 주시면 정말로 좋죠. 저를 생각해 주셔서 감사합니다, 왓슨 교수님.

Listening Skills

Professor: Marty, could I speak with you for a moment, please?
Student: Sure, Professor Watson. What can I do for you?
Professor: Are you still looking for a job for the summer?
Student: Yes, I am. I haven't had any luck so far though.

• Exercise 5 • p.84

정답 Q1 Ⓐ   Q2 Ⓓ
스크립트 🎧 05-11

M Student: So, Professor Blaire, how do you like the presentation I wrote? I'm looking forward to giving it this Friday.
W Professor: Everything you wrote here is fine.
M: Great.
W: But . . .
M: Uh, oh. But what?
W: Well, you didn't write about the topic I gave you. You were supposed to follow the directions precisely.
M: Oh, sorry. I just found a different topic I liked better, so I thought I would make my presentation about it.
W: That's not acceptable.
M: Why not?
W: You have to follow my instructions, Jason. I gave you that topic for a reason. Your presentation should be on it.
M: Are you sure I can't keep this topic?
W: This is not a matter for discussion.
M: Okay, but, uh . . . Today is Tuesday. Friday is just three days away.
W: Right.
M: How am I supposed to prepare my presentation by then?
W: If you had done it on the right topic, you wouldn't have that problem, would you?
M: Er, yes . . . I see your point.
W: Good luck.

해석

M Student: 그러면, 블레어 교수님, 제가 작성한 발표문에 대해서 어떻게 생각하세요? 이번 주 금요일 발표를 고대하고 있거든요.
W Professor: 자네가 여기에 쓴 모든 내용이 좋아요.
M: 다행입니다.
W: 그렇지만…
M: 아, 이런. 그렇지만 무엇인가요?
W: 음, 자네는 내가 준 주제에 대해 쓰지 않았어요. 지시 사항을 정확히 따랐어야 해요.
M: 아, 죄송해요. 더 마음에 드는 다른 주제를 마침 찾게 되어서 그에 대해서 발표를 하면 된다고 생각했어요.
W: 그건 용납되지 않아요.
M: 왜 안 되나요?
W: 내 지시를 따라야 해요, 제이슨. 이유가 있어서 그 주제를 준 거예요. 자네의 발표는 그것에 관한 것이어야 해요.
M: 이 주제로 하면 정말 안 되는 건가요?
W: 이건 논의할 대상이 아니에요.
M: 알겠습니다, 하지만, 어… 오늘이 화요일이네요. 금요일은 고작 3일 남았는데요.
W: 맞아요.
M: 그때까지 제가 어떻게 발표를 준비할 수 있을까요?
W: 제대로 된 주제에 대해 준비했다면 그런 문제를 겪지 않을 테죠, 그렇죠?
M: 으, 네… 무슨 말씀인지 알겠어요.
W: 행운을 빌어요.

Listening Skills

Student: Are you sure I can't keep this topic?
Professor: This is not a matter for discussion.
Student: Okay, but, uh . . . Today is Tuesday. Friday is just three days away.
Professor: Right.

• Exercise 6 • p.85

정답 Q1 Ⓒ   Q2 Ⓓ
스크립트 🎧 05-13

W Professor: Hello, Timothy. I got your message from my secretary. What can I do for you?
M Student: Professor Perry. We're halfway through the semester. How is my grade looking?
W: Let me see . . . Timothy Fabian . . . Well, it appears to be pretty good.
M: Really? What does "pretty good" mean?
W: You have a high B average.
M: A high B? But I need an A to keep my scholarship.
W: An A, huh?
M: Yes.
W: Well, you have the rest of the semester. Try to step it up some. That's all you need to do.
M: I know. But the school will be checking my grades next week.
W: I see. Well, in that case . . . You could do some extra work. Your average is about an eighty-eight.
M: Really? That would be great.
W: Give me a four-page paper by Wednesday.
M: What's the topic?
W: Something on, um, how about the moon?
M: Sounds good.
W: I won't give you a grade though. But I will give you two bonus points.
M: Thanks, Professor Perry.

해석

W Professor: 안녕, 티모시. 조교한테 메시지를 받았어요. 내가 도와줄 게 뭔가요?
M Student: 페리 교수님. 학기의 반이 지나가고 있는데요. 제 성적이 어떤가요?
W: 어디 봅시다… 티모시 페이비안… 음, 꽤 좋은데요.
M: 정말인가요? "꽤 좋은" 게 어떤 의미일까요?

W: 평균 B 이상이군요.
M: B 이상이요? 하지만 저는 장학금을 계속 받으려면 A가 필요해요.
W: A라, 말이죠?
M: 네.
W: 자, 학기가 남아 있어요. 좀 더 분발하도록 노력해보세요. 자네가 해야 할 일은 그것뿐이에요.
M: 알고 있습니다. 하지만 학교에서는 다음 주에 제 성적을 확인할 거예요.
W: 그렇군요. 음, 그런 경우… 추가 과제를 할 수 있어요. 자네의 평균이 88점 정도 되거든요.
M: 정말인가요? 그러면 좋을 것 같아요.
W: 수요일까지 4쪽짜리 보고서를 써 오세요.
M: 주제는 무엇인가요?
W: 어떤 거냐면, 음, 달에 대한 건 어떤가요?
M: 좋습니다.
W: 그렇다고 해도 학점을 줄 수는 없어요. 하지만 2점을 추가점으로 줄게요.
M: 감사합니다, 페리 교수님.

Listening Skills

Professor: Your average is about an eighty-eight.
Student: Really? That would be great.
Professor: Give me a four-page paper by Wednesday.
Student: What's the topic?

• Exercise 7 •   p.86

정답 Q1 Ⓐ   Q2 Ⓐ
스크립트 🎧 05-15

M Professor: Are you on your way to class, Amber?
W Student: Actually, I'm coming to see you.
M: I have class in ten minutes.
W: This won't take long.
M: Okay. What's going on?
W: I think I left my textbook in your classroom yesterday. I took your English literature class at 2:00 PM yesterday.
M: Did you? Did you check the room?
W: No, it's locked.
M: Well, I have the key. I can check really quickly since the room is right here.
W: Are you sure you have time?
M: Oh, don't worry about that. Okay. Go in and check. I bet it is still there.
W: It is. I can see the book from here. It's still on my desk. What a relief. It's an expensive book.
M: Amber, can you do me a favor?
W: Sure.
M: I have to run. Can you lock the door and give me the key tomorrow? I have to get to class.
W: Sure thing. Go ahead. I'll make sure it's locked.

해석
M Professor: 수업에 가는 길인가요, 앰버?
W Student: 사실, 저는 교수님을 뵈러 가는 길이에요.
M: 나는 10분 후에 수업이 있는데요.

W: 오래 걸리지 않는 일이에요.
M: 알겠어요. 무슨 일이죠?
W: 제가 어제 교재를 교수님 교실에 두고 온 것 같아요. 저는 어제 오후 2시에 교수님의 영문학 수업을 들었습니다.
M: 그랬나요? 교실을 확인해 봤나요?
W: 아뇨, 잠겨 있었어요.
M: 음, 나에게 열쇠가 있어요. 교실이 바로 여기니까 빨리 확인해 볼게요.
W: 시간이 괜찮으시겠어요?
M: 아, 걱정 말아요. 됐어요. 들어가서 확인해 봐요. 분명 거기에 아직도 있을 거예요.
W: 정말이네요. 여기서 책이 보여요. 아직 제 책상 위에 있네요. 다행이에요. 비싼 책이거든요.
M: 앰버, 부탁 한 가지 해도 될까요?
W: 물론이죠.
M: 난 서둘러야 할 것 같아요. 문을 잠그고 내일 열쇠를 주겠어요? 난 수업에 가야 해요.
W: 물론이죠. 어서 가세요. 제가 확실히 잠글게요.

Listening Skills

Student: Actually, I'm coming to see you.
Professor: I have class in ten minutes.
Student: This won't take long.
Professor: Okay. What's going on?

• Exercise 8 •   p.87

정답 Q1 Ⓓ   Q2 Ⓒ
스크립트 🎧 05-17

M Professor: Did you enjoy the lecture?
W Student: Yes. It was very interesting.
M: I'm glad. Can you help me with something?
W: Uh, sure.
M: Can you help me lug some of these books? I can't carry them all to my office.
W: No problem. Some of these are really ancient, aren't they?
M: They sure are. I bought this one in college. I was about your age.
W: And you kept it for this long?
M: Sure. I keep all the books I buy.
W: Wow. Your office must be like a library.
M: Yes, kind of. My home is full of even more books.
W: I usually sell my books. That is, after the class is over.
M: Yes. Most students do the same. I understand it. You need the cash.
W: That's right.
M: Do you unload them all?
W: No, I don't. I keep the ones I like. I actually have a small library in my apartment.

해석
M Professor: 강의가 마음에 들었나요?
W Student: 네. 아주 재미있었어요.
M: 기쁘네요. 나를 좀 도와줄 수 있나요?

W: 아, 그럼요.
M: 이 책들 중 일부를 옮기는 걸 도와줄래요? 나 혼자서는 모두 연구실로 옮길 수가 없네요.
W: 문제없습니다. 어떤 책들은 아주 오래되었네요, 그렇지 않나요?
M: 확실히 그래요. 이 책은 내가 대학 다닐 때 산 거예요. 내가 자네 나이 정도였을 때죠.
W: 그러면 이렇게 오랫동안 가지고 계신 거예요?
M: 물론이에요. 난 내가 사는 책은 모두 가지고 있어요.
W: 와, 교수님의 연구실은 정말 도서관 같겠네요.
M: 그래요, 그런 편이죠. 우리집은 훨씬 더 많은 책으로 꽉 차 있어요.
W: 저는 대개 책을 팔아요. 그러니까, 수업이 끝난 다음에요.
M: 맞아요. 대부분의 학생들이 그렇게 하죠. 이해해요. 학생들은 돈이 필요하잖아요.
W: 맞아요.
M: 책을 모두 처분하나요?
W: 아니요, 그렇지는 않아요. 좋아하는 책들은 가지고 있어요. 사실 제 아파트에도 작은 도서관이 있답니다.

Listening Skills

Student: And you kept it for this long?
Professor: Sure. I keep all the books I buy.
Student: Wow. Your office must be like a library.
Professor: Yes, kind of.

Vocabulary Review   p.88

A 1 ecstatic
   2 tutoring
   3 texts
   4 run
   5 lug

B 1 Ⓒ   2 Ⓐ   3 Ⓑ   4 Ⓒ   5 Ⓐ

C 1 Ⓐ   2 Ⓓ   3 Ⓐ   4 Ⓑ   5 Ⓒ

D 1 aced
   2 step it up
   3 ancient
   4 luck
   5 intricate

Practice Test   p.90

1 Ⓒ   2 Ⓑ   3 Ⓐ

스크립트 🎧 05-19

W Professor: Good morning, Stewart. Thanks for coming in.
M Student: Good morning, Professor Maddux.
W: I have a question to ask you. What are your plans for the summer?
M: I'm not sure yet. Why?
W: You know I'm the director of undergraduate students, right?
M: Yes.
W: I want to start a website for undergrads. You know, to help students, especially new ones, answer common questions, provide phone numbers, and do other similar things.
M: That's a great idea.
W: Well, I hope you can give me a hand.
M: Me?
W: Sure. Why not?
M: Oh, I would love to help you out.
W: The thing is that I want to start the project this summer. That's why I asked if you are going to be here.
M: I see.
W: I want to work on it every day. That way, the website will be ready for the fall semester.
M: I've got it. Well, I'm still undecided about summer.
W: I completely understand. All I want you to do is think about it. Of course, I'll pay you for your work, Stewart.
M: Thanks. I'll definitely give it some thought.

해석
W Professor: 좋은 아침이에요, 스튜어드. 와 줘서 고마워요.
M Student: 안녕하세요, 매덕스 교수님.
W: 자네에게 물어볼 게 있어요. 여름에 무슨 계획이 있나요?
M: 아직 확실하지 않습니다. 왜 그러시죠?
W: 내가 학부생 지도 교사라는 것을 알고 있지요, 그렇죠?
M: 네.
W: 나는 학부생들을 위한 웹사이트를 하나 개설하고 싶어요. 알겠지만, 학생들, 특히 신입생들을 돕는 건데, 자주 묻는 질문에 답하거나, 전화번호를 제공해주고, 기타 그런 비슷한 일들을 하려고요.
M: 좋은 생각입니다.
W: 음, 자네가 나를 좀 도와주었으면 해요.
M: 제가요?
W: 그럼요. 안 될 이유가 없죠?
M: 아, 저도 교수님을 도와드리고 싶어요.
W: 문제는 내가 그 프로젝트를 이번 여름에 시작하고 싶다는 거예요. 그래서 자네가 여기에 올 수 있는지 물어본 거고요.
M: 그렇군요.
W: 나는 그 프로젝트에 매일 매달리고 싶어요. 그래야 웹사이트가 가을 학기에 맞게 준비될 테니까요.
M: 이해했어요. 음, 전 여름에 대해 아직 결정한 것이 없어서요.
W: 그렇고 말고요. 내가 원하는 것은 그것에 대해 한 번 생각해 보라는 거예요. 물론, 일에 대한 보수를 줄 예정이에요, 스튜어드.
M: 감사합니다. 그 부분에 대해 꼭 생각해 보겠습니다.

CHAPTER 6 Physiology

Understanding TOEFL Question Types & Listening Skills
p.94

1 Question Types ▶ Sample Question

스크립트 ∩ 06-01

W Professor: We call it the circulatory system. It <u>is</u> <u>made</u> <u>up</u> <u>of</u> the <u>heart</u> and <u>blood</u> <u>vessels</u>. There are <u>two</u> <u>main</u> <u>kinds</u> of <u>blood</u> <u>vessels</u>. They are arteries and veins. <u>First</u>, the <u>heart</u> <u>pumps</u> <u>blood</u> <u>away</u> from the heart <u>in</u> <u>arteries</u>. These <u>blood</u> <u>cells</u> <u>have</u> <u>oxygen</u> in them. They are <u>bright</u> <u>red</u>. Then, the <u>heart</u> <u>pumps</u> <u>blood</u> <u>back</u> to it <u>through</u> <u>veins</u>. This blood looks <u>dark</u> <u>red</u> as it <u>doesn't</u> <u>carry</u> <u>any</u> <u>oxygen</u>.

해석

W Professor: 우리는 그것을 순환계라고 부릅니다. 순환계는 심장과 혈관으로 이루어져 있습니다. 두 가지 주요한 종류의 혈관이 있습니다. 동맥과 정맥이죠. 먼저 심장은 피를 펌프질해 심장에서 동맥으로 내보냅니다. 이 혈액 세포들 안에는 산소가 있습니다. 그 혈액 세포들은 선홍색을 띱니다. 그러고 나서 심장은 피를 다시 펌프질해 정맥을 통해 심장으로 다시 보냅니다. 이 피는 산소를 운반하지 않기 때문에 검붉은 빛을 띱니다.

2 Listening Skills ▶ Check-Up

1 <u>First</u>, the heart pumps blood away from the heart in arteries.
2 <u>Then</u>, the heart pumps blood back to it through veins.

• Exercise 1 •
p.96

정답 Q1 ⓓ Q2 ⓑ

스크립트 ∩ 06-03

M Professor: Let's <u>take</u> <u>a</u> <u>look</u> <u>at</u> <u>the</u> <u>muscles</u> in our bodies, class. Sound good? Okay. Now, um, there are <u>three</u> <u>basic</u> <u>kinds</u>: cardiac, skeletal, and smooth.
Everyone, look at the screen . . . Okay . . . <u>First</u>, look at this image. This is a view of <u>a</u> <u>cardiac</u> <u>muscle</u>. It is a <u>heart</u> <u>muscle</u>. It's also an involuntary muscle. This means that <u>it</u> <u>works</u> <u>automatically</u>. Humans <u>don't</u> <u>control</u> <u>it</u> by thinking.
Now, the <u>second</u> image . . . Okay, next are <u>skeletal</u> <u>muscles</u>. These are a kind of <u>voluntary</u> <u>muscles</u>. These are the muscles we use <u>for</u> <u>movement</u>. They are, <u>for</u> <u>example</u>, in our <u>arms</u> and <u>legs</u>. They are <u>very</u> <u>important</u>.
Next, the <u>third</u> image. The last ones are <u>smooth</u> <u>muscles</u>. They are <u>involuntary</u>, like cardiac muscles. They are found, for example, <u>in</u> <u>the</u> <u>stomach</u>.

해석

M Professor: 우리 몸의 근육에 대해 살펴봅시다, 여러분. 재밌어 보이죠? 좋아요. 그렇다면, 음, 기본적으로 3가지 종류가 있어요: 심근, 골격근, 그리고 평활근이 있지요.

모두들, 화면을 보세요… 좋아요… 첫째로, 이 이미지를 보세요. 이것은 심근의 모습입니다. 심장의 근육이죠. 또한 불수의(不隨意)근이기도 합니다. 이것은 근육이 자동적으로 움직인다는 의미입니다. 사람이 생각을 하여 근육을 조절할 수 없습니다.

이번에는, 두 번째 이미지입니다… 자, 다음은 골격근입니다. 이것은 수의(隨意)근의 일종이지요. 이 근육들은 우리가 움직이는 데 사용하는 근육입니다. 예를 들어, 우리의 팔과 다리에 있는 근육이지요. 이 근육들은 아주 중요합니다.

다음은 세 번째 이미지입니다. 마지막 이미지들은 평활근입니다. 이 근육은 심근과 마찬가지로 불수의근입니다. 이 근육들은, 예를 들자면 위장에서 볼 수 있습니다.

Listening Skills

1 <u>First</u>, look at this image.
2 Now, the <u>second</u> image . . . Okay, next are skeletal muscles.

• Exercise 2 •
p.97

정답 Q1 ⓑ Q2 ⓑ

스크립트 ∩ 06-05

W Professor: The <u>bones</u> in the human body have <u>three</u> <u>basic</u> <u>purposes</u>. Some, <u>for</u> <u>example</u>, such as the backbone or spinal column, <u>provide</u> <u>support</u>. They <u>allow</u> <u>us</u> <u>to</u> <u>stand</u> <u>upright</u> and tall.
<u>Another</u> <u>main</u> <u>function</u> of bones is <u>protection</u>. Bones like your ribs in the ribcage <u>protect</u> <u>important</u> <u>organs</u>. Actually, the ribs are kind of like armor, uh, like <u>a</u> <u>protective</u> <u>vest</u>. <u>Furthermore</u>, <u>the</u> <u>backbone</u> <u>protects</u> the spinal cord. The spinal cord allows <u>the</u> <u>brain</u> <u>to</u> <u>communicate</u> <u>with</u> the rest of your body.
The brain is <u>one</u> <u>of</u> <u>the</u> <u>most</u> <u>important</u> <u>organs</u> in the body. <u>The</u> <u>skull</u> <u>protects</u> this sensitive organ <u>from</u> dangerous <u>bumps</u> and <u>knocks</u>.
<u>Lastly</u>, the bones are <u>blood</u> <u>machines</u>. <u>Inside</u> <u>your</u> <u>bones</u> is bone marrow. This substance <u>makes</u> <u>new</u> <u>red</u> and <u>white</u> <u>blood</u> <u>cells</u> in people's bodies.

해석

W Professor: 사람 몸의 뼈는 기본적으로 3가지 기능을 가지고 있습니다. 예를 들어, 등뼈나 척추와 같은 어떤 뼈는 지탱을 돕습니다. 이 뼈들은 우리가 똑바로 서게 해줍니다.

뼈의 또 다른 주요 기능은 보호입니다. 흉곽의 갈비뼈와 같은 뼈들은 중요한 장기들을 보호합니다. 사실 갈비뼈는 갑옷, 아, 마치 방탄조끼와 같은 종류입니다. 더 나아가 등뼈는 척수를 보호합니다. 척수는 뇌가 신체의 나머지 부분들과 소통하게 해줍니다.

뇌는 신체에서 가장 중요한 장기 중 하나입니다. 두개골은 이 민감한 장기를 위험한 충격과 충돌에서 보호합니다.

마지막으로, 뼈는 혈액 공장입니다. 뼈 안에는 골수가 있습니다. 이 물질은 우리 몸 안에 새로운 적혈구와 백혈구를 만들어냅니다.

Listening Skills

1 Some, <u>for</u> <u>example</u>, such as the backbone or spinal column, provide support.

2 Another main function of bones is protection.

• Exercise 3 • ———————————————— p.98

정답 Q1 Ⓑ   Q2 Ⓒ
스크립트 🎧 06-07

M Professor: The human heart is actually a large muscle. Well, it's really like a large muscle pump. Um, hang on a second. It is more like two pumps. The right part of the heart gets blood from the rest of the body and pumps it into the lungs. The left side does the opposite. It gets blood from the lungs and pumps it out to the rest of the body.
Now, let's go a little deeper. Inside the heart are four chambers. They're like little rooms in the heart. There are two chambers in each side. The name of the top chambers is atria. They fill with blood coming from the body and the lungs. The bottom chambers are ventricles. They pump blood to the lungs and the rest of the body. Everyone got it . . . ? Great.

해석
M Professor: 인간의 심장은 사실상 커다란 근육입니다. 그러니까, 정말로 하나의 커다란 근육 펌프와 같습니다. 음, 잠시만요. 두 개의 펌프에 좀 더 가깝겠네요. 심장의 우측 부분은 우리 몸의 다른 부분에서 피를 받아들여 그 피를 폐로 펌프질해 내보냅니다. 좌측 부분은 그 반대입니다. 그것은 폐에서 피를 받아 몸의 나머지 부분으로 그 피를 펌프질해 내보냅니다.
그럼, 좀 더 자세히 살펴봅시다. 심장 안에는 4개의 실(室)이 있습니다. 그것은 심장 안에 있는 작은 방들과 같습니다. 양쪽에 두 개씩 있습니다. 위쪽에 있는 방의 이름은 심방입니다. 심방은 우리 몸과 폐에서 들어오는 피로 채워집니다. 아래쪽에 있는 방은 심실입니다. 심실은 피를 폐와 우리 몸의 나머지 부분으로 펌프질해 내보냅니다. 여러분 다 알아들었나요…? 좋습니다.

Listening Skills

1 Um, hang on a second.
2 Now, let's go a little deeper.

• Exercise 4 • ———————————————— p.99

정답 Q1 Ⓑ   Q2 Ⓐ
스크립트 🎧 06-09

W Professor: Think about that slice of pizza you had for lunch. Or that fried chicken. Whatever. What happens to it? Yes, I'm talking about the digestive process. You know, the digestive system.
First, saliva, um, spit, begins to break down the food in your mouth. As a result, it becomes softer and easier to swallow. Second, the food enters your throat, or esophagus. This is the tube leading to your stomach. Small muscles help push the food down to your stomach. However, the esophagus serves another important purpose. It makes sure that food doesn't go into your windpipe, the breathing tube leading to your lungs. That's pretty important, huh? Finally, the food enters the stomach. The stomach stores the food and breaks it down more into a liquid substance.

해석
W Professor: 여러분이 점심으로 먹은 그 피자 한 조각을 생각해보세요. 아니면 닭튀김도 좋고요. 무엇이든 상관없습니다. 그 음식에 무슨 일이 일어나고 있나요? 그래요, 저는 소화 과정에 대해 이야기하려고 합니다. 모두 알고 있는, 그 소화 과정 말이에요.
먼저, 타액, 그러니까, 침이 여러분의 입에서 음식을 분해하기 시작합니다. 그 결과, 음식은 부드러워져 삼키기 쉬워집니다. 다음으로, 음식이 목구멍, 즉 식도로 들어갑니다. 이것은 위장으로 이어지는 관입니다. 작은 근육들이 음식을 밀어 위까지 내려가게 해줍니다. 하지만 식도는 또 다른 중요한 목적도 수행합니다. 식도 때문에 음식은 확실히, 폐로 이어지는 호흡 관인 기도로 넘어가지 않게 됩니다. 그것은 정말 중요합니다, 그렇지 않을까요? 마지막으로 음식이 위장으로 들어갑니다. 위는 음식을 저장했다가 그 음식을 더 분해해 액체 상태로 만듭니다.

Listening Skills

1 However, the esophagus serves another important purpose.
2 Third, the food enters the stomach.

• Exercise 5 • ———————————————— p.100

정답 Q1 Ⓒ   Q2 Ⓐ
스크립트 🎧 06-11

M Professor: Let me cover the immune system now. This is what keeps you healthy. The immune system basically fights germs, viruses, bacteria, and other harmful organisms. It tries to keep them out of the body. If they get in the body, it attempts to kill them.
First, the immune system has several parts. The skin is the outer part of it. It keeps pathogens—you know, germs and other harmful things—out of your body. There's also mucus in the nose and throat. If pathogens get past the skin, mucus can capture them and remove them.
What happens if pathogens get inside the body? Well, white blood cells try to kill them. These cells can go anywhere in your body. They fight infections, diseases, sicknesses, and other problems. Some white blood cells also recognize previous pathogens, such as viruses. So if you get a virus a second time, the immune system creates antibodies. They then fight and kill the virus.

해석
M Professor: 이제 면역 체계를 다루도록 하죠. 면역 체계는 건강을 유지시켜 줍니다. 면역 체계는 기본적으로 병균, 바이러스, 박테리아, 그리고 기타 해로운 물질들과 싸웁니다. 면역 체계는 이들이 신체 내로 들어오지 못하게 막으려고 합니다. 만약 이들이 신체 내로 들어오는 경우에는 면역 체계가 이들을 없애려고 합니다.
먼저, 면역 체계는 몇 가지 부분으로 이루어져 있습니다. 피부는 면역 체계의 바깥쪽 부분입니다. 피부는 병원균이—알다시피, 병균 및 기타 해로운 존재들이—신체로 들어오는 것을 막아 주죠. 또한 코와 목구멍에는 점액이 존재합니다. 병원균이 피부를 지나 들어오면 점액이 이들을 포획해 제거할 수 있습니다.
병원균이 체내로 들어오면 어떻게 될까요? 음, 백혈구가 이들을 없애려고 합니다. 이들 세포는 신체 내 어디든 돌아다닐 수 있습니다. 이들은 감염병, 질병, 질환, 그리고 기타 문제들과 싸웁니다. 어떤 백혈구는 바이러스와 같이 이전에 들어온 병원균 또한 인식합니다. 따라서 바이러스가 두 번째로 유입되면, 면역 체계가 항체를 생성합니다. 그러면 이들이 바이러스와 싸워서 물리치죠.

Listening Skills

1 <u>Let me</u> cover the immune system now.
2 <u>First</u>, the immune system has several parts.
3 <u>Well</u>, white blood cells try to kill them.

• Exercise 6 • — p.101

정답 Q1 ⓒ Q2 ⓑ
스크립트 🎧 06-13

W Professor: <u>Babies don't come with</u> a full set of teeth. <u>However</u>, by the time babies are six to twelve months old, <u>teeth begin to appear</u>. At the <u>age of three</u>, most children have <u>a full set of their first teeth</u>. We call these primary, or baby, teeth. Ultimately, children have <u>twenty primary teeth</u>. <u>However</u>, they are <u>only temporary</u>.
As kids turn five or six years old, their primary teeth <u>start to fall out</u>. Well, they don't just fall out. <u>Adult teeth</u> in the gums begin to <u>push them out</u>. We call adult teeth <u>permanent teeth</u>. By the age of twelve or thirteen, most kids have <u>all of their permanent teeth</u>. There are twenty-eight in all. That's <u>eight more than</u> the first set. But this <u>isn't the end of</u> tooth development. <u>Later</u>, perhaps between the ages of eighteen and twenty-one, some young adults <u>develop wisdom teeth</u>. Notice, class, that I said some. <u>Some young adults never develop</u> wisdom teeth.

해석
W Professor: 아기는 아래위 치아를 모두 갖추고 태어나지 않습니다. 그러나 아기가 6개월에서 12개월이 되는 시기에는, 이가 나기 시작합니다. 3세가 되면, 대부분의 아이들이 아래위 유치를 모두 갖게 됩니다. 우리는 이를 유치, 혹은 젖니라고 부릅니다. 기본적으로 아이들은 20개의 유치를 가지고 있습니다. 그러나 유치는 일시적일 뿐입니다.
어린이가 5세 내지 6세가 되면, 유치가 빠지기 시작합니다. 음, 이가 단순히 빠지기만 하는 것은 아닙니다. 잇몸 속에 있던 성치가 밖으로 나오기 시작하는 거죠. 우리는 이러한 성치를 영구치라고 부릅니다. 12-13세 정도가 되면, 대부분의 아이들이 영구치를 모두 가지게 됩니다.
모두 합하여 28개의 치아가 있습니다. 유치보다 8개가 더 많은 거죠. 그러나 이것이 치아 발달의 끝이 아닙니다. 이후에, 아마도 18세에서 21세 사이에 어떤 젊은 성인의 경우에는 사랑니가 납니다. 여러분, 제가 어떤이라고 한 말에 주목하세요. 어떤 젊은 성인의 경우에는 사랑니가 전혀 나지 않습니다.

Listening Skills

1 <u>However, by the time</u> babies are six to twelve months old, teeth begin to appear.
2 <u>Ultimately</u>, children have twenty primary teeth. <u>However</u>, they are only temporary.
3 <u>Later</u>, perhaps between the ages of eighteen and twenty-one, some young adults develop wisdom teeth.

• Exercise 7 • — p.102

정답 Q1 ⓑ Q2 ⓒ
스크립트 🎧 06-15

M Professor: The <u>skin is the largest organ</u> in the body. Really. It <u>holds all of the inside stuff</u> together. The skin also <u>protects us</u> and <u>keeps us the right temperature</u>. And it <u>allows</u> us the <u>sense of touch</u>.
Okay. There are <u>three layers</u> to our skin. Let's start with <u>the top layer</u>. <u>The part that we can see</u> is the epidermis. Actually, it <u>is made up of</u> dead skin cells. They are <u>tough</u> and <u>strong</u>. <u>Every couple</u> of weeks, they <u>rub off</u>. More dead skin cells <u>replace them</u>. <u>Next</u> is the dermis. It <u>contains nerves</u> and <u>blood vessels</u>. <u>This layer</u> allows us <u>to feel things</u> like hot water and cool breezes. The sweat glands are <u>in the dermis as well</u>. We <u>sweat through small openings</u> in the skin. These openings <u>are called</u> pores. <u>Sweat</u> helps us <u>cool down</u> on hot days. <u>Last</u> is <u>a layer of fat</u>. It <u>keeps us warm</u>. It is also <u>where hair starts to grow</u>.

해석
M Professor: 피부는 몸에서 가장 넓은 부분을 차지하는 기관입니다. 정말 넓습니다. 그것은 신체 내부의 모든 요소를 감싸고 있습니다. 피부는 또한 우리를 보호하고 우리가 적정한 체온을 유지하게 해줍니다. 그리고 우리가 촉감을 느낄 수 있게 해줍니다.
봅시다. 우리의 피부에는 세 겹의 층이 있습니다. 가장 위쪽의 층부터 시작해봅시다. 우리가 볼 수 있는 피부층을 표피라고 합니다. 사실 표피는 죽은 피부 세포로 이루어져 있습니다. 그것은 단단하고 강합니다. 표피는 2-3주마다 벗겨집니다. 다른 죽은 피부 세포가 이를 대체합니다. 다음 층은 진피입니다. 진피에는 신경과 혈관이 있습니다. 이 진피층은 우리가 뜨거운 물과 시원한 바람과 같은 것을 느낄 수 있게 해줍니다. 땀샘도 마찬가지로 진피층에 있습니다. 우리는 피부의 작은 구멍을 통해 땀을 배출합니다. 이러한 구멍을 모공이라고 합니다. 더운 날 땀을 흘리면 체온을 낮출 수 있습니다. 마지막은 지방층입니다. 지방층은 우리 몸을 따뜻하게 유지해줍니다. 또한 체모가 자라기 시작하는 곳이기도 합니다.

Listening Skills

1 <u>Let's start</u> with the top layer.
2 <u>Actually</u>, it is made up of dead skin cells.
3 <u>Last</u> is a layer of fat.

• Exercise 8 • — p.103

정답 Q1 ⓑ Q2 ⓐ
스크립트 🎧 06-17

W Professor: <u>In general</u>, human beings <u>have five senses</u>. One is <u>sight</u>. This is the <u>ability to see things</u>. We <u>use our eyes to see</u>. <u>However</u>, some people <u>cannot</u>. We <u>call this blindness</u>. Another sense is <u>hearing</u>. Take this word down in your notes, class: audition. The experts <u>use this word for hearing</u>. It could be on your test. Hint, hint . . .
Now, we hear <u>with our two ears</u>. People with the <u>inability to hear</u> are <u>deaf</u>. Everyone with me . . .? Great. Next is <u>the sense of smell</u>. The nose is the <u>main organ</u> for <u>smell</u>. Some experts

believe the sense of smell is the strongest.
We have two more senses to discuss. One is the sense of taste. The organ we use for taste is the tongue. Finally, we have the sense of touch. It depends on pressure for feeling and sensation. And, yes, the skin is the main organ we use for this sense.

해석
W Professor: 일반적으로 인간에게는 오감이 있습니다. 하나는 시각입니다. 이것은 사물을 볼 수 있는 능력입니다. 우리는 눈을 통해 봅니다. 그러나 어떤 사람은 볼 수 없습니다. 우리는 이것을 시각장애라고 부릅니다. 또 다른 감각은 청각입니다. 이 단어를 노트에 적으세요, 여러분: 청각(audition)이요. 전문가들은 청력(hearing)이라는 말 대신 이 단어를 사용합니다. 시험에 나올 수도 있어요. 힌트예요, 힌트 …
자, 우리는 두 귀로 듣습니다. 들을 수 없는 사람들을 청각장애인이라고 합니다. 모두 잘 이해하고 있나요…? 좋아요. 다음은 후각입니다. 코는 냄새를 맡는 주요 기관이지요. 어떤 전문가들은 후각이 가장 강하다고 생각합니다.
두 가지 감각을 더 이야기해야 합니다. 하나는 미각입니다. 우리가 맛을 느끼기 위해 사용하는 기관은 혀입니다. 마지막으로, 우리는 촉각을 가지고 있습니다. 촉각은 느낌과 감각에 대한 자극에 따라 반응합니다. 그리고, 맞아요, 피부가 이 감각에 사용되는 주요 기관입니다.

Listening Skills

1 We have two more senses to discuss.
2 One is the sense of taste.
3 Finally, we have the sense of touch.

Vocabulary Review   p.104

A
1 sensation
2 stuff
3 full
4 recognized
5 Whatever

B 1 Ⓒ   2 Ⓐ   3 Ⓒ   4 Ⓐ   5 Ⓓ

C 1 Ⓐ   2 Ⓑ   3 Ⓒ   4 Ⓑ   5 Ⓑ

D
1 ability
2 pores
3 bump
4 breaks down
5 permanent

Practice Test   p.106

1 Ⓑ   2 Ⓒ   3 Tendons: ②, ③   Ligaments: ①, ④
4 Ⓐ

스크립트 🎧 06-19

M Professor: Without tendons or ligaments, we couldn't move. Together with muscles, they give us the ability to walk, talk, lift things, move things, and do just about any physical activity.
First, let's discuss tendons. These are connective tissues that connect or attach muscles to bones. Tendons are fairly flexible and very strong and tough. However, sometimes we can injure our tendons, and this can cause major problems. A common tendon injury occurs at the heel of the foot. We call this tendon the Achilles tendon. It connects the heel with the calf, which is a lower-leg muscle. The Achilles is the largest tendon in the human body.
Now, let me discuss ligaments. Similar to tendons, they are connective tissues, but unlike tendons, they attach bones to bones. So ligaments basically form the joints in our bodies. Let me give you some examples. Um, well, your elbows are a good example of where ligaments attach the bones of in arms. Your knees are another good example. Moreover, ligaments are elastic. That is, they can stretch, but injuries can occur if they stretch too much.

해석
M Professor: 힘줄 또는 인대가 없으면, 우리는 움직이지 못할 것입니다. 근육과 함께, 힘줄과 인대는 우리가 걷고, 말하고, 물건을 들어올리고, 물건을 나르는 등 신체적인 활동이라면 무엇이든 바로 할 수 있게 해줍니다.
먼저, 힘줄에 대해 이야기해 봅시다. 이것은 결합조직으로, 근육을 뼈에 연결하거나 붙어 있게 합니다. 힘줄은 상당히 유연하면서도 매우 강하고 튼튼합니다. 그러나 때때로 힘줄을 다칠 수 있고, 이는 심각한 문제를 초래할 수 있습니다. 흔히 있는 힘줄 부상은 발뒤꿈치에서 일어납니다. 우리는 이 힘줄을 아킬레스건이라고 부릅니다. 그것은 발뒤꿈치를 종아리, 즉 다리 아래쪽 근육과 연결합니다. 아킬레스건은 인체에서 가장 큰 힘줄입니다.
이번에는, 인대에 대해 이야기해 봅시다. 힘줄과 비슷하게 인대도 결합조직이지만, 힘줄과는 또 다르게 뼈와 뼈를 연결합니다. 그러니까 인대는 기본적으로 우리 몸의 관절을 형성합니다. 몇 가지 예를 들어보겠습니다. 음, 그러니까, 팔꿈치가 좋은 예가 되는데, 팔꿈치의 인대로 인해 팔에 뼈들이 붙어 있는 것입니다. 무릎도 또 다른 좋은 예입니다. 더 나아가 인대는 탄력이 있습니다. 다시 말하자면, 인대는 늘어날 수 있는데, 하지만 너무 많이 늘어나면 다칠 수도 있습니다.

CHAPTER 7 Oceanography

Understanding TOEFL Question Types & Listening Skills
p.110

1 Question Types ▶ Sample Question
Ⓑ

스크립트 🎧 07-01

W Professor: The Great Barrier Reef <u>is</u> in <u>serious peril</u>. The <u>largest</u> <u>coral</u> <u>reef</u> in the world is <u>dying</u>. Some experts think it <u>will die by 2027</u>. Remember, everyone, that coral reefs are <u>living</u> <u>things</u>. They <u>aren't</u> <u>just</u> <u>big</u> <u>rocks</u> in the ocean. And <u>warmer</u> <u>waters</u> are the <u>main</u> <u>cause</u> of this sad situation. The reef <u>needs</u> <u>fish</u> <u>to</u> <u>live</u>. Some fish <u>look</u> <u>for</u> <u>new</u> <u>homes</u> when the <u>water</u> <u>gets</u> <u>warm</u>.

해석

W Professor: 그레이트 배리어 리프는 심각한 위기에 처해 있습니다. 세계에서 가장 큰 산호초가 죽어가고 있습니다. 어떤 전문가들은 2027년이면 그것이 멸종할 거라고 생각합니다. 여러분, 산호초는 살아 있는 생명체라는 것을 기억하세요. 그것은 단지 바닷속의 큰 바위덩어리가 아닙니다. 그리고 수온 상승이 이 슬픈 상황의 주요 원인입니다. 산호초가 살려면 물고기들이 필요합니다. 어떤 물고기들은 수온이 올라가면 새로운 서식지를 찾아 나섭니다.

2 Listening Skills ▶ Check-Up

1 leaf – (reef)   2 (think) – sink
3 leads – (needs) 4 (fish) – pish

• Exercise 1 •
p.112

정답 Q1 True: ①, ③, ④ False: ② Q2 Ⓓ

스크립트 🎧 07-03

M Professor: We all know about <u>volcanoes</u>. You probably saw <u>the news report</u> about the one that just <u>erupted</u> <u>in</u> <u>Indonesia</u>. Well, volcanoes do <u>not</u> <u>just</u> <u>exist</u> <u>on</u> <u>land</u>. There are also <u>underwater</u> volcanoes. Now, uh, here's <u>something</u> <u>interesting</u> about underwater volcanoes. When they <u>erupt</u>, the lava <u>encounters</u> <u>water</u>. This usually makes the lava <u>cool</u> <u>off</u> and <u>harden</u>. <u>Over time</u>, the volcano <u>continues to erupt</u>. The lava <u>gets</u> <u>hard</u>. So the volcano <u>rises</u> <u>higher</u> <u>and</u> <u>higher</u> under the water. If it <u>erupts</u> <u>enough</u>, the volcano will <u>rise</u> <u>above</u> <u>the</u> <u>sea</u>. This <u>creates</u> <u>an</u> <u>island</u>. There are <u>lots</u> <u>of</u> <u>volcanic</u> <u>islands</u> around the world. There are many islands <u>in</u> <u>Hawaii</u>. They are all <u>the</u> <u>result</u> <u>of</u> <u>volcanic</u> <u>eruptions</u>. A new island just <u>formed</u> <u>in</u> <u>the</u> <u>Pacific</u> <u>Ocean</u>. Let me show you some pictures.

해석

M Professor: 우리 모두 화산에 대해 알고 있습니다. 여러분들은 아마도 얼마 전 인도네시아에서 분출한 화산에 관한 뉴스 보도를 보았을 겁니다. 음, 화산은 땅에만 존재하는 것이 아닙니다. 해저 화산도 존재하죠. 자, 아, 해저 화산에 관한 흥미로운 점을 알려 드릴게요. 이들이 분출하면, 용암과 물이 만나게 됩니다. 이렇게 되면 보통 용암이 식어서 굳습니다. 시간이 지나면서, 화산은 계속해서 분출합니다. 용암은 단단해집니다. 그로 인해 바닷속에서 화산은 점점 더 높아집니다. 화산이 충분히 분출을 하면 그것은 바다 위로 솟아 오르게 됩니다. 이로써 섬이 만들어집니다. 전 세계에 많은 화산섬이 존재합니다. 하와이에는 많은 섬들이 있죠. 이들은 모두 화산 분출의 결과물입니다. 얼마 전에도 태평양에 새로운 섬이 만들어졌습니다. 사진을 몇 장 보여 드리겠습니다.

Listening Skills

1 views – (news)   2 (land) – rand
3 (harden) – pardon 4 (rise) – vise

• Exercise 2 •
p.113

정답 Q1 Ⓑ Q2 Marianas Trench: ①, ② Mount Everest: ③, ④

스크립트 🎧 07-05

W Professor: <u>The deepest place</u> on the Earth <u>that we know about</u> is the Marianas Trench. We can find it <u>in the North Pacific Ocean</u> <u>near Guam</u>. <u>Its maximum depth</u> is nearly seven miles deep. And it's <u>still growing</u>, so it's <u>getting deeper</u>.

Think of it like this. Mount Everest is <u>the tallest mountain</u> in the world. The Marianas Trench is <u>more than a mile deeper</u>, making it <u>much bigger than</u> Mount Everest. <u>Why</u> is it <u>so deep</u>? <u>It has to do with</u> plate tectonics. Continental plates and oceanic plates are always <u>crashing together</u> or <u>moving apart</u>. The oceanic plate near the trench is <u>much heavier</u>, so it is <u>going down into the Earth</u>. <u>At the same time</u>, the continental plate in the area is <u>going up toward the surface</u>. Their actions <u>have resulted in</u> the Marianas Trench.

해석

W Professor: 우리가 알고 있는 지구상에서 가장 깊은 곳은 마리아나 해구입니다. 괌 근처의 북태평양에서 그것을 발견할 수 있습니다. 그곳의 가장 깊은 부분은 거의 7마일에 달합니다. 그리고 그것은 지금도 성장하고 있어서, 더 깊어지고 있습니다.

이렇게 생각해 봅시다. 에베레스트산이 지구상에서 가장 높은 산이죠. 마리아나 해구는 1마일 더 깊기 때문에, 에베레스트산보다 훨씬 더 큰 것입니다. 왜 그렇게 깊을까요? 그것은 판구조론과 관련이 있습니다. 대륙판과 해양판은 항상 서로 충돌하거나 떨어져 이동합니다. 해구 근처의 해양판은 훨씬 더 무거워서, 지구 안쪽으로 내려갑니다. 동시에 그 지역의 대륙판은 지구 표면을 향해 올라갑니다. 이들의 작용이 마리아나 해구를 만들어 낸 것입니다.

Listening Skills

1 (depth) – death   2 (bigger) – figure
3 (plates) – planes 4 trash – (crash)

• Exercise 3 •   p.114

정답 Q1 ⓒ   Q2 Stony: ②   Soft: ①, ③, ④

스크립트 🎧 07-07

W Professor: There are many types of shallow corals. But there are deep types of corals, too. Deep corals do not need sunlight like their shallow relatives.
There are three main types of deep corals. They are stony, soft, and black corals. Please make note of them, class. Okay. Stony corals are very rocky and large. They can live for a long time. Next are soft corals. They are very colorful. Pinks and reds are most common. They come in a multitude of shapes and sizes. One example of them is the sea fan. It's very light and flowing. It's quite beautiful, actually. Last of all are black corals. They are often orange or tan with a tough black skeleton. Many of them can live longer than 100 years.

해석
W Professor: 많은 종류의 얕은 물에 사는 산호가 있습니다. 하지만 깊은 곳에 사는 산호류도 있습니다. 깊은 물에 사는 산호는 얕은 물에 사는 동족 산호처럼 햇빛을 필요로 하지 않습니다.
깊은 물에 사는 산호에는 주로 세 가지 종류가 있습니다. 돌산호류, 연산호류, 각산호류입니다. 이 이름들을 필기하세요, 여러분. 자. 돌산호류는 정말 단단하고 크기가 큽니다. 이들은 수명이 깁니다. 다음은 연산호류입니다. 그것은 색채가 매우 다양합니다. 분홍색과 붉은색이 가장 일반적입니다. 연산호류는 모양과 크기가 다양합니다. 그중 한 예는 부채산호입니다. 그것은 아주 얇고 하늘거립니다. 그것은 실제로 아주 아름답습니다. 마지막으로는 각산호류가 있습니다. 각산호류는 검은색의 거친 골격을 가지며 주로 주황색이나 황갈색입니다. 각산호 중 다수가 100년 이상 살 수 있습니다.

Listening Skills

1 (not) – lot   2 freeze – (please)
3 crass – (class)   4 right – (light)

• Exercise 4 •   p.115

정답 Q1 ⓓ   Q2 True: ②, ③   False: ①, ④

스크립트 🎧 07-09

M Professor: This is a picture of an iceberg. Icebergs are basically huge chunks of ice floating in the ocean. Many of them can be quite large. Some can be more than 100 meters high. They might be several kilometers long, too. And here's something interesting. Only a small part of an iceberg is actually visible. Most of its bulk is hidden beneath the water. That's why icebergs are so dangerous. Throughout history, many ships have hit icebergs and sunk. The *Titanic* is the most famous one, of course.
Most icebergs come from glaciers. They break off where glaciers meet the ocean. Then, they float on the water. Some of them drift for thousands of kilometers. These icebergs often drift to warm waters and melt. Others stay in cold areas for years and years.

해석
M Professor: 이것은 빙산의 사진입니다. 빙산은 기본적으로 바다에 떠 있는 거대한 얼음 덩어리입니다. 많은 빙산들이 꽤 클 수 있습니다. 어떤 빙산들은 높이가 100미터 이상이 될 수도 있습니다. 길이가 몇 킬로미터에 이르는 것도 있을 수 있습니다. 그리고 흥미로운 점이 있습니다. 빙산의 극히 일부분만이 실제로 눈에 보입니다. 빙산 부피의 대부분은 물속에 숨겨져 있습니다. 빙산이 매우 위험한 이유가 바로 이러한 점 때문입니다. 역사를 통해 많은 선박들이 빙산과 충돌해 가라앉았습니다. 물론 *타이타닉*호가 가장 유명하죠.
대부분의 빙산은 빙하에서 생깁니다. 빙하가 바다와 만나는 곳에서 빙산이 떨어져 나오죠. 그 후 빙산은 물 위를 떠다닙니다. 그중 일부는 수천 킬로미터를 이동합니다. 이러한 빙산들은 종종 따뜻한 수역까지 떠내려와서 녹습니다. 여러 해 동안 추운 지역에 머물러 있는 빙산들도 있습니다.

Listening Skills

1 (visible) – risible   2 (sunk) – sump
3 (drift) – drip   4 warn – (warm)

• Exercise 5 •   p.116

정답 Q1 ⓑ   Q2 Flood Tide: ①, ②   Ebb Tide: ③, ④

스크립트 🎧 07-11

W Professor: Tides are simply the rising and falling of the ocean's surface. The attraction of the sun and the moon creates tides. Tides happen about every twelve hours or so. There are basically two types of tides: flood and ebb tides.
How do tides work? Okay. Think about a time you were at the beach. Say you were building a sandcastle. After around thirty minutes or so, you probably noticed the water was getting closer and closer to your sandcastle. This was a flood tide. The water was coming in and advancing up the beach. Is everyone with me . . . ? Now, at a certain time, the water went as far up the beach as it could. That was a high tide. Then, the cycle changed, and the tide began to recede. That means it started to withdraw from the beach. We call this the ebb tide. Later, the level of the ocean stopped falling. We call this low tide. Then, the cycle repeated again and again.

해석
W Professor: 조수는 간단하게는 해수면이 오르내리는 현상입니다. 태양과 달의 인력이 조수를 만듭니다. 조수는 12시간 정도마다 일어납니다. 조수에는 기본적으로 두 가지 종류가 있습니다: 밀물과 썰물이 그것입니다.
조수는 어떻게 작용할까요? 자. 여러분이 바닷가에 있었던 때를 생각해 보세요. 여러분이 모래성을 만들고 있었다고 합시다. 대략 30여분이 지나자, 아마도 물이 여러분의 모래성 쪽으로 점점 더 가까워지고 있는 것을 발견했을 겁니다. 이것이 밀물이었습니다. 물이 밀려와서 해안 위로 차오르고 있었습니다. 모두 이해하고 있나요…? 이제, 어떤 시점에는, 물이 해안 위로 올라올 수 있을 만큼 차올랐습니다. 그것이 만조였습니다. 그러고 난 뒤 주기가 바뀌어, 조수가 물러나기 시작했습니다. 그것은 조수가 해안을 빠져나가기 시작했다는 것을 의미합니다. 이것을 썰물이라고 부릅니다. 이후에, 바다의 수위가 더 이상 빠지지 않습니다. 이것을 간조라고 부릅니다. 그러고 나면, 이 주기는 되풀이되어 반복되었습니다.

Listening Skills

1 (tide) – lied
2 bar – (far)
3 never – (level)
4 (low) – row

• Exercise 6 •
p.117

정답 Q1 Ⓐ Q2 Red Sea: ②, ④ Black Sea: ①, ③

스크립트 🎧 07-13

M Professor: I want to focus on two inland seas today: the Red Sea and the Black Sea. Let's start with the Red Sea. Everyone, take a look at the map in your book on page 244. Now, find the Red Sea . . . It's between Saudi Arabia and Africa. It has one of the highest salt contents of all the oceans on the Earth. Some experts presume its name comes from the red mountains located nearby.

Let's move on to the Black Sea. See if you can find it in your text. It is located directly north of Turkey in Southeastern Europe. It has a lower salt content than the Red Sea. In addition, the Black Sea is very abyssal. This makes its waters look dark. Some experts believe this is why it was named the Black Sea. Are there any questions so far, class?

해석

M Professor: 오늘은 두 내륙해에 초점을 맞춰 보고자 합니다: 바로 홍해와 흑해입니다. 홍해부터 시작해 봅시다. 모두 교재 244쪽의 지도를 보세요. 이제, 홍해를 찾아보세요… 홍해는 사우디아라비아와 아프리카 사이에 있습니다. 그것은 지구상의 모든 바다 중에서 소금 함량이 가장 높은 바다 중 하나입니다. 어떤 전문가들은 그 이름이 근처에 위치한 붉은 산들에서 유래한다고 추정합니다.

흑해로 넘어가 봅시다. 교재에서 흑해를 찾을 수 있는지 확인해 보세요. 흑해는 바로 유럽의 동남쪽에 있는 튀르키예 북부에 위치해 있습니다. 흑해는 홍해보다는 소금 함량이 낮습니다. 그에 더해 흑해는 아주 깊은 심해입니다. 그래서 물이 어두워 보입니다. 어떤 전문가들은 이것이 흑해라는 이름을 갖게 된 이유라고 생각합니다. 지금까지 질문이 있나요, 여러분?

Listening Skills

1 bogus – (focus)
2 (look) – rook
3 expels – (experts)
4 lame – (name)

• Exercise 7 •
p.118

정답 Q1 Ⓐ Q2 Rogue Waves: ①, ③ Tsunamis: ②, ④

스크립트 🎧 07-15

W Professor: We once thought rogue waves were just legends. In other words, we thought that they didn't exist. However, modern research proves they do actually exist. We also call them monster waves. They are giant waves that suddenly occur. That is, they form for no real reason.

Now, let me contrast them with the better-known tsunamis. It's clear that huge underwater earthquakes cause tsunamis. But rogue waves seem to appear spontaneously. They can threaten ships on the ocean surface. They are like huge walls of water. Tsunamis, on the other hand, do not appear on the surface like rogue waves. They exist underwater and do their damage once they hit land. Is everyone clear on this . . .? Perfect.

Oh, there's another important difference between rogue waves and tsunamis. Rogue waves simply don't ramble as far. Sometimes they travel for a few miles or so. However, tsunamis often travel thousands and thousands of miles before striking land.

해석

W Professor: 우리는 한때 로그 웨이브(무법자 파도)가 전설일 뿐이라고 생각했습니다. 다시 말하면, 그것이 존재하지 않는다고 생각했습니다. 하지만, 현대의 연구는 그것이 실제로 정말 존재한다고 증명합니다. 우리는 그것을 몬스터 웨이브(괴물 파도)라고 부르기도 합니다. 그것은 갑자기 발생하는 거대한 파도입니다. 말하자면, 그것은 아무런 실제 원인 없이 형성됩니다.

이제, 그것을 조금 더 잘 알려진 쓰나미와 비교해 봅시다. 해저의 거대한 지진이 쓰나미를 발생시킨다는 것은 명백합니다. 그러나 로그 웨이브는 자연발생적으로 나타나는 것처럼 보입니다. 그것은 해수면에 떠 있는 배들에게 위협적일 수 있습니다. 그것은 마치 물로 만들어진 거대한 벽과 같습니다. 반면에, 쓰나미는 로그 웨이브처럼 수면 위에 나타나지 않습니다. 그것은 해저에서 발생하고 그것이 육지를 강타해야 피해가 발생합니다. 모두들 이것에 대해 이해하고 있나요…? 좋아요.

아, 로그 웨이브와 쓰나미 사이에는 또 다른 중요한 차이점이 있습니다. 로그 웨이브는 그렇게 멀리 퍼지지 않습니다. 가끔씩 몇 마일 정도 이동합니다. 그러나 쓰나미는 종종 수천 마일을 이동하여 육지를 강타합니다.

Listening Skills

1 sought – (thought)
2 vogue – (rogue)
3 (few) – view
4 mires – (miles)

• Exercise 8 •
p.119

정답 Q1 Ⓓ Q2 Blue Whale: ② Whale Shark: ①, ③, ④

스크립트 🎧 07-17

M Professor: We know that the blue whale is the largest living thing on the Earth. We also know that it is a mammal. But what about fish? Who can tell me the largest fish on the Earth . . .? Nobody . . .? Actually, it shares the same name as the blue whale. It is the whale shark.

The whale shark isn't a typical shark though. It is pretty sluggish because of its size. It can reach up to around fifty feet in length. It also has miniscule teeth, unlike many man-eating sharks. Whale sharks do not feed on other fish. Well, they might eat some tiny ones now and then. But they usually feed on plankton and shellfish. They're basically immense, lazy feeding machines. In addition, unlike some species of sharks, they're very gentle. They are even playful with divers at times. Isn't that amazing, class? Well, I think it is.

해석

M Professor: 우리는 대왕고래가 지구상에서 가장 큰 생물이라는 것을 알고 있습니다. 우리는 또한 그것이 포유류라는 것도 알고 있습니다. 그렇다면 물고기는 어떨까요? 지구상에 가장 큰 물고기에 대해 말해줄 수 있는 사람 있나

요…? 아무도 없나요…? 사실, 그것은 대왕고래와 같은 이름을 나눠 갖고 있습니다. 그것은 고래상어입니다.

그렇지만 고래상어는 전형적인 상어는 아닙니다. 그것은 그 크기 때문에 꽤 굼뜹니다. 고래상어는 길이가 약 50피트까지 자랄 수 있습니다. 또한 많은 식인 상어들과는 달리, 아주 작은 이빨을 가지고 있습니다. 고래상어는 다른 물고기들을 먹지 않습니다. 음, 아마도 이따금씩은 아주 작은 물고기들을 먹을 수는 있을 것입니다. 하지만 그들은 주로 플랑크톤과 조개류를 먹습니다. 그들은 기본적으로 거대하고 게으른, 먹깨비죠. 게다가 어떤 상어종과는 다르게, 그들은 아주 신사적입니다. 심지어 가끔은 다이버들과 함께 놀기도 합니다. 놀랍지 않나요, 여러분? 음, 저는 그렇다고 생각해요.

Listening Skills

1 plume – ⓑlue
2 sing – ⓣhing
3 ⓕeed – bead
4 ⓝow – low

Vocabulary Review   p.120

Ⓐ 1 rambled
2 miniscule
3 directly
4 cycles
5 drift

Ⓑ 1 Ⓑ 2 Ⓐ 3 Ⓓ 4 Ⓒ 5 Ⓒ

Ⓒ 1 Ⓐ 2 Ⓒ 3 Ⓐ 4 Ⓓ 5 Ⓑ

Ⓓ 1 legend
2 sluggish
3 multitude
4 spontaneously
5 presumed

Practice Test   p.122

1 Ⓑ 2 Atlantic Ocean: 2, 4 Pacific Ocean: 1, 3
3 Ⓐ 4 Ⓓ

스크립트 🎧 07-19

M Professor: The Pacific and Atlantic oceans are the two largest oceans in the world. However, the Pacific is about twice as big as the Atlantic. It holds nearly fifty percent of the world's seawater. The Atlantic holds just over twenty percent. Another difference between the two is that the Pacific is much deeper than the Atlantic.

Moving on, the Atlantic occupies an area between the east coast of the Americas and the west coast of Europe and Africa. Everyone, please take a look at the map on page ninety-seven in your text. Do you see it . . . ? Very good.

In addition, please note the line in the middle of the map of the world. It wraps around the world. We call this the equator. It splits the Earth in two. Oceans are the warmest near the equator. The equator also separates the North Atlantic and South Atlantic oceans. Now, the Pacific Ocean stretches between the west coast of the Americas and the east coast of Asia. Of course, these two great oceans have to meet somewhere, don't they? Off the southern tip of South America at Cape Horn, they come together as one.

해석

M Professor: 태평양과 대서양은 세계에서 가장 큰 두 바다입니다. 그러나 태평양이 대서양보다 두 배 가까이 더 큽니다. 태평양은 지구 해수의 거의 50%를 차지합니다. 대서양은 20%를 약간 넘게 차지할 뿐입니다. 둘 사이의 또 다른 차이점은 태평양이 대서양보다 훨씬 더 깊다는 점입니다.

좀 더 짚어보자면, 대서양은 아메리카 대륙의 동쪽 해안과, 유럽과 아프리카의 서쪽 해안 사이의 영역을 차지합니다. 모두 교재의 97쪽에 있는 지도를 보세요. 보이나요…? 아주 좋아요.

추가로, 세계 지도 한가운데 있는 선에 주목해주세요. 그 선은 세계를 빙 둘러쌉니다. 이것을 적도라고 부릅니다. 적도는 지구를 둘로 나눕니다. 바다는 적도 근처에서 가장 따뜻합니다. 적도는 또한 북대서양과 남대서양을 나눕니다. 자, 태평양은 아메리카 대륙의 서쪽 해안과 아시아의 동쪽 해안 사이에 펼쳐져 있습니다. 물론, 이 두 개의 대양은 어딘가에서 만날 것입니다, 그렇지 않을까요? 남아메리카의 남쪽 끝단에 위치한 혼 곶에서 두 대양이 하나로 만납니다.

CHAPTER 8 Endangered Animals

Understanding TOEFL Question Types & Listening Skills
p.126

1 Question Types ▶ Sample Question

스크립트 🎧 08-01

W Professor: The polar bear is the largest of all bears. Actually, it's the biggest land carnivore on the planet. Carnivores are meat eaters. It weighs between 650 and 1,350 pounds. Big, huh? In addition, its average length is between eight and ten feet. But that's when it's on all four legs. A standing male might be thirteen feet tall. It's also a superior swimmer and catches fish well. Some polar bears can swim for thirty miles at one time.

해석

W Professor: 북극곰은 모든 곰들 중 가장 큰 곰입니다. 사실, 지구에 사는 육지 동물 중 가장 큰 육식동물이지요. 육식동물이란 고기를 먹는 동물을 말합니다. 북극곰은 무게가 650파운드에서 1,350파운드 사이에 이릅니다. 아주 크죠, 그렇죠? 게다가 북극곰의 평균 길이는 8피트에서 10피트 사이에 이릅니다. 그런데 네 발로 서 있을 때 그 정도입니다. 두 발로 선 수컷 곰은 그 키가 13피트인 경우도 있습니다. 북극곰은 또한 뛰어난 헤엄치기 선수이면서 물고기도 잘 잡습니다. 어떤 북극곰은 한 번에 30마일을 헤엄쳐 갈 수 있습니다.

2 Listening Skills ▶ Check-Up

1 It weighs between 650 and 1,350 pounds.
2 A standing male might be thirteen feet tall.
3 Some polar bears can swim for thirty miles at one time.

• Exercise 1 •
p.128

정답 Q1 Ⓒ   Q2 Ⓐ
스크립트 🎧 08-03

M Professor: Alligators might be scary, but they are amazing creatures. Some species can live for seventy or even eighty years. The average length of a female is about 8.2 feet. Males average a bit more at around 11.2 feet. They also have huge, powerful jaws. Inside are between seventy-four and eighty large teeth. New teeth replace old ones during their lives. Some alligator experts believe the average alligator goes through 2,000 or even 3,000 teeth in one lifetime. That's a lot of teeth.
I forgot to mention something to you. Alligators have four big front teeth that you can't see if their jaws are closed. These teeth aren't visible, unlike the crocodile's front teeth. There are several other deviations between crocodiles and alligators. Let me discuss them . . .

해석

M Professor: 앨리게이터 악어는 아주 무서울지 모르지만, 그러나 그들은 놀라운 생물입니다. 어떤 종은 70년 혹은 심지어 80년을 살 수 있습니다. 암컷의 평균 길이는 8.2피트 정도입니다. 수컷은 평균이 그보다 조금 더 커서 약 11.2피트 정도입니다. 앨리게이터 악어는 또한 크고 강력한 턱을 가지고 있습니다. 그 안에는 74개에서 80개의 큰 이빨이 있습니다. 생애 동안, 새 이빨이 낡은 이빨을 대체하며 자랍니다. 어떤 앨리게이터 악어 전문가들은 앨리게이터 악어가 평균적으로 일생 동안 2,000개 혹은 심지어 3,000개의 이빨을 거친다고 생각합니다. 엄청난 수의 이빨이죠.
중요한 것을 말해주는 것을 잊었네요. 앨리게이터 악어에게는, 턱이 닫혀 있으면 잘 보이지 않는 4개의 커다란 앞니가 있습니다. 이 이빨들은 크로커다일 악어의 앞니와는 다르게 보이지 않습니다. 크로커다일 악어와 앨리게이터 악어 사이에는 몇 가지 다른 차이점들이 있습니다. 그것에 대해 설명해드리겠습니다…

Listening Skills

1 Males average a bit more at around 11.2 feet.
2 Inside are between seventy-four and eighty large teeth.
3 The average alligator goes through 2,000 or even 3,000 teeth in one lifetime.

• Exercise 2 •
p.129

정답 Q1 Ⓐ   Q2 Ⓑ
스크립트 🎧 08-05

W Professor: Bull sharks are perhaps some of the world's most dangerous sharks. They like to feed in shallow waters. They are even found in rivers. Sometimes they even swim in freshwater rivers. A few years ago, some fishermen snagged a bull shark more than 2,000 miles up the Amazon River.
Males can grow to be about 6.8 feet long. They can weigh as much as 196 pounds. However, females get even bigger! They can reach 11.7 feet in length and weigh nearly 700 pounds. Now that's a big shark.
And how about their hunting technique? Well, they are usually—but not always—solo hunters. They hunt just about everything—even other sharks! Bull sharks are highly territorial, too. This means that they protect the area they live in. They'll attack anything that crosses into their territory.

해석

W Professor: 황소상어는 아마도 세계에서 가장 위험한 상어종일 것입니다. 그들은 얕은 물에서 서식하기를 좋아합니다. 심지어는 강에서 발견되기도 합니다. 때로는 심지어 담수인 강에서 헤엄치기도 합니다. 몇 년 전, 몇몇 어부들이 아마존강 상류 2,000마일 이상 지점에서 황소상어 한 마리를 잡았습니다. 수컷은 6.8피트 정도까지 자랄 수 있습니다. 무게는 196파운드만큼 나갈 수 있습니다. 하지만, 암컷은 훨씬 더 크게 자랍니다! 암컷은 길이가 11.7피트에 이를 수 있으며 무게는 거의 700파운드까지 나갑니다. 지금으로서는 정말 큰 상어입니다.
그러면 그들의 사냥 기술은 어떨까요? 음, 그들은 보통은—항상 그런 것은 아니지만—혼자서 사냥을 합니다. 그들은 그냥 모든 것을 사냥합니다.—심지어는 다른 상어도요! 황소상어는 또한 영역을 매우 중시합니다. 이 말은 그들이 자신들이 서식하는 지역을 지킨다는 의미입니다. 그들은 자신의 영역을 침범

해 넘어오는 무엇이든 공격할 것입니다.

Listening Skills

1 Males can grow to be about 6.8 feet long.
2 They can weigh as much as 196 pounds.
3 They can reach 11.7 feet in length.

• Exercise 3 • ———————————— p.130

정답 Q1 Ⓐ   Q2 Ⓒ
스크립트 🎧 08-07

M Professor: There are many birds of prey. These are predatory birds. One you probably know of is the bald eagle. It lives in North America. Actually, it is the national bird of the United States.
Anyway, the bald eagle is quite large. The length of its body is usually between seventy-two and ninety-five centimeters. That's for an adult. Its wingspan is normally between 167 and 223 centimeters. Yeah, that's pretty big. Oh, and it usually weighs about 3.7 to 6.4 kilograms.
And how about its nest? Well, the bald eagle builds the largest nest of any North American bird. These nests are enormous! They can be more than four meters deep. Some are even 2.4 to 2.7 meters wide. In addition, a single nest can weigh as much as one ton. Amazing!

해석

M Professor: 많은 종류의 맹금류 새들이 있습니다. 이들은 포식조류입니다. 아마 여러분이 아는 종류 중 하나는 흰머리수리일 것입니다. 그것은 북아메리카에 서식합니다. 실제로, 그것은 미국의 국조입니다.
어쨌든, 흰머리수리는 아주 큽니다. 그 몸 길이는 보통 72센티미터에서 95센티미터 사이에 이릅니다. 이것은 다 자란 성조의 경우입니다. 날개 길이는 보통 167센티미터에서 223센티미터 사이에 달합니다. 맞아요, 꽤 큽니다. 아, 그리고 무게는 3.7킬로그램에서 6.4킬로그램 정도 나갑니다.
그러면 그것의 둥지는 어떨까요? 음, 흰머리수리는 북아메리카에 있는 모든 새 중 가장 큰 둥지를 짓습니다. 이 둥지들은 정말 거대합니다! 그 깊이가 4미터 이상이 될 수도 있습니다. 어떤 것은 심지어 넓이가 2.4미터에서 2.7미터에 이릅니다. 게다가 하나의 둥지는 거의 1톤만큼의 무게가 나갈 수 있습니다. 정말 놀랍습니다!

Listening Skills

1 The length of its body is usually between seventy-two and ninety-five centimeters.
2 Its wingspan is normally between 167 and 223 centimeters.
3 It usually weighs about 3.7 to 6.4 kilograms.

• Exercise 4 • ———————————— p.131

정답 Q1 Ⓑ   Q2 Ⓐ
스크립트 🎧 08-09

M Professor: Let's move on to the killer whale, which is often called an orca. Some populations, or pods, feed on other fish. However, some populations munch on animals such as seals. It really depends on the pod and the region it is in.
The orca is mainly black with a white belly, or underside. Males can be almost thirty feet in length. Many orcas weigh more than 12,000 pounds. The largest orca ever recorded weighed 17,636 pounds. It was caught off the coast of Japan. Even orca babies are big. Just so you know, we call them calves. At birth, they can weigh more than 500 pounds.
An orca lives a fairly long life, too. On average, it lives to be about fifty years old. However, some can live to be eighty or even ninety years of age.

해석

M Professor: 보통 범고래라고 부르는 살인자 고래로 넘어가 봅시다. 어떤 개체, 즉 무리들은 다른 물고기들을 먹습니다. 그러나 어떤 개체들은 물개와 같은 동물들을 먹습니다. 그것은 그 무리와 그 무리가 있는 지역에 따라 정말로 다릅니다.
범고래는 주로 검은색이고 배쪽, 즉 아래쪽이 흰색입니다. 수컷은 길이가 거의 30피트에 달할 수 있습니다. 많은 범고래들이 무게가 12,000파운드 이상 나갑니다. 가장 큰 범고래로 기록된 것은 무게가 17,636파운드였습니다. 그것은 일본 연안에서 잡혔습니다. 심지어 범고래의 새끼들도 큽니다. 참고로 말하자면, 새끼는 calves라고 부릅니다. 새끼들은 날 때부터 무게가 500파운드 넘게 나갑니다.
범고래는 꽤 오래 살기까지 합니다. 평균적으로 50년 정도까지 삽니다. 그러나 어떤 것은 80년, 심지어는 90년까지도 살 수 있습니다.

Listening Skills

1 The largest orca ever recorded weighed 17,636 pounds.
2 At birth, they can weigh more than 500 pounds.
3 It lives to be about fifty years old.

• Exercise 5 • ———————————— p.132

정답 Q1 Ⓑ   Q2 Ⓓ
스크립트 🎧 08-11

W Professor: Komodo dragons are very large reptile predators. Today, they are found only on a few islands in Indonesia. Komodo dragons are carnivores. This means that they are mainly meat eaters.
They are silent hunters. They hide from their prey and then, at the last minute, run and attack. They also have an excellent— I mean keen—sense of smell. They can smell prey up to nearly seven miles away. They are very adroit reptiles, too. Some can run about 12.5 miles per hour.
Western scientists first saw Komodo dragons in 1910. Today, scientists estimate there are between 4,500 and 5,000 Komodo dragons left in the wild. They are therefore considered a threatened species. Earthquakes and habitat loss are two main reasons they are in danger of extinction.
Now, are they dangerous? Sure, they intimidate people. And if you get too close to one, it might attack. So it's smart to keep a safe distance from them.

해석

W Professor: 코모도왕도마뱀은 아주 큰 파충류 포식동물입니다. 오늘날, 코모도왕도마뱀은 인도네시아의 몇몇 섬에서만 발견됩니다. 코모도왕도마뱀은 육식 동물입니다. 이 말은 이들이 주로 고기를 먹는다는 뜻입니다.

그들은 소리 없는 사냥꾼입니다. 그들은 먹잇감을 피해 숨어 있다가, 마지막 순간에 달려가 공격합니다. 그들은 또한 아주 훌륭한—예민할 정도의—후각을 지니고 있습니다. 그들은 거의 7마일이나 떨어진 곳까지도 먹잇감의 냄새를 맡을 수 있습니다. 그들은 매우 명민한 파충류이기도 합니다. 어떤 코모도왕도마뱀은 약 시속 12.5마일의 속도로 달릴 수 있습니다.

서양의 과학자들이 코모도왕도마뱀을 처음 본 때는 1910년이었습니다. 오늘날, 과학자들은 야생 상태로 남아 있는 코모도왕도마뱀의 수가 4,500마리에서 5,000마리 사이로 추정합니다. 그래서 그들은 멸종 위기 종으로 여겨집니다. 지진과 서식지 감소가 그들이 멸종 위기에 놓이게 된 두 가지 주요 원인입니다. 자, 코모도왕도마뱀은 위험할까요? 물론, 그들은 사람들을 위협합니다. 그리고 여러분이 너무 가까이 다가가면 그것은 공격할지도 모릅니다. 그러므로 그들로부터 안전한 거리를 유지하는 것이 현명합니다.

Listening Skills

1 They can smell prey up to nearly seven miles away.
2 Some can run about 12.5 miles per hour.
3 Western scientists first saw Komodo dragons in 1910.

• Exercise 6 • ─────────────── p.133

정답 Q1 Ⓐ Q2 Ⓓ
스크립트 🎧 08-13

W Professor: Lions typically grow to be about 272 kilograms. They are the second largest cat after the tiger. The average weight of the tiger is a tad more.
Lions hunt in groups. We call this cooperative hunting. They like to hunt large prey. They prefer large mammals such as wildebeests, zebras, and buffaloes. They circle and stalk their prey. Then, they attack. They must be pretty close to their prey before they attack. Sure, they can run fast. Top recorded speeds are close to forty miles per hour. However, they do not have the best endurance. This is why they must be fairly close to their prey.
In general, kind of like pet cats, lions are pretty lazy. They are not active for about twenty hours a day. Nighttime is their most active time. And most of their hunting happens around dawn. They also spend about two hours a day walking and then nearly sixty minutes a day eating.

해석

W Professor: 사자는 일반적으로 272킬로그램 정도까지 자랍니다. 그들은 호랑이가 다음으로 두 번째로 큰 고양잇과 동물입니다. 호랑이의 평균 무게는 약간 더 많이 나갑니다.

사자는 집단을 이루어 사냥을 합니다. 이것을 협동 사냥이라고 부릅니다. 그들은 큰 먹잇감을 사냥하는 것을 좋아합니다. 그들은 야생영양, 얼룩말, 버펄로와 같은 크기가 큰 포유동물을 선호합니다. 그들은 먹잇감을 둘러싸고 그것에 몰래 접근합니다. 그런 다음, 공격합니다. 공격하기 전에는 먹잇감에 꽤 가깝게 접근해야 합니다. 물론, 그들은 빠르게 달릴 수 있습니다. 가장 빠르게 기록된 속도는 시속 40마일에 가깝습니다. 그러나 그들은 최상의 지구력을 갖추지는 못했습니다. 이 때문에 그들은 먹잇감에 상당히 가까이 다가가야 합니다.

일반적으로, 반려동물로 키우는 고양이와 비슷하게, 사자는 꽤 게으릅니다. 그들은 하루에 거의 20시간 동안은 움직이지 않습니다. 밤이 그들이 가장 활동적인 때입니다. 그리고 대부분의 사냥이 새벽 즈음에 이루어집니다. 그들은 또한 하루 2시간 정도를 돌아다니는 데 보내고 하루에 거의 60분 정도를 먹는 데 씁니다.

Listening Skills

1 Lions typically grow to be about 272 kilograms.
2 They are not active for about twenty hours a day.
3 Then they spend nearly sixty minutes a day eating.

• Exercise 7 • ─────────────── p.134

정답 Q1 Ⓑ Q2 Ⓑ
스크립트 🎧 08-15

M Professor: Another bird of prey is the owl. There are more than 200 species of owls. It's a solitary predator. This means that it hunts by itself. It is also a nocturnal predator. This means that it hunts mainly at night.
You can find owls pretty much everywhere on the planet. That is, except areas of severe cold like Antarctica. Now, two things help the owl become a very successful predator. One is its sight. It can see far-off prey very clearly. It has trouble with things close to it though. Second is its unique head. It is able to turn its head 135 degrees. This means it can see behind itself without moving its body. It simply quietly rotates its head more than forty-five degrees.
Oh, there's one more thing. Its feather coloring helps it blend in with the environment. This lets it surprise its prey. You could say it has excellent camouflage in the wild.

해석

M Professor: 또 다른 맹금류는 올빼미입니다. 200종 이상의 올빼미들이 존재합니다. 올빼미는 고독한 포식자입니다. 이것은 올빼미가 혼자서 사냥한다는 의미입니다. 올빼미는 또한 야행성 사냥꾼입니다. 이것은 올빼미가 주로 밤에 사냥한다는 것을 의미합니다.

지구상의 거의 모든 곳에서 올빼미를 찾아볼 수 있습니다. 그러니까, 남극대륙과 같이 극심하게 추운 곳을 제외한 곳에서요. 자, 올빼미를 매우 뛰어난 사냥꾼이 되도록 도와주는 두 가지가 있습니다. 하나는 시력입니다. 올빼미는 멀리 떨어져 있는 먹잇감을 아주 정확하게 볼 수 있습니다. 그렇지만 가까이에 있는 사물에는 어려움을 겪습니다. 두번째는 올빼미의 독특한 머리입니다. 올빼미는 머리를 135도 돌릴 수 있습니다. 이것은 올빼미가 몸을 돌리지 않고도 자기 뒤에 있는 것을 볼 수 있다는 것을 의미합니다. 올빼미는 머리를 45도 각도 이상 조용히 회전시킬 뿐입니다.

아, 한 가지 더 있습니다. 올빼미의 깃털 색은 올빼미가 주변 환경과 잘 섞이도록 도와줍니다. 이 때문에 먹잇감을 깜짝 놀라게 하죠. 올빼미는 야생에서 아주 뛰어난 위장술을 가졌다고 말할 수 있습니다.

Listening Skills

1 There are more than 200 species of owls.
2 It is able to turn its head 135 degrees.

3 It simply quietly rotates its head more than forty-five degrees.

• Exercise 8 • — p.135

정답 Q1 ⓑ   Q2 ⓓ

스크립트 🎧 08-17

W Professor: This is the rhinoceros. People often just call it the rhino. There are five different types of rhinos on the planet today. They live in Africa, India, and Indonesia. Most people recognize rhinos because of their horns. Some types have one horn while others have two.
Sadly, the rhino is an endangered species today. Many people kill them for their horns. They believe special medicine can be made from the horns. As a result, there are only around 30,000 rhinos in the wild today.
In general, rhinos are peaceful creatures. However, they can attack people. You see, rhinos don't have good eyesight. And they get scared easily. When they are scared, they attack. And they're huge creatures. Some can weigh up to 2,500 kilograms. They can also run more than forty kilometers an hour. So you had better be careful around rhinos. They can be extremely dangerous if you aren't careful. They have even been known to kill people.

해석
W Professor: 이것이 코뿔소입니다. 사람들은 보통 그것을 라이노(rhino)라고만 부릅니다. 오늘날 지구상에는 다섯 가지 다른 종의 코뿔소가 있습니다. 이들은 아프리카, 인도, 그리고 인도네시아에서 서식합니다. 대부분의 사람들은 뿔 때문에 코뿔소를 알아봅니다. 어떤 종은 뿔이 하나인 반면 두 개의 뿔을 가지고 있는 것들도 있습니다.
안타깝게도 코뿔소는 현재 멸종 위기종입니다. 많은 사람들이 뿔을 얻기 위해 이들을 죽이고 있죠. 그들은 이 뿔로 특별한 약을 만들 수 있다고 생각합니다. 그 결과 오늘날 야생에는 불과 약 30,000마리의 코뿔소만 존재합니다.
일반적으로 코뿔소는 평화로운 동물입니다. 하지만 사람들을 공격할 수 있습니다. 알겠지만, 코뿔소는 시력이 좋지 않습니다. 그리고 쉽게 겁을 먹죠. 코뿔소는 겁을 먹으면 공격을 합니다. 그리고 이들은 덩치가 큰 동물입니다. 어떤 것은 무게가 2,500킬로그램까지 나갈 수 있습니다. 코뿔소는 또한 시속 40킬로미터 이상을 달릴 수 있습니다. 그래서 코뿔소가 주변에 있다면 조심하는 편이 좋습니다. 조심하지 않으면 이들은 극도로 위험할 수 있습니다. 코뿔소가 사람을 사망에 이르게 한 경우도 알려져 있습니다.

Listening Skills

1 As a result, there are only around 30,000 rhinos in the wild today.
2 Some can weigh up to 2,500 kilograms.
3 They can also run more than forty kilometers an hour.

Vocabulary Review — p.136

Ⓐ 1 peaceful
   2 severe
   3 dawn
   4 intimidate
   5 keen

Ⓑ 1 ⓒ   2 ⓒ   3 ⓓ   4 ⓐ   5 ⓑ

Ⓒ 1 ⓐ   2 ⓓ   3 ⓑ   4 ⓐ   5 ⓒ

Ⓓ 1 dangerous
   2 superior
   3 national
   4 fairly
   5 attack

Practice Test — p.138

1 ⓓ   2. ⓑ   3 Gray Foxes: ①, ②   Red Foxes: ③, ④
4 ⓓ

스크립트 🎧 08-19

M Professor: I want to begin with gray foxes today. They live mainly in North America, but we can also find them in South America. Well, they're mainly in the northern part of South America. They are one of the most common species in the Americas. Now, there's something unique about gray foxes. You see, they have the unique ability to climb trees. Most other foxes can't or won't do this. The reasons they climb trees are to escape predators and to gather food. They also usually live in mountainous areas with a lot of brush, but they also live in swampy areas.
Now, I want to move on to red foxes. They are close relatives of gray foxes. In general, red foxes are a bit bigger than gray foxes. The two types tend to share habitats, but gray foxes tend to be more dominant. They are more aggressive than red foxes. In addition, red foxes like to live in hilly areas, and we can find them near streams and in wetlands. Furthermore, red foxes, unlike gray foxes, are able to live close to humans.

해석
M Professor: 저는 오늘 회색여우로 강의를 시작할까 합니다. 그들은 주로 북아메리카에 살지만, 남아메리카에서도 발견할 수 있습니다. 음, 남아메리카에서는 주로 북부 지역에 서식합니다. 그들은 아메리카 대륙에서는 아주 흔한 종 중 하나입니다. 자, 회색여우에게는 독특한 점이 있습니다. 보세요, 나무를 타는 독특한 능력이 있습니다. 대부분의 다른 여우들은 이렇게 할 수도 없고 하려고 하지도 않습니다. 그들이 나무에 오르는 이유는 포식자들을 피하고 먹이를 모아두기 위해서입니다. 그들은 또한 수풀이 우거진 산악 지대에서 주로 살지만, 늪지대에서 살기도 합니다.
이제 붉은여우로 넘어가 볼까 합니다. 붉은여우는 회색여우의 가까운 동족입니다. 일반적으로 붉은여우는 회색여우보다는 약간 더 큽니다. 이 두 종은 서식지를 공유하는 경향이 있지만, 회색여우가 우위를 차지하는 경향이 있습니다. 회색여우는 붉은여우보다 더 공격적입니다. 그에 더해서 붉은여우는 언덕 지대에서 사는 것을 좋아하고 개울과 늪지 근처에서도 찾아볼 수 있습니다. 더 나아가 붉은여우는 회색여우와는 다르게 사람과 가깝게 지낼 수 있습니다.

Actual Test

Actual Test 1
p.142

1 ⓒ 2 Ⓐ 3 Ⓓ 4 ⓒ 5 Ⓑ 6 ⓒ 7 ⓒ
8 General Severe Weather: ②, ④ Localized Severe Weather: ①, ③   9 Ⓑ

스크립트 🎧 09-01

W Student: Good afternoon, Professor Tomlinson. Are you busy now?
M Professor: Well, I was about to go home. But I'm not in a hurry. What can I do for you, Cindy?
W: Thanks so much, sir. I appreciate it. This won't take long.
M: Sure.
W: So, uh, I'm here about the midterm exam.
M: That's what I thought.
W: You know, uh, my grade was a lot lower than I had expected. I'm not sure why my score was so low.
M: Did you bring the test with you?
W: Yes, I've got it here . . . Uh, here you are . . .
M: Thanks. Let me take a look . . . Ah, okay. I remember now.
W: Yes?
M: Well, this was an essay test. You were supposed to write comprehensive answers to the questions. But you wrote very short answers instead.
W: Oh, I see.
M: Take a look at question one. Most students wrote two or three hundred words for their answers. But you wrote just one sentence. That's not an essay. You did the same thing for two other questions.
W: I guess I misunderstood the directions.
M: Well, try to pay closer attention the next time. I know you understand the course material. But you need to show me that you understand on the test.
W: Yes, sir. I'll do a better job on the final exam.
M: Great. Study hard and follow the directions. Then, I'm sure your test will be much better.

해석

W Student: 안녕하세요, 톰린슨 교수님. 지금 바쁘신가요?
M Professor: 음, 막 집에 가려던 참이었어요. 하지만 급한 일은 없어요. 무엇을 도와줄까요, 신디?
W: 정말 고맙습니다, 교수님. 감사해요. 오래 걸리지 않을 거예요.
M: 알겠어요.
W: 그러니까, 어, 저는 중간고사 때문에 왔어요.
M: 그런 것 같았어요
W: 아시겠지만, 어, 제 성적이 예상보다 훨씬 더 낮아서요. 제 점수가 왜 그렇게 낮은지 잘 모르겠어요.
M: 시험지를 가지고 왔나요?
W: 네, 여기 가지고 왔어요… 아, 여기요…
M: 고마워요. 좀 볼게요… 아, 그래요. 이제 기억나네요.
W: 그렇죠?
M: 음, 이번에는 에세이 시험이었잖아요. 자네는 질문에 대해 종합적인 답안을 작성해야 했어요. 하지만 그 대신 답안을 매우 짧게 썼죠.
W: 아, 그렇군요.
M: 1번 문제를 보세요. 대부분의 학생들이 200개에서 300개의 단어로 답안을 작성했어요. 하지만 자네는 한 문장만 썼죠. 그건 에세이가 아니에요. 다른 두 문제의 경우에도 똑같이 했고요.
W: 제가 지침을 잘못 이해한 것 같네요.
M: 음, 다음 번에는 좀 더 주의하도록 하세요. 자네가 수업 내용을 잘 이해하고 있는 건 알아요. 하지만 시험에서는 자네가 잘 이해하고 있다는 점을 내게 보여주어야 해요.
W: 네, 교수님. 기말고사에서는 더 잘할게요.
M: 좋아요. 열심히 공부하고 지침을 잘 따르세요. 그러면 분명 시험 결과가 훨씬 더 좋을 거예요.

스크립트 🎧 09-02

W Professor: That storm last night was intense, wasn't it? According to the weather report, we got three inches of rain in just two hours. Lots of trees were blown down by the wind, too.
Today, I want to talk about severe weather like last night's thunderstorm. What is severe weather? It's basically any type of weather event that can damage buildings, kill people, and cause disruptions to daily life. There are many kinds of severe weather. There are thunderstorms, of course. Hurricanes and typhoons are severe weather. So are blizzards, ice storms, and hailstorms. And let's not forget tornadoes. They are extremely dangerous.
We can divide severe weather into two groups. The first is general severe weather. The second is localized severe weather. General severe weather happens over a broad area. It includes hurricanes, typhoons, and blizzards. Localized severe weather is more restricted. It includes tornadoes as well as sudden downbursts of rain. Most hailstorms are localized weather, too.
Severe weather can be extremely dangerous. A single typhoon or hurricane can kill thousands of people. It may injure many more and destroy buildings due to wind and flooding. Tornadoes can flatten entire towns. Hundreds of people can die because of one tornado. Hailstorms can cause a tremendous amount of damage, especially to cars.
Fortunately, we can predict severe weather. So people can get to places of safety. Their property may be damaged, but they will be okay. Let me give you an example of how a tornado warning saved many lives recently.

해석

W Professor: 어젯밤의 폭풍이 강력하지 않았나요? 일기 예보에 따르면 단 두 시간 만에 3인치의 비가 내렸더군요. 바람에 의해 많은 나무들이 쓰러지기도 했고요.
오늘은 어젯밤의 천둥과 같은 악천후에 대해 이야기를 하고자 합니다. 악천후란 무엇일까요? 이는 기본적으로 건물에 피해를 입히고, 사람들의 목숨을 앗아가고, 일상 생활에 지장을 줄 수 있는 모든 날씨 현상입니다. 많은 유형의 악천후가 존재합니다. 물론 천둥이 있고요. 허리케인과 태풍도 악천후입니다. 눈보라, 진눈깨비, 그리고 우박도 마찬가지입니다. 그리고 토네이도(회오리바람)

도 잊지 맙시다. 이러한 것들은 매우 위험하죠.
악천후는 두 가지 범주로 나눌 수 있습니다. 첫 번째는 일반적인 악천후입니다. 두 번째는 국지적인 악천후입니다. 일반적인 악천후는 넓은 지역에 걸쳐 발생합니다. 여기에는 허리케인, 태풍, 눈보라가 포함됩니다. 국지적인 악천후는 이보다 제한적입니다. 여기에는 토네이도뿐 아니라 갑작스러운 폭우도 포함됩니다. 대부분의 우박 역시 국지적인 악천후입니다.
악천후는 매우 위험할 수 있습니다. 단 한 차례의 태풍이나 허리케인 때문에 수천 명의 사람들이 목숨을 잃을 수 있습니다. 바람과 홍수로 인해 더 많은 사람들이 부상을 입고 건물들이 파괴될 수 있습니다. 토네이도는 마을 전체를 무너뜨릴 수 있습니다. 한 차례의 토네이도로 수백 명이 목숨을 잃을 수도 있죠. 우박은, 특히 차량에, 막대한 피해를 입힐 수 있습니다.
다행히도 우리는 악천후를 예측할 수 있습니다. 그에 따라 사람들이 안전한 곳으로 대피할 수 있죠. 재산상의 피해는 입을 수도 있지만 사람들은 괜찮을 것입니다. 최근 토네이도 경보로 인해 많은 사람들이 목숨을 지켰던 한 가지 사례를 알려 드리죠.

Actual Test 2

p.146

1 ⓒ   2 Ⓐ   3 Ⓑ   4 Ⓑ   5 Ⓓ   6 ⓒ
7 True: ②, ③, ④   False: ①   8 Ⓐ   9 Ⓐ

스크립트 🎧 09-03

W Librarian: Excuse me. You seem like you're having a tough time. Can I help you with something?
M Student: Oh, hello. You're a librarian?
W: That's right.
M: Great. I've got a problem.
W: You can't find a book?
M: It's worse than that. There are several books I'm looking for. But they're either already checked out or not available.
W: What's your topic?
M: It's castles in France during the Middle Ages. It's for a history class.
W: Hmm . . . I don't think we have too many books on that subject.
M: I have a list of books I want. I checked the library's online catalog. Of the ten books I need, the library doesn't have six of them. That's not good at all.
W: What about the other four?
M: Three are checked out. One is supposed to be available, but I couldn't find it on the shelves.
W: That's strange. Which is the missing one?
M: It's this one here on the list . . . The book written by Claude Desmond.
W: I'm not familiar with it. But I'll let everyone know we need to find it.
M: Thanks. Now, uh, what about the other books?
W: You have a couple of options. First, you can recall the books that are checked out. That means they must be returned within ten days. Then, you can check them out.
M: My paper isn't due until two months from now.
W: Great. So you'll be able to use those books. As for the others, you can use the interlibrary loan program. That means you can request the books from other schools.
M: I've never heard of this program. Can you tell me more about it, please?

해석

W Librarian: 실례합니다. 문제가 있으신 것 같은데. 도와 드릴까요?
M Student: 아, 안녕하세요. 사서 선생님이신가요?
W: 맞아요.
M: 잘 됐네요. 문제가 있어요.
W: 책을 찾지 못하겠나요?
M: 그것보다 더 좋지 않은 문제예요. 제가 찾고 있는 책이 몇 권 있는데요. 하지만 이미 대출이 되었거나 아니면 대출을 할 수가 없더군요.
W: 주제가 뭐죠?
M: 중세 시대 프랑스의 성들이요. 역사 수업에 필요하거든요.
W: 흠… 그러한 주제의 책은 그다지 많이 보유하고 있지 않은 것 같군요.
M: 제가 원하는 책들의 목록이 있어요. 도서관의 온라인 도서 목록을 확인했고요. 제가 필요한 10권의 책 중에서 6권은 도서관에 없더군요. 큰일이에요.
W: 나머지 4권은요?
M: 3권은 대출되었어요. 한 권은 대출이 가능하다고 되어 있는데, 서가에서 찾을 수가 없었어요.
W: 이상하네요. 없는 책이 어떤 것이죠?
M: 여기 목록에 있는데… 클로드 데즈몬드가 쓴 책이에요.
W: 잘 모르는 책이네요. 하지만 다른 사람들에게 그 책을 꼭 찾아야 한다고 알릴게요.
M: 고맙습니다. 그럼, 아, 나머지 책들은요?
W: 학생에게는 두 가지 옵션이 있어요. 먼저, 대출된 책에 대해 회수 요청을 할 수 있어요. 그러면 10일 내에 책이 반납되어야 한다는 뜻이에요. 그런 다음에 학생이 대출을 할 수 있어요.
M: 제 보고서는 지금부터 2달 후에 제출하면 돼요.
W: 잘 됐네요. 그러면 그 책들을 이용할 수 있을 거예요. 나머지 책들에 대해서는, 도서관 상호 대출 프로그램을 이용할 수 있어요. 학생이 다른 학교에 그 책들을 요청할 수 있다는 뜻이에요.
M: 이 프로그램에 대해서는 들어본 적이 없네요. 그것에 대해 좀 더 설명해 주시겠어요?

쇼크립묘 🎧 09-01

M Professor: In 1856, a skeleton was dug up in the Neander Valley in Germany. People realized it was a new kind of human. They called it the Neanderthal after where it was dug up. Since then, anthropologists have found many more Neanderthal skeletons. They have found Neanderthal artifacts and art, too. So we know quite a bit about Neanderthals now.
First, Neanderthals lived mostly in Europe. They also lived in parts of southwest and central Asia. They appeared around 400,000 years ago. They disappeared approximately 40,000 years ago. They are considered our closest human relative today.
Neanderthals averaged around 1.50 to 1.75 meters in height. Adults weighed between sixty-four and eighty-two kilograms. They also had very large brains. We believe their brains let them speak. We know they hunted large animals in groups, so they were definitely able to communicate with one another. Ah, yes, they ate meat. They also ate various plants and mushrooms. Those that lived near the sea ate shellfish and caught fish, too.

Now, uh, as I said, they disappeared around 40,000 years ago. Why? Nobody knows for sure. They didn't die out because of cold weather. They were well adapted to living in frigid temperatures. They didn't die out because of warm weather either. They lived in warm regions such as Spain and Italy. Some anthropologists believe modern humans made them go extinct. You see, modern humans left Africa around 50,000 years ago and headed into Europe. They may have encountered Neanderthals. It's likely the two fought, and Neanderthals were the losers.

해석

M Professor: 1856년, 독일의 네안데르 계곡에서 해골 하나가 발굴되었습니다. 사람들은 이것이 새로운 종의 인류라는 점을 알게 되었습니다. 그것이 발굴된 장소의 이름을 따서 그것을 네안데르탈인이라고 불렀습니다. 그때부터 인류학자들은 더 많은 네안데르탈인의 유골을 발견하고 있습니다. 네안데르탈인의 유물과 그림 또한 발견되고 있습니다. 따라서 우리는 현재 네안데르탈인에 대해서는 꽤 알고 있는 편입니다.

먼저, 네안데르탈인은 주로 유럽에서 살았습니다. 그들은 서남아시아 및 중앙아시아의 일부 지역에서도 살았습니다. 이들은 약 40만년 전에 등장했습니다. 4만년 전쯤 사라졌고요. 그들은 현생 인류와 가장 가까운 인류로 여겨지고 있습니다.

네안데르탈인의 평균 신장은 약 1.5미터에서 1.75미터였습니다. 성인들의 경우 몸무게가 64킬로그램에서 82킬로그램 사이였습니다. 또한 뇌가 매우 컸습니다. 이러한 뇌로 인해 그들이 말을 했을 것으로 생각됩니다. 무리를 지어 커다란 동물을 사냥했다는 점이 알려져 있기 때문에 그들은 분명 서로 의사소통을 할 수 있었을 것입니다. 아, 그래요, 그들은 고기를 먹었습니다. 또한 다양한 식물과 버섯류들도 먹었죠. 바다 근처에 살았던 네안데르탈인은 조개도 먹고 물고기도 잡았습니다.

자, 아, 얘기한 대로, 이들은 약 4만년 전에 사라졌습니다. 왜일까요? 확실한 것은 아무도 모릅니다. 추운 날씨 때문에 소멸한 것은 아니었습니다. 그들은 추운 날씨에 사는 것에 잘 적응해 있었죠. 따뜻한 날씨 때문에 소멸한 것도 아니었습니다. 스페인과 이탈리아와 같은 따뜻한 지역에서도 살았으니까요. 어떤 인류학자들은 현생 인류 때문에 그들이 멸종했을 것으로 생각합니다. 알겠죠, 현생 인류는 약 5만년 전에 아프리카를 떠나 유럽으로 향했어요. 이들은 네안데르탈인과 우연히 만났을 것입니다. 양측이 충돌을 해서 네안데르탈인이 패했을 가능성이 있습니다.

Actual Test 3   p.150

1 Ⓐ 2 Ⓓ 3 Ⓒ 4 Ⓑ 5 Ⓓ 6 Ⓑ, Ⓓ
7 Mammals: ①, ④ Marsupials: ②, ③ 8 Ⓐ 9 Ⓒ

스크립트 🎧 09-05

W Student: Professor Moore, you have office hours now, right?
M Professor: I sure do, Tina. What do you want to talk about?
W: I'm having some problems with the final paper.
M: What kinds of problems?
W: Well, actually, I don't have a topic. I can't think of anything.
M: All right. I asked everyone to choose a topic we discussed this semester.
W: That's right. We studied lots of interesting things, but, uh, I just don't know what to write about.
M: Why don't you tell me what you liked? I mean, what topics did you enjoy learning about?
W: Hmm . . . I loved the lecture on jellyfish. I also liked the lecture on deep-sea creatures.
M: Anything else?
W: Sharks. It was fascinating to learn about sharks.
M: Okay. Which of the three topics you mentioned did you like the most?
W: Oh . . . that's a tough one. I guess deep-sea creatures. I really found them interesting.
M: That's good. Was there a particular creature you liked learning about?
W: I thought the lanternfish was interesting. I also liked learning about the octopus. I never knew it could shoot ink as a defense mechanism.
M: Hmm . . . I think we've found your topic.
W: We have?
M: Yes. I want you to write about the defenses deep-sea creatures have. Choose three or four animals. Then, describe how they protect themselves from predators. That's it.
W: Oh, wow. That sounds like a cool topic. Um . . . how do you think I should start?
M: If I were you, I'd go to the library.
W: Great idea. I've got time before my next class starts. Thanks so much for helping, Professor Moore. See you in class tomorrow.

해석

W Student: 무어 교수님, 지금 집무 시간이시죠, 그렇죠?
M Professor: 그래요, 티나. 무슨 얘기가 하고 싶은가요?
W: 기말 보고서와 관련해 문제가 좀 있어서요.
M: 어떤 문제죠?
W: 음, 실은 주제를 정하지 못하겠어요. 아무것도 떠오르지가 않아요.
M: 알겠어요. 내가 모두에게 이번 학기에 우리가 논의했던 한 가지 주제를 선택하라고 요청했죠.
W: 맞아요. 흥미로운 것들을 많이 배웠지만, 어, 무엇에 대해 써야 할지 잘 모르겠어요.
M: 어떤 것이 마음에 들었는지 얘기해 볼래요? 내 말은, 어떤 주제를 배울 때가 재미있었나요?
W: 흠… 해파리에 관한 강의가 재미있었어요. 심해 생물에 관한 강의도 좋았고요.
M: 또 있나요?
W: 상어요. 상어에 대해 배우게 돼서 정말 좋았어요.
M: 그래요. 자네가 언급한 세 가지 주제 중에서 뭐가 가장 좋았죠?
W: 아… 어려운데요. 심해 생물인 것 같아요. 정말 흥미롭다고 느꼈어요.
M: 좋아요. 재미있게 배웠던 생물이 따로 있었나요?
W: 랜턴피쉬가 흥미롭다고 생각했어요. 문어에 대해 배운 것도 좋았고요. 문어가 방어 수단으로써 먹물을 발사하는지는 정말 몰랐어요.
M: 흠… 주제를 찾은 것 같군요.
W: 찾았다고요?
M: 그래요. 자네가 심해 생물이 가지고 있는 방어 수단에 대해 글을 쓰면 좋겠네요. 서너 종의 동물을 선택하세요. 그런 다음 이들이 포식자들로부터 스스로를 보호하는 방법에 대해 설명하세요. 그럼 끝이죠.
W: 아, 와. 멋진 주제 같아요. 음… 제가 어떻게 시작하면 좋을까요?

M: 내가 자네라면 도서관에 갈 것 같은데요.
W: 좋은 생각이에요. 다음 수업이 시작하기 전까지 시간이 있어요. 도와 주셔서 정말 감사합니다. 무어 교수님. 내일 수업시간에 뵐게요.

스크립트 09-06

W Professor: Mammals are animals such as humans, dogs, cows, horses, and dolphins. They are warm-blooded animals that have skin covered with hair. They provide their young with milk and have a backbone. Mammals can grow to large sizes, like whales, elephants, and hippos.

Now, uh, there is a group of mammals called marsupials. Marsupial is spelled M-A-R-S-U-P-I-A-L, by the way. There are around 330 species of marsupials. Most live in Australia and South America. They include the kangaroo, the koala, and the wombat. Ah, there's one marsupial in North America. It's the possum.

Marsupials share many similarities with mammals. For instance, they have all of the characteristics of mammals I just mentioned. But there are also a few differences. For example, mammals give birth to well-developed young. When marsupials give birth, their young are not fully developed. They are blind and lack both back legs and ears. Obviously, they need to develop more. A marsupial female has a pouch in her stomach. The babies climb into the pouch, where they can drink their mother's milk. They continue to develop in the pouch.

There are some other differences. Let me see . . . Marsupials have more teeth than regular mammals. However, they only grow one set of teeth their entire lives. Marsupials have a lower body temperature than mammals. And they have lower metabolic rates.

Okay. That's enough for now. Why don't we take a break? When we come back, I'm going to show you a short film on marsupials.

해석

W Professor: 포유류는 인간, 개, 소, 말, 그리고 돌고래와 같은 동물들입니다. 포유류는 온혈 동물로서 털로 덮인 피부를 지니고 있죠. 이들은 새끼에게 젖을 먹이며 척추를 가지고 있어요. 포유류는 고래, 코끼리, 하마처럼 몸이 거대하게 자라기도 합니다.

자, 아, 유대류라고 불리는 포유류 집단이 있습니다. 유대류의 철자는 참고로, M-A-R-S-U-P-I-A-L이에요. 약 330종의 유대류가 존재합니다. 대부분은 오스트레일리아와 남아메리카에서 서식하죠. 유대류에는 캥거루, 코알라, 웜뱃이 포함됩니다. 아, 북아메리카에도 유대류가 하나 있어요. 바로 주머니쥐입니다.

유대류는 포유류와 많은 유사성을 공유합니다. 예를 들어, 유대류는 제가 방금 말한 포유류의 모든 특성들을 지니고 있죠. 하지만 몇 가지 차이점도 존재합니다. 예를 들어 포유류는 충분히 발달한 상태의 새끼를 낳습니다. 유대류가 새끼를 낳는 경우에는, 새끼들이 완전히 발달해 있지 않아요. 눈이 보이지 않고 뒷다리와 귀도 가지고 있지 않죠. 분명 더 발달해야 합니다. 유대류의 암컷은 배에 주머니가 있습니다. 새끼들은 주머니 속으로 기어들어가는데, 여기에서 어미의 젖을 받아 먹습니다. 새끼들은 그 주머니 속에서 발달을 이어 나갑니다.

다른 차이점들도 존재합니다. 봅시다… 유대류는 일반적인 포유류보다 이빨이 더 많습니다. 하지만 평생 단 한 번의 치열만 자랍니다. 유대류는 포유류보다 체온이 더 낮습니다. 그리고 대사율도 더 낮습니다.

좋아요. 이만하면 충분히 설명한 것 같군요. 잠시 쉬는 것이 어떨까요? 다시 돌아와서 유대류에 관한 짧은 영상을 보여 드리겠습니다.